Bravo!

The Philadelphia

Orchestra

Cookbook II

Bravo!

Printed in the USA by

WIMMER
The Wimmer Companies, Inc.
Memphis

2

Bravo!

Table of Contents

Bravo!

Dedication

Founded in 1900, the Orchestra was first led by Fritz Scheel and then by Carl Pohlig. Leopold Stokowski, appointed third Music Director in 1912, built the Orchestra into a world-class ensemble during years of exciting growth and experimentation, marked by many world premieres and achievements in broadcasting and recording.

Eugene Ormandy, serving an unprecedented 44 years as fourth Music Director, gave distinguished leadership to the Orchestra, which continued to meet with international critical acclaim. Extensive tours in the United States and abroad and an extraordinary recording schedule were highlights of his tenure.

Appointed in 1980, Riccardo Muti, continuing the Orchestra's tradition of presenting new works, became a leader in promoting new American music as well as operatic repertoire. During his 12-year term, Muti and the Orchestra explored new territory artistically as well as geographically, visiting 88 cities in 21 countries around the world.

Maestro Wolfgang Sawallisch, who became Music Director in 1993, has demonstrated his mastery as a conductor and has infused new energy and luster into Orchestra performances. Philadelphia audiences have given him their enthusiastic support and applaud his superb musicianship. To Maestro Sawallisch we dedicate ***BRAVO! The Philadelphia Orchestra Cookbook II***.

Bravo!

Cookbook Committees

First Edition Committee

Editors Lois Garaventi
Lois Renthal

Art Editor Mary Anne Justice

Computer Holly Luff
Sue Reichel

Testing Peggy Kippax
Judy MacGregor
Connie Mayock

Marketing Betsy Rainey

Orchestra Vignettes Alice Ahrens
DeAnn Clancy
Peggy Kippax
Margery Lee

Current Committee

Co-Chairs Lois Renthal
Susie Robinson

Treasurer Sandy Ringo
Asst. Treasurer Mary Anne Justice

Marketing Kathryn Simich

Publicity Betsy Rainey

Sales Alice Ahrens
Holly Luff

With sincere appreciation we thank the many people who so generously donated their time and talent to ensure the excellence of this book. We are particularly grateful to Sam Maitin for his inspirational creativity. Special thanks for their valuable expertise go to the committee who created our first cookbook. Initially published in 1980, it continues to sell successfully. Finally, we thank all the members of The West Philadelphia Committee for boundless support and encouragement. Their collective efforts have made this project a reality.

Lois Garaventi and Lois Renthal

Every member of The West Philadelphia Committee promotes and sells ***BRAVO! The Philadelphia Orchestra Cookbook II***.

Explanation of Symbols

QED Recipes that can be prepared in 30 minutes or less – Quick, Easy, and Delicious

Recipes contributed by musicians

Recipes contributed by chefs, restaurants, or catering services

Recipes with a low-cholesterol, low-fat content

Tips

Bravo!

The West Philadelphia Committee
for The
Philadelphia Orchestra

Sydney Stevens, Chairman

Alice Ahrens
Carol Barker
Lyle Beatty
Elia Buck
Joan Calhoun
DeAnn Clancy
Rika Cornwell
Betsy Crowell
Alice Cullen
Karen Cunningham
Betsy D'Angelo
Evie Day
Winnie Doherty
Barbara Erdman
Jane Hastings
Joan Holmes
Helen Justi
Mary Anne Justice
Sandy Kay
Jane Kelly
Peggy Kippax
Janet Klaus
Sandy Kress

Nancy Lander
Margery Lee
Holly Luff
Judy MacGregor
Pat McCarter
Connie Mayock
Ingrid Morsman
Barbara Noone
Carol Pendergrass
Lynn Pohanka
Betsy Rainey
May Belle Rauch
Sue Reichel
Lois Renthal
Sandy Ringo
Susie Robinson
Cackie Rogers
Kathryn Simich
Mary Lee Stallkamp
Susie Thorkelson
Kristine Walters
Nonie Williams

Sustaining Members
Lee Annenberg
Debbie Balis
Joan Borden
Jane Copeland
Jackie Counselman
Dorothea Haff
Dottie Halbkat
Dolores Hess
Lynn Ivey
Anne Kellett
Patti Kirkpatrick
Barbara Linder
Betty Lloyd
Martha Miller
Pat Quigg
Didi Rieger
Barkie Supplee
Holly Wendt
Honorary Members
Connie Begien
Anne Krout
Lucile Lewis
Doris Roberts
Joyce Stein

The purpose of The West Philadelphia Committee for The Philadelphia Orchestra is to advance the interests of The Philadelphia Orchestra.

Bravo!

Sam Maitin

Sam Maitin, a Philadelphia artist with a national and international reputation as a painter, sculptor, printmaker, and collagist, who is also noted for his involvement with book design, created the painting for the cover of **Bravo!**, the collages for the section dividers, and all graphic design for the book. Maitin's work is in public and private collections in the United States, Europe, and Japan. He has been honored with major exhibitions in Europe, Israel, Japan, and Mexico, as well as in the United States, and is the recipient of many honors, awards, and grants, including a Guggenheim Foundation Fellowship.

Initially, we asked Sam Maitin to design the cover and the section dividers for the cookbook. When we saw his preliminary sketches, it became obvious that we must have Sam's work throughout the book. So, to his collaborations on book design with artists such as Joan Miro, Marino Marini, and Jean Dubuffet, we asked him to add one with the editors of **BRAVO! The Philadelphia Orchestra Cookbook II**. With characteristic creativity, enthusiasm, and generosity, he has applied his unique talent to the design of his first cookbook.

Barbecued Chicken with Dill Mustard Sauce

Easy	Yield: 36 skewers (8 to 10 servings)
Do ahead	Preparing: 20 minutes
	Baking: 20 minutes

3 whole chicken breasts, skinned and boned

Barbecue Sauce:
½ cup ketchup
¼ cup lemon juice (reconstituted may be used)
2 tablespoons vinegar

Dill Mustard Sauce:
1 cup sweet mustard
1 cup sour cream

36 wooden skewers

¼ cup brown sugar
2 tablespoons Worcestershire sauce
1 teaspoon dry mustard

½ cup chopped fresh dill

Barbecue Sauce: In a small saucepan, whisk all ingredients together and simmer for 15 minutes. (Sauce may be frozen for several weeks.)
Dill Mustard Sauce: Mix all ingredients together. Cover and refrigerate until ready to use. Will keep for 3 days. Makes 2 cups.
Chicken: Preheat oven to 350°. Pour enough barbecue sauce into baking dish to cover bottom. Dip chicken in sauce so both sides are coated. Cover dish with foil and bake for 20 minutes. Allow chicken to cool in sauce (or refrigerate overnight in sauce). Before serving, cube chicken into bite-size pieces and thread two pieces onto a skewer. Serve at room temperature with Dill Mustard Sauce.

Note: Looks attractive on a tray covered with lettuce.

Sedgwick Clams

Easy	Yield: 8 to 10 servings
Do ahead	Preparing: 20 minutes
	Baking: 30 minutes
	May be doubled

2 cans (7 ounces) minced clams
1 cup bread crumbs
1 cup grated Swiss cheese
1 teaspoon fresh lemon juice

½ stick butter, melted
1 small onion, chopped
1 teaspoon oregano

Preheat oven to 350°. Grease a small flat casserole. Mix all ingredients together, place in casserole, and bake for 30 minutes. Serve with crackers.

Bravo!

Cheese Straws

Average	*Yield: 60 straws*
Do ahead	*Preparing: 15 minutes plus 30 minutes*
Freeze	*Chilling: Overnight*
	Baking: 15 minutes

1½ cups flour
1 teaspoon seasoned salt
¼ teaspoon dry mustard
1 stick (¼ pound) margarine

3½ tablespoons cool water
5 ounces sharp Cheddar cheese,
   grated

In a bowl, combine flour, salt, and mustard. Cut in the margarine until there is a cornmeal consistency. Add grated cheese and mix the same way. Add the water gradually and mix until it forms a ball. Do not make it too wet. Divide into two equal balls and refrigerate overnight in a tightly-closed plastic bag. Remove balls from refrigerator and allow them to sit for 30 minutes before rolling out. Preheat oven to 350°. Place a ball between two sheets of wax paper and roll out, turning the paper around, until the dough is as thin as you like (the thinner the better) in a rectangular shape. With a sharp knife or pastry wheel, cut the dough into 5-inch strips and lay them on a lightly greased cookie sheet. Bake at 350° for 10 minutes on the middle rack, and 5 minutes on the top rack. The time of cooking will depend on the thickness of the strips. They will be lightly colored when done. Remove from oven and allow to cool on a rack before storing in a tightly closed container.

Note: For a variation in shape, the straws may be twisted before baking.

Cheese Sticks

Easy	*Yield: Varies according to need*
Partial do ahead	*Preparing: 20 minutes*
	Baking: 10 to 15 minutes
	May be doubled or tripled

White bread, pre-sliced, crust
   removed, cut into 1-inch fingers
Canola oil

Olive oil
Parmesan cheese, grated
Romano cheese, grated

Dip bread fingers into a mixture of equal parts of canola oil and olive oil. Dust with a mixture of equal parts of the cheeses. Allow them to dry on waxed paper. Preheat oven to 350°. Bake fingers for 10 to 15 minutes, or until golden brown.

Jimmy Duffy & Sons, Inc., Berwyn, PA

Spinach Balls by Natalie and Sue

Easy
Do ahead
Freeze

Yield: 60 balls
Preparing: 30 minutes
Baking: 15 minutes

2 (10-ounce) packages frozen, chopped spinach
2 cups crushed Pepperidge Farm stuffing
1 medium onion, chopped finely
½ cup grated Parmesan cheese

½ cup grated mozzarella cheese (or 1 cup Parmesan only)
4 eggs, lightly beaten
½ cup soft margarine
Dash garlic salt
Dash thyme

Defrost spinach and squeeze dry. Preheat oven to 350°. Mix all ingredients and form into balls about 1½ inches in diameter. (If not cooking immediately, flash freeze balls and save them in a freezer bag until required.) If cooking immediately, place balls on a baking tray; place on top rack of a 350° oven for 15 minutes. To obtain a light brown top, leave oven door open, and broil for 1 or 2 minutes more. Watch that they do not burn! May be made ahead and reheated in a microwave. Good served with Sweet Hot Mustard Sauce (see page 239).

Pita-Chile

Average
Partial do ahead

Yield: 48 pieces
Preparing: 30 minutes

1 package pita bread (6 pockets)
¼ cup butter or margarine, softened
2 cloves garlic, pressed
1 bottle Tuscany peppers (or green chilies)

1 green sweet pepper, seeds and membrane removed
¼ pound thinly sliced Gruyère cheese

Preheat oven to 350°. Cut pita pockets into quarters and split each quarter horizontally to make 48 pieces. Squeeze the garlic over the butter and mix thoroughly. Spread this mixture over the pita wedges. Place on a cookie sheet and bake for about 3 minutes until lightly toasted. In a food processor, finely chop the green pepper and the Tuscany peppers. Spread this mixture on the pita toasts and cover each with sliced cheese. When ready to serve, turn on broiler; broil just until cheese is melted. Watch carefully. Serve immediately.

Note: This may be prepared before broiling and held for up to 1 hour at room temperature.

Bravo!

Piquant Palmiers

Easy
Do ahead
Freeze

Yield: 12 pieces
Preparing: 10 minutes
Baking: 12 minutes
May be doubled

QED

1 package (8 ounces) frozen puff
  pastry, thawed
4 tablespoons tomato purée

4 tablespoons grated Parmesan
  cheese
Freshly ground pepper

Roll out pastry into a rectangle 12 x 10 inches. Lightly spread pastry with tomato purée and sprinkle with Parmesan cheese and pepper. Roll up from the two narrow edges so that the rolls meet in the middle. Trim off the edges and slice remainder into twelve pieces. Place cut side down on a greased baking sheet, leaving room for expansion. Press down slightly to flatten. Preheat oven to 425° and bake for 12 minutes or until lightly browned.

Sausages Arabella

Easy
Do ahead
Freeze

Yield: 65 to 72 balls
Preparing: 20 minutes

1 pound mild ground sausage
1 pound hot ground sausage
1 jar (8 ounces) chutney, finely
  chopped

¼ cup dry sherry
1 cup sour cream

Mix both sausages well and shape into 1-inch balls. Fry until cooked through. Pour off grease, saving the brown bits stuck to frying pan. Remove sausage balls from pan. Combine all other ingredients in pan and warm thoroughly. Add sausage balls. Place in chafing dish or heated serving dish; serve with toothpicks.

Hot Crab, Artichoke and Jalapeño Dip
with Pita Triangles

Average
Do ahead

Yield: 10 servings (128 pita triangles)
Preparing: Dip, 30 minutes/Pita, 20 minutes
Baking: Dip, 25 to 30 minutes/Pita, 10 minutes
May be doubled

Dip:
1 large green bell pepper, chopped
1 tablespoon vegetable oil
2 (14-ounce) cans artichoke hearts, drained and finely chopped
2 cups mayonnaise
½ cup thinly sliced scallions
½ cup chopped pimiento or roasted pepper
1 cup freshly grated Parmesan cheese
1½ tablespoons fresh lemon juice

4 teaspoons Worcestershire sauce, or to taste
2 pickled jalapeño peppers, or to taste, seeded and minced (wear rubber gloves)
1 teaspoon celery salt
1 pound crabmeat, picked over
⅓ cup sliced almonds, lightly toasted
Baked Pita Triangles (see recipe)

In a small heavy skillet, cook the bell pepper in the oil over moderate heat, stirring until it is softened. Cool. In a large bowl, combine the cooked bell pepper, artichokes, mayonnaise, scallions, pimiento, Parmesan cheese, lemon juice, Worcestershire sauce, jalapeño peppers, and celery salt. Stir until thoroughly mixed; gently fold in the crab. Transfer mixture to a buttered baking or chafing dish and sprinkle with sliced almonds. The dip may be made ahead to this point, covered, and refrigerated for 24 hours. To serve, bake in a preheated 375° oven for 25 to 30 minutes, or until the top is golden and the mixture is bubbly. Serve hot with Pita Triangles.

Pita Triangles:
8 large pita bread pockets   ½ cup melted butter

Preheat oven to 375°. Cut each pita into eight wedges and split each wedge into two triangles. Arrange the triangles in a tight layer in a jelly-roll pan, rough side up. Brush them lightly with melted butter and bake in the upper third of the preheated oven for 10 to 12 minutes or until they are crisp and golden. Allow to cool in the pan and store in an airtight container at room temperature.

Note: Leftover triangles are a delicious accompaniment to soup.

Bravo!

Jake's Jumbo Lump Crabcakes

Complicated   Yield: 8 servings
Preparing: 30 minutes
Chilling: 1 hour
Cooking: 15 minutes

3 to 4 Idaho potatoes*
2 pounds jumbo lump crabmeat
7 ounces shrimp, peeled
  and deveined
2 egg whites

3 ounces plus 1 tablespoon
  heavy cream
1 cup chopped scallions (white
  and green)
1 tablespoon soft butter
Salt and pepper to taste

Pick over crabmeat, keeping all pieces as large as possible. Purée shrimp with egg whites and half of the cream. Lightly sauté the scallions in the soft butter and add to the shrimp mixture. Add salt and pepper to taste. Whip the remaining cream and gently fold into the shrimp mixture. Using a #12 ice cream scoop, place crabcakes on a cookie sheet and refrigerate 1 hour. Peel potatoes and grate with the large holes of a standard grater. Do not allow potatoes to mash back together. Gently coat each crabcake with grated potato. Sauté cakes in clarified butter over moderately high heat in a non-stick pan until they are golden on both sides.

Note: Boil the potatoes until they are almost cooked and allow them to stand overnight.

Jake's, Manayunk, PA

Crab Dip

Easy   Yield: 8 to 10 servings
Preparing: 15 minutes
Baking: 35 minutes

8 ounces cream cheese, softened
18 ounces jumbo lump crabmeat
1 clove garlic, minced
½ cup mayonnaise
2 teaspoons confectioners' sugar

1 teaspoon dry mustard
⅛ teaspoon seasoned salt
¼ cup sherry
½ cup toasted slivered almonds

Preheat oven to 350°. Pick over crabmeat to remove any shell or cartilage. Mix together all ingredients. Place in a baking dish and bake for 30 to 40 minutes until bubbly. Serve with crackers.

Crabmeat Quesadillas

Average	*Yield: 80 pieces*
Do ahead	*Preparing: 45 minutes*
Freeze	*Baking: 20 minutes*
	May be doubled or tripled

8 ounces crabmeat, flaked
  and picked over
½ cup sour cream
3 green onions, chopped
3 tablespoons canned, chopped
  green chilies
1 tablespoon fresh lemon juice
1 tablespoon chopped fresh cilantro

1 teaspoon chili powder
¼ teaspoon ground red pepper
20 flour tortillas (7-inch size)
¾ cup shredded Cheddar cheese
¾ cup shredded Monterey Jack
  cheese
1 large egg white, lightly beaten
Vegetable oil for cooking

In a medium bowl, combine crabmeat, sour cream, green onions, chilies, lemon juice, cilantro, chili powder, and red pepper. Take out one tortilla, leaving others wrapped, and spread 2 tablespoons crabmeat in the middle, leaving a 1-inch border. Sprinkle crabmeat mixture with 1 tablespoon each of Cheddar and Jack cheese. Brush edge of tortilla with egg white and cover with a second tortilla, pressing edges tightly to seal. Cover with a damp towel to keep moist. Repeat with remaining tortillas. Lightly grease a large frying pan and heat over medium high. Add one tortilla and cook until golden, about 1 minute on each side. Drain on paper towels. Repeat with remaining tortillas, greasing pan when necessary. May be made ahead. Cool completely; wrap individually and freeze for up to 1 month. To serve, defrost, if necessary. Preheat oven to 350°. Place tortillas on a cookie sheet and bake for 10 minutes, or until heated through. Cut each into eight wedges. Serve warm. These are also good served as an accompaniment to soup or salad as a luncheon combination.

Drunken Hot Dogs

Easy	*Yield: 12 servings*
	Preparing: 10 minutes
	Baking: 1 hour

1 pound hot dogs
¾ cup bourbon
½ cup brown sugar
1½ cups ketchup

1 tablespoon chopped onion
Pinch oregano
½ teaspoon rosemary

Preheat oven to 350°. Cut the hot dogs into bite-sized pieces and place in a 10 x 6 x 2-inch baking dish. Combine all other ingredients and pour over hot dogs. Bake in a 350° oven, uncovered, for 1 hour. Serve hot, with toothpicks, right from the baking dish.

Bravo!

Smoked Fish Spread

Easy Yield: 6 to 8 servings
Do ahead Preparing: 15 minutes
  May be doubled or tripled

Q E D

½ pound smoked fish (salmon,
  bluefish, etc.)
1 medium onion, finely minced
1 tablespoon capers
2 teaspoons fresh dill
  (or 1 teaspoon dried)

¼ cup sour cream (or low-fat yogurt)
¼ cup mayonnaise
Freshly ground black pepper
Chopped fresh parsley
Rye or pumpernickel bread or
  unsalted whole grain crackers

By hand, chop fish, removing any fat or skin. In a medium bowl, mix fish with
onion, capers, dill, sour cream (or yogurt), and mayonnaise. Blend well.
Refrigerate until serving time. Place in a serving dish garnished with freshly
ground pepper and chopped parsley. Serve with thinly-sliced rye or pumpernickel bread or unsalted whole-grain crackers.

Artichoke Pizza Appetizer

Easy Yield: 24 pieces
  Preparing: 45 minutes
  Baking: 10 minutes (twice)

2 (8-ounce) cans refrigerated dinner
  rolls
1 (14-ounce) can artichoke hearts,
  drained and chopped
1 (7-ounce) package Italian salad
  dressing mix

¾ cup mayonnaise
¼ cup grated Parmesan cheese
1½ cups grated Cheddar cheese
Paprika

Preheat oven to 350°. On an ungreased cookie sheet, spread out rolls, pinching
them together to make one large rectangle. Bake for 10 minutes or until golden
brown. Allow to cool completely. In a medium bowl, mix together the artichoke hearts, salad dressing mix, mayonnaise, Parmesan cheese and 1 cup
Cheddar cheese, reserving the rest of the Cheddar for later. Spread the mixture
onto the crust. Sprinkle with remaining ½ cup Cheddar cheese and paprika.
Bake for 10 minutes; cut into squares while hot. Serve warm.

Gruyère Puff in Mushroom Crust

Average   *Yield: 6 servings as a luncheon dish*
Preparing: 1 hour

Mushroom Crust:
3 cups finely chopped mushrooms
  (about 12 ounces)
1 large clove garlic, finely chopped

2 tablespoons margarine
¼ cup dry bread crumbs
1 egg white

Gruyère Filling:
1 small onion, sliced
2 tablespoons margarine
2 tablespoons flour
¼ teaspoon dry mustard
1 cup skim milk

1 cup shredded Gruyère cheese
  (4 ounces)
2 eggs, separated
1 egg white
1 tablespoon snipped fresh chives

Mushroom Crust: Preheat oven to 375°. Spray a 9 x 1¾-inch pie plate with non-stick cooking spray. In a 10-inch non-stick skillet over medium heat, melt 2 tablespoons margarine; cook mushrooms and garlic for about 5 minutes, or until most of the moisture has evaporated. Cool slightly; stir in bread crumbs. Beat 1 egg white until stiff peaks form. Fold into mushroom mixture and spread in greased pie plate. Bake in 375° oven for about 10 minutes, or until edge begins to brown and crust is set. Reduce oven heat to 350°.
Filling: In a 1-quart non-stick saucepan, heat 2 tablespoons margarine over low heat. Add onions and cook for about 3 minutes, or until onion is softened but not brown. Stir in flour and mustard; blend. Remove from heat. Stir in milk, return to heat, and bring to a boil, stirring constantly. Continue to stir and boil for 1 minute. Remove from heat. Add cheese and stir until it has melted. Beat 3 egg whites until stiff but not dry. Beat 2 egg yolks until light and lemon-colored. Stir egg yolks into cheese mixture. Fold in beaten egg whites and add chives. Spread in mushroom crust and bake in preheated 350° oven, uncovered, for 30 minutes, or until golden brown and cracks look dry. Serve immediately. Good also with a salad for lunch.

Bravo!

Chicken Wings

Easy
Do ahead

Yield: 8 to 10 servings
Preparing: 15 minutes
Baking: 1½ to 2 hours
May be doubled

3 pounds chicken wings
½ cup chicken broth
⅓ cup soy sauce
3 tablespoons brown sugar
3 tablespoons vinegar

1 teaspoon ground ginger
2 tablespoons sherry (optional)
Pinch garlic powder
Pinch MSG (optional)
Dash pepper

Wash and disjoint chicken wings, discarding tops. Mix together all ingredients except MSG and pepper. Marinate chicken for at least 2 hours in this mixture. Preheat oven to 325°. In a baking tray large enough to hold all chicken in one layer, place chicken and marinade; sprinkle with MSG and pepper. Bake for 1 to 2 hours, or until fairly dry. Serve at room temperature.

Ceviche-Marinated Fish

Average

Yield: 6 servings
Preparing: 20 minutes
Marinating: About 4 hours

2 pounds firm white fish or scallops
2 cups fresh lemon juice
2 cups chopped onions
½ cup tomato purée
½ cup tomato juice
1 tablespoon salt
15 green stuffed olives, sliced

2 tablespoons Worcestershire sauce
1 teaspoon Tabasco sauce
2 jalapeño chili peppers
3 firm tomatoes, chopped
3 avocados, halved, pit removed
Parsley

Cut fish into ½-inch chunks and marinate in the lemon juice for 4 hours in the refrigerator, until fish is opaque. Pour off half the liquid. Add all other ingredients except avocados; mix thoroughly. To serve as a first course, place fish in the hollow of the avocado and sprinkle with parsley. May be served on crackers as an appetizer.

Mussels, Steamed on the Half Shell

Easy Yield: 8 servings
Preparing: 45 minutes
May be doubled or tripled

Bicarbonate of soda	**1 sprig thyme**
2 quarts live mussels	**¼ bay leaf**
2 tablespoons chopped shallots	**5 tablespoons butter**
2 sprigs parsley	**1 cup dry white wine**

Place mussels in a large bowl and cover with cold water to which bicarbonate of soda has been added (one pinch to one quart); allow to soak for ½ hour. Scrub mussels thoroughly, trim, and scrape. Heat 2 tablespoons butter in a large saucepan and add shallots, parsley, thyme, and bay leaf. Add cleaned mussels; pour in white wine. Bring to a boil and cook, covered, over high heat until mussels are fully open (5 to 10 minutes). Remove them from the liquid. Take one shell from each mussel and discard. Loosen mussel in remaining half shell and place in a serving bowl. Keep hot. Remove parsley, thyme, and bay leaf from the cooking liquid and swirl in the remaining 3 tablespoons of butter. Pour over mussels. Sprinkle with chopped parsley and serve with toothpicks.

Cheddar-Stuffed Mushrooms

Easy Yield: 1 to 1½ dozen
Do ahead Preparing: 30 minutes
Baking: 20 to 25 minutes
May be doubled

1 pound medium-size mushrooms	**½ cup chopped walnuts**
3 tablespoons melted butter	**¼ cup chopped parsley**
1 cup chopped onion	**¼ teaspoon salt**
1 cup soft bread crumbs	**¼ teaspoon ground black pepper**
1 cup shredded Cheddar cheese	

With a damp cloth gently clean mushrooms and remove the stems. Chop stems and set aside. Lightly brush the top only of the mushrooms and set them upside down on a lightly greased shallow pan. Heat the remaining butter in a frying pan and lightly sauté the onions and mushroom stems until the onions are translucent (about 3 minutes). Add remaining ingredients, remove from heat, and mix lightly. Spoon the onion mixture into the mushroom caps. (May be made ahead to this point, and set aside until ready.) Preheat oven to 350°. Bake for 20 to 25 minutes, or until hot. Serve immediately.

Bravo!

Marinated Onions

Easy Yield: 8 to 10 servings
Do ahead Preparing: 15 minutes
  Marinating: 3 days

3 pounds onions, sliced very thinly
1 cup malt vinegar
1 cup olive oil
1 teaspoon dry mustard

1 teaspoon salt
1 teaspoon pepper
Cream cheese (optional)
Crackers

Place the sliced onions in a large glass or plastic container with a lid. Mix together the vinegar, oil, mustard, salt, and pepper, and pour over onions. Allow to marinate in the refrigerator for 3 days, turning several times. The onions will become limp. To serve, remove as many onions as needed from the marinade and place on crackers with cream cheese. Without cream cheese, serve as a side dish with meat, or on a bed of lettuce as a salad.

Greg's Easy Does It

Easy Yield: 6 to 8 servings
Do ahead Preparing: 10 minutes
  May be doubled

12 ounces cream cheese, at room
  temperature
2 tablespoons mayonnaise
1 teaspoon finely grated onion
Garlic powder to taste

Chili sauce
6 to 8 ounces lump crabmeat or
  cooked small shrimp
Plain crackers

In a food processor or by hand, thoroughly blend cream cheese, mayonnaise, onion, and garlic powder. Spread mixture in a low-sided 8-inch serving dish. Spread over the top a thick layer of chili sauce and top with crabmeat or shrimp. Serve at room temperature with crackers.

Cheesy Sausage Puffs

Easy
Do ahead

Freeze

Yield: 54 pieces
Preparing: 10 minutes
Chilling: 1½ hours (approximately)
Baking: 15 to 20 minutes

1 package (8 ounces) frozen puff pastry sheets, thawed 1 egg 1 tablespoon milk	12 ounces fresh pork sausage ⅓ cup grated Parmesan cheese Poppy or sesame seeds

Unfold pastry sheets and cut each into 3 strips (9¼ x 3¼ inches), using the dough's natural folds as a guide. In a small bowl, beat egg with milk until blended. Brush each strip of pastry with this glaze. Divide sausage into six equal portions and form a roll, ¾-inch in diameter, down the center length of each pastry strip. Sprinkle cheese over sausage. Fold pastry over sausage and pinch the edges tightly together with a fork to seal. Brush with glaze and sprinkle with seeds. Refrigerate until firm. (May be frozen at this stage, wrapped well. Allow to thaw before continuing.) Cut each strip into nine pieces each about 1-inch long. Arrange on a baking sheet lined with brown paper (may use grocery bag, but NOT one from recycled paper). Refrigerate until firm (about 1 hour). (May also be frozen at this point.) Preheat oven to 400°. Bake until sausage is cooked, about 15 to 20 minutes. Serve warm.

Santa Fe Shrimp

Average
Partial do ahead

Yield: 50 pieces
Preparing: 40 minutes
Chilling: Overnight
Cooking: 8 minutes

2 pounds medium shrimp (about 50) 3 large red bell peppers, roasted (making 2 cups) 1 tablespoon finely chopped garlic	2 tablespoons cilantro, washed and dried ½ cup olive oil, plus 2 tablespoons Pinch salt and pepper

Peel and devein the shrimp and set aside in a bowl. To make the marinade, place the roasted peppers, garlic, cilantro, ½ cup olive oil, salt, and pepper in a food processor; blend thoroughly. Pour over shrimp; cover; and refrigerate overnight. Bring to room temperature before cooking. Over medium-high heat in 2 tablespoons oil, sauté the shrimp in batches until they turn pink (about 2 minutes). Keep warm until all are cooked. Serve on skewers with a little of the marinade drizzled on top, if desired.

Culinary Concepts, Philadelphia, PA

Bravo!

Scallops in Mustard Dill Sauce

Easy — Yield: Serves 8
Do ahead — Preparing: 30 minutes
May be doubled or tripled

2½ pounds bay scallops or sea
   scallops halved and quartered
½ cup Dijon mustard
4 teaspoons dry mustard
2 tablespoons sugar
½ cup white wine vinegar

⅔ cup vegetable oil
½ cup chopped fresh dill
Salt and Tabasco sauce to taste
Lettuce leaves
4 ripe avocados

Poach scallops in water until just opaque (about 5 minutes), being careful not to overcook. Do not boil. Rinse under cold water, drain, and refrigerate. Combine mustards and sugar. Stir in vinegar and gradually add oil, stirring constantly so as not to separate. Add dill, salt, and Tabasco sauce. Combine with scallops and refrigerate. Line plates with lettuce leaves, halve avocados, and fill with scallop mixture. Accompany with toast points. As a variation, this dish may be served as an hors d'oeuvre with toothpicks and crackers.

Bean Dip — Spicy and Low-Fat

Easy — Yield: 6 servings (1½ cups)
Do ahead — Preparing: 15 minutes
May be doubled or tripled

1 can (15½ ounces) kidney beans,
   drained and rinsed
2 cloves garlic, pressed
1 teaspoon chili powder
3 tablespoons fresh lime juice
1 tablespoon vegetable oil

1 teaspoon cumin
½ cup medium-hot salsa
1 tablespoon water
2 green onions, minced
Cilantro sprigs

Purée all ingredients, except green onions and cilantro, in a food processor. Place in a serving dish and garnish with green onion and cilantro sprigs. Surround with tortilla chips.

Deviled Cheese Bites

Average   Yield: 30 to 36
Do ahead   Preparing: 20 minutes
Chilling: 2 to 3 hours
May be doubled or tripled

2 (4½-ounce) cans deviled ham
16 ounces cream cheese
1 cup chopped pecans
4 ounces blue cheese

Onion powder to taste
Chopped fresh parsley
Miniature pretzel sticks

With electric mixer, combine ham, cheese, pecans, cheese, and onion powder. Chill 2 to 3 hours. Form mixture into small balls; roll in parsley. Refrigerate. Just before serving, place balls on a serving tray and insert pretzel into the center of each.

Mock Pâté de Foie Gras

Easy   Yield: 6 servings
Do ahead   Preparing: 30 minutes

¼ cup chopped onions
½ pound chicken livers
1 tablespoon butter
¼ cup light- or no-fat mayonnaise
1 tablespoon prepared horseradish

½ teaspoon paprika
½ teaspoon salt
Crackers
Crudites (optional)

Melt butter in skillet and sauté onions until translucent. Add chicken livers and cook until centers are pink. Transfer to a food processor fitted with a steel blade; process until smooth. Add mayonnaise, horseradish, paprika, and salt. Process until thoroughly mixed. Place in a crock, covered, and allow to stand in the refrigerator for 1 day to improve flavor. Garnish with parsley. Serve with crackers or crudites.

Bravo!

Sage Derby Cheese

Easy   Yield: 8 servings
Do ahead   Preparing: 10 minutes

1 (8-ounce) package cream cheese, softened
1 tablespoon dried, crumbled sage leaves

2 tablespoons chopped green onions
2 tablespoons poppy seeds

In a food processor fitted with a steel blade, thoroughly mix cream cheese, sage, and onions. Refrigerate until firm and easy to handle; form cheese into a small wheel and press poppy seeds onto all sides. Serve with crackers

Tuna Pâté

Easy   Yield: 8 to 10 servings
Do ahead   Preparing: 10 minutes
Chilling: At least 3 hours or overnight

1 (8-ounce) package cream cheese, softened
2 (7-ounce) cans tuna, packed in water, drained

2 tablespoons chili sauce
2 tablespoons chopped parsley
1 teaspoon instant minced onion
½ teaspoon Tabasco sauce

Mix all ingredients in a bowl. Pack into an oiled 4-cup mold. Chill at least 3 hours. Unmold onto a serving plate and serve with crackers.

Note: Pretty when packed into a fish mold. Cut a green olive slice for eye and a slice of pimiento for mouth. Garnish with parsley. Also makes a good sandwich if there are leftovers.

Cheese Toasts

Easy   Yield: 20 pieces (approximately)
Preparing: 10 minutes
Baking: 2 minutes
May be doubled or tripled

1 baguette French bread
1 cup coarsely grated Parmesan cheese

½ cup mayonnaise

Slice bread ¼-inch thick. Mix cheese and mayonnaise and spread on one side of each slice. Place on a cookie sheet and broil about 4 inches away from the heat for about 2 minutes, watching carefully that it does not burn. The toasts are ready when they are bubbly and beginning to brown. Serve hot.

Irene's Oyster Crackers

Easy   Yield: 12 servings
Do ahead   Preparing: 10 minutes

1 package dry Ranch dressing
¾ cup mild olive oil
1 tablespoon chopped fresh dill

1 teaspoon lemon pepper
½ teaspoon garlic salt (optional)
1 (8-ounce) box small oyster crackers

Place the Ranch dressing, oil, dill, lemon pepper, and optional garlic salt in a large bowl and mix well with a fork or a whisk. Add the oyster crackers and quickly, with your hands or a large spoon, mix thoroughly to coat as evenly as possible. Place one paper lunch bag inside another to make two double bags; put half the mixture into each bag. Fold the tops tightly and shake well. Set aside for several hours. Remove from bags and store in an airtight container.

Ginger Dip

Easy   Yield: 2 cups
Do ahead   Preparing: 10 minutes
            Chilling: 24 hours

1 cup sour cream
1 cup mayonnaise
2 tablespoons finely chopped
   crystallized ginger

⅓ cup chopped parsley
1 (6-ounce) can water chestnuts,
   drained and finely chopped
1 tablespoon soy sauce

Combine all ingredients and refrigerate for 24 hours or overnight. Serve with crackers, celery, carrot sticks, chips, etc.

Bravo!

Shrimp Canapé

Average *Yield: 12 serving*
Partial do ahead *Preparing: 30 minutes*

3 to 4 ounces cooked shrimp (reserve 2 for garnish), finely chopped
1 to 2 tablespoons peeled and finely chopped Granny Smith apple
1 tablespoon finely chopped green bell pepper
1 tablespoon finely chopped red bell pepper

Tomato slices
Mayonnaise, to taste
Butter mashed with anchovy paste, to taste
Canapé toast
1 to 2 hard-boiled eggs

Mix shrimp, apple, peppers, and mayonnaise. Spread toast with anchovy butter, place a slice of tomato on the toast, and top with shrimp spread. Garnish with a bit of whole shrimp and finely chopped egg yolk.

Vivian's Cumin Cheese Wafers

Average *Yield: 4 dozen*
Do ahead *Preparing: 15 minutes*
Freeze *Chilling: At least 4 hours*
  Baking: 10 to 15 minutes
  May be doubled

½ cup butter or margarine
½ pound sharp Cheddar cheese, shredded
1 teaspoon salt

½ teaspoon cayenne pepper
1 teaspoon cumin
1 cup flour

In a large bowl, cream butter or margarine. Add cheese and beat until mixture is very light. Beat in salt, cayenne, and cumin. Blend in flour. On wax paper, shape the dough into a smooth roll about 2 inches in diameter, wrap tightly, and refrigerate for at least 4 hours or up to 3 days. Preheat oven to 375°. With a very sharp knife, cut roll into ¼-inch slices and bake on an ungreased cookie sheet for 10 to 15 minutes, or until the edges are golden brown. Place on wire racks to cool. Stored in an airtight container, these wafers will keep up to 2 weeks. They may be frozen.

Pecan Brie Tarts

Average

Yield: 36 tarts
Preparing: 30 minutes
Baking: 10 minutes for cases
5 minutes for filling

---

1 (11-ounce) package pie crust mix
¼ pound Brie cheese

¼ cup ground pecans

Preheat oven to 375°. Prepare pie crust mix according to directions. Divide into 36 balls and press into 2-inch tart pans. Press up sides, making a small cup. Prick sides and bottom with a fork. Bake until crisp and lightly brown (8 to 10 minutes). Remove from baking pan. Cut Brie into 36 ½-inch squares. Place a square of cheese in each tart shell. Sprinkle with ground pecans. Bake on a cookie sheet until Brie melts and starts to bubble (about 5 minutes). Watch closely.

Note: Tarts may be assembled up to 1 hour ahead and allowed to stand at room temperature. Bake when ready to serve.

Shrimp Pita Wedges

Average
Do ahead

Yield: 72 pieces
Preparing: 1 hour
Baking: 10 minutes

½ pound shrimp, cooked and cleaned
2 tablespoons fresh lemon juice
1 (8-ounce) package cream cheese, softened
1 cup shredded sharp Cheddar cheese
4 green onions, chopped

2 cloves garlic, minced
2 tablespoons chopped fresh parsley
1 teaspoon cumin
1 teaspoon chili powder
6 pita bread rounds, split and cut into wedges

Sprinkle lemon juice over the cooked shrimp, cover, and chill for 30 minutes. In a food processor fitted with a steel blade, combine all ingredients, except the pita bread, and process until smooth (about 1 minute), scraping bowl sides occasionally. Preheat oven to 350°. Place pita wedges on baking sheets and spread with shrimp mixture. Bake for 10 minutes, or until bubbly. Garnish with more parsley if desired. Serve hot.

Note: 1) Shrimp mixture may be made ahead and kept in the refrigerator, covered, for up to 2 days. Warm slightly to make spreading easy. 2) The wedges may be spread and frozen, then brought to room temperature before final baking.

Bravo!

Shrimp in Dill Mayonnaise

Average
Do ahead

Yield: 8 servings
Preparing: 45 minutes
Chilling: At least 6 hours or overnight
May be doubled

2 pounds shrimp, peeled
  and deveined
4 tablespoons fresh snipped dill
2 tablespoons fresh parsley leaves,
  finely chopped

½ cup mayonnaise
1 teaspoon Dijon mustard
1 medium onion, thinly sliced
Lettuce leaves
Sprigs of dill for garnish (optional)

In a large saucepan bring salted water to a boil. Add the shrimp; when the water returns to a boil, remove pan from heat and allow to stand for 2 minutes. Drain shrimp and slice them in half lengthwise. Combine the dill, parsley, mayonnaise, mustard, and onion; mix well. Transfer the onion mixture to a large plastic bag. Add shrimp and shake gently until shrimp are evenly coated. Chill for at least 6 hours or overnight. Serve over lettuce leaves, garnished with dill sprigs.

Note: An excellent, do-ahead first course for a Thanksgiving dinner.

Eggplant Antipasto

Easy
Do ahead

Yield: 3 cups
Preparing: 20 minutes
Cooking: 40 minutes
Chilling: Overnight

3 cups peeled eggplant,
  cut in ½-inch cubes
⅓ cup chopped green pepper
1 medium onion, chopped
¾ cup sliced fresh mushrooms
2 cloves garlic, crushed
⅓ cup olive oil
1 (6-ounce) can tomato paste

¼ cup water
1 teaspoon oregano
2 tablespoons wine vinegar
½ cup sliced, stuffed green olives
1 teaspoon salt
⅛ teaspoon freshly ground black
  pepper

Put eggplant, green pepper, onion, mushrooms, garlic, and oil in a skillet and cook, covered, over low-to-moderate heat, for 10 minutes, stirring occasionally. Add tomato paste, water, oregano, vinegar, olives, salt, and pepper; simmer, covered, until eggplant is tender, about 30 minutes. Transfer to a covered container and refrigerate overnight to blend flavors. Serve on a lettuce leaf as a first course, or as a dip with saltines.

Fresh Vegetable Pizza

Easy
Do ahead

Yield: 60 appetizers
Preparing: 30 minutes
Baking: 14 to 19 minutes
May be doubled or tripled

2 cans (8 ounces) crescent dinner rolls
8 ounces sour cream
1 to 2 tablespoons horseradish
¼ teaspoon salt
⅛ teaspoon pepper

2 cups fresh mushrooms, chopped
1 cup small broccoli flowerets
½ cup chopped green bell pepper
½ cup chopped green onions
1 cup chopped, seeded tomatoes

Preheat oven to 375°. Separate dough into four long rectangles. Place rectangles crosswise on ungreased 15 x 10 x 1-inch baking sheet. Press over bottom and 1 inch up sides. Seal perforations. Bake 14 to 19 minutes until golden brown. Cool completely. Blend sour cream, horseradish, salt, and pepper. Spread over crust. Top with remaining ingredients. Cut into small pieces. Store in refrigerator.

Note: May also add grated carrot, shredded cheese, etc.

Sun-Dried Tomato Brie

Easy

Yield: Depends on size of Brie
Preparing: 15 minutes
Baking: 5 to 10 minutes

1 wheel Brie, any size, chilled
Oil-packed sun-dried tomatoes

Thinly sliced prosciutto

Preheat oven to 350°. Slice chilled Brie in half horizontally and cut off the top rind. Mince enough sun-dried tomatoes to cover bottom half of Brie. Place top half over tomato layer. Place 3 or 4 prosciutto slices on top of cheese. Place on a baking sheet and bake, watching carefully, until cheese is soft and begins to melt.

Bravo!

Crabmeat and Shrimp in Phyllo

Average
Partial do ahead

Yield: 8 servings
Preparing: 30 minutes
Baking: 10 minutes

8 ounces cream cheese, softened
Pinch salt
Pinch white pepper
1 teaspoon lemon juice
3 ounces jumbo lump crabmeat,
  picked over

3 ounces peeled, deveined, lightly
  poached, and diced shrimp
1 package Phyllo sheets
Melted butter

Optional sauce:
1 cup mayonnaise
Chopped fresh parsley

Snipped fresh chives
Chopped fresh tarragon

Beat cream cheese, salt, pepper, and lemon juice until smooth and creamy. Gently fold in crab and shrimp. Following the directions on the box of phyllo, brush 3 sheets of phyllo with melted butter and place on top of each other. Cut these sheets into 4 long strips. Place 1 heaping tablespoon of the crab mixture on the corner of each strip and fold into triangles (flag style). Brush tops lightly with melted butter to seal. Repeat until all crab mixture is used. Preheat oven to 350°. Place triangles on a baking tray and bake for 10 minutes, or until golden brown. Serve warm.

Note: This appetizer may be held in the refrigerator for up to 3 days and may be accompanied by mayonnaise flavored with fresh herbs or served alone.

The Skippack Roadhouse and 4022 Rotisserie, Skippack, PA

Taco Cheese Dip

Easy

Yield: 8 to 10 servings
Preparing: 20 minutes

Q E D

8 ounces cream cheese, softened
1 pint sour cream
1 jar (12 ounces) chunky-style salsa
1 tomato, chopped

1 green bell pepper, chopped
Sliced black olives, to taste
1 package (12 ounces) taco-flavored
  cheese, shredded

Cream together cream cheese and sour cream. Add remaining ingredients, except cheese, and pour into a serving dish. Sprinkle with cheese. Serve with taco chips.

Cheese Shrimp Soufflé

Easy Yield: 12 servings
Preparing: 10 minutes
Baking: 30 minutes

1 can (4.5 ounces) shrimp	**1 teaspoon snipped chives**
8 ounces cream cheese, softened	**2 tablespoons mayonnaise**
½ teaspoon garlic salt	**1 tablespoon fresh lemon juice**

Preheat oven to 350°. Mix all ingredients together. Put into a baking dish. Bake for 30 minutes. Top with lemon wedges, parsley, and paprika.
Serve warm with crackers.

Japanese Chicken Wings

Easy Yield: 6 to 8 servings
Do ahead Preparing: 15 minutes
Marinating: 1 hour or overnight
Baking: 1 hour
May be doubled

2 pounds chicken wings	**¼ teaspoon crushed red pepper**
½ cup soy sauce	**(optional)**
½ cup dry sherry or sake	**1 garlic clove, crushed**
½ cup sugar	**1½ teaspoons grated fresh ginger root**

Cut wings into three parts and discard wing tips, saving them for stock or some other use. Mix together the soy sauce, sherry, sugar, red pepper, garlic, and fresh ginger, and pour over chicken to coat well. Allow to marinate for at least 1 hour at room temperature, or in the refrigerator overnight, turning occasionally. Preheat oven to 375°. Put chicken and marinade in a pan large enough to hold all in one layer, and bake, uncovered, for 1 hour, turning once. Serve warm or cold.

Bravo!

Brie with Sun-Dried Tomatoes II

Easy Yield: 6 servings
Do ahead Preparing: 10 minutes
Standing: 1 hour

1 pound Brie, chilled
2 tablespoons minced parsley
2 tablespoons freshly ground
Parmesan cheese

4 oil-packed sun-dried tomatoes,
drained and minced (reserve 1
tablespoon oil)
6 cloves garlic, minced and mashed
1 teaspoon dried basil, crumbled

Remove rind from Brie with a sharp knife. Place Brie on a serving plate. In a small bowl, combine parsley, Parmesan cheese, tomatoes, garlic, basil, and reserved oil. Spread over Brie. Let stand for at least 1 hour before serving. Serve with crackers.

Pinwheels

Easy Yield: 35 to 40
Do ahead Preparing: 10 minutes
Freeze Baking: 15 to 20 minutes
Chilling: At least 1 hour
May be doubled or tripled

1 pound small Kielbasa sausage,
finely chopped or ground, divided

1 package (17¼ ounces) frozen puff
pastry dough, thawed
1 cup hot and sweet mustard, divided

In a skillet, brown sausage over medium heat. Drain well. Unfold one sheet of pastry dough; spread with ½ cup mustard. Spread half of sausage over mustard. Roll up, jelly-roll fashion. Seal well. Repeat with second sheet of pastry. Wrap tightly in plastic wrap; refrigerate at least 1 hour. Preheat oven to 450°. Cut rolls into ½-inch thick slices. Place on ungreased baking sheets. Bake 15 to 20 minutes, or until puffed and golden. Do not burn bottoms. Serve warm or at room temperature. Extra mustard can be used for dipping.
Can be frozen before baking.

Heavenly Spiced Pecans

Easy
Do ahead

Yield: 4 cups
Preparing: 5 minutes
Baking: 30 minutes
May be doubled

3 tablespoons butter
3 tablespoons Worcestershire sauce
½ teaspoon salt
½ teaspoon cinnamon

¼ teaspoon cayenne pepper
¼ teaspoon Tabasco sauce
Dash ground cloves
4 cups shelled pecan halves

Preheat oven to 300°. In a 9-inch square baking pan, melt the butter and stir in all the other ingredients except the nuts. Add the pecans and toss well for 2 or 3 minutes until all the nuts are completely coated. Bake for 30 minutes, tossing once after 15 minutes, or until nuts are crisp and slightly browned. Be careful not to burn them. When they are done, resist the temptation to taste until they are cool! The house smells heavenly while these are cooking.

Galette de Crabe Le Bec-Fin (Crab Cake)

Average

Yield: 10 portions
Preparing: 30 minutes
Cooking: 15 minutes

1 bunch scallions
1 teaspoon butter
1 pound jumbo lump crabmeat, picked over
14 ounces peeled, deveined large shrimp
2 eggs

1 pint heavy cream
Salt and pepper to taste
2 tablespoons Dijon mustard
1 tablespoon Worcestershire sauce
1 tablespoon Tabasco sauce
1 tablespoon light oil

Place bowl of food processor in the refrigerator to chill. Cross cut the scallions, the white and some green, ⅛-inch thick. Melt the butter in a small pan, add the scallions, and stir to coat. Cover and cook gently for 2 or 3 minutes, until scallions are tender but not browned. Mix scallions with the picked-over crabmeat. Set aside. Put the shrimp in the very cold food processor bowl and process on high about 1 minute. Scrape down sides of bowl and add the eggs. Process on high until mixture is smooth and shiny (about 2 minutes). Scrape bowl down. Process again; while the machine is running, slowly add the cream. Scrape bowl down. Process one more time to make sure the cream is incorporated. Add mustard, Tabasco, and Worcestershire; mix well. Add salt and pepper to taste. Fold this mixture into the crab and scallions. In a non-stick pan over medium-high heat, sauté the mixture in ½-cup portions, cooking approximately 2 minutes on each side. Serve immediately.

Le Bec-Fin, Philadelphia, PA

Bravo!

Insalata Bianca with or without Carpaccio

Average Yield: 8 servings
Partial do ahead Preparing: 30 minutes

1 head white curly endive
1 bulb fennel
3 stalks celery
1 daikon (Chinese white radish)
½ pound filet of beef sliced
 ¼-inch thick

2 ounces lemon juice
6 ounces olive oil
Salt and pepper to taste
¼ pound solid piece
 of Parmesan cheese
Lemon wedges

Wash endive and tear into small pieces. Set aside. Remove coarse outer layer of fennel and the stalk. Slice paper thin the fennel (lengthwise), celery (horizontally), and daikon. Set aside. (There should be equal quantities of endive to vegetables.) Place filet slices between two pieces of plastic wrap, and pound gently with mallet until paper thin. Keep in the plastic, refrigerated, until ready to serve. Dressing: Blend the lemon juice and olive oil and add salt and pepper to taste. With a carrot peeler, shave the Parmesan to make delicate curls. Set aside. When ready to serve, toss the salad ingredients with the dressing. Peel one piece of the plastic wrap from the beef and center on the plate, smoothing and shaping with your fingers. Remove top piece of plastic. Season lightly with salt and freshly ground pepper. Place a small mound of insalata bianca on top of the carpaccio, decorate with Parmesan curls, and serve with half a lemon.

Note: The success of this salad requires everything to be sliced paper thin.

Orso Restaurant, New York, NY

Top toasted rye rounds with a thin slice of onion, a dash of mayonnaise, and a slice of Swiss cheese. Broil until the cheese melts.

Breads

Muffins

and Brunch

Drumrolls

Bravo!

The Philadelphia Sound

Approaching its centenary, The Philadelphia Orchestra can be proud of its musical heritage. Each of its six Music Directors has made a unique and significant contribution to its success: Fritz Scheel (1900-1907) with his organizational skill and musicianship; Carl Pohlig (1907-1912) with his expansion of the Orchestra; Leopold Stokowski (1912-1941) with his bold innovation and musical exploration of contemporary composers; Eugene Ormandy (1936-1980) with his renewed attention to the classical repertoire; Riccardo Muti (1980-1992) with his expansion of the Orchestra's range to include a greater emphasis on American music and on operatic repertoire; and Wolfgang Sawallisch (1993-present) with his enthusiasm for all periods of music, especially the classical and romantic European repertoire and early 20th century works.

Many distinguished guest conductors have occupied the podium of The Philadelphia Orchestra including Abbado, Beecham, Giulini, Leinsdorf, Mitropoulos, Munch, Szell, Toscanini, and Walter. Fine young conductors, such as Reiner and Rodzinsky, apprenticed with The Philadelphia Orchestra. William Smith served for many years as a talented Associate Conductor. Assistant Conductor André Raphel Smith was recently appointed; the Orchestra's Principal Second Violin Luis Biava was named Conductor in Residence; and Bernard Rands is Composer in Residence. Charles Dutoit is summer Music Director at the Mann Music Center and the Saratoga Performing Arts Center.

Several prominent composers, including Casals, Kreisler, and Rachmaninoff, established close relationships with The Philadelphia Orchestra: Rachmaninoff called the Philadelphians his "very favorite orchestra." World and national premieres of works by Prokofiev, Shostakovich, Sibelius, Stravinsky, Strauss, and many others have been given by the Orchestra. Numerous works by contemporary composers such as Barber, Bartok, Copland, Hindemith, Menotti, Persichetti, Rands, and Rochberg have entered the orchestral repertory.

Talented singers, pianists, conductors, and instrumentalists have contributed to the glorious presence that is The Philadelphia Orchestra. We are especially proud of Philadelphia artists such as Marian Anderson, Anna Moffo, Peter Serkin, Susan Starr, André Watts, and Efrem Zimbalist. We are the fortunate beneficiaries of a rich and remarkable legacy of orchestral brilliance.

Cranberry-Orange Bread

Easy
Do ahead
Freeze

Yield: 1 loaf
Preparing: 20 minutes
Baking: 1¼ hours
May be doubled

2 cups flour
¼ teaspoon salt
2 teaspoons baking powder
4 tablespoons butter (unsalted)
¾ cup plus 1 tablespoon sugar

1 tablespoon diced orange zest
1 egg
⅔ cup fresh orange juice
2 cups cranberries
1 cup chopped walnuts

Preheat oven to 350°. Butter a 9 x 5 x 3-inch loaf pan and line bottom with buttered parchment. Combine flour, salt, and baking powder. Cut in butter with a pastry blender. Add the ¾ cup sugar and orange zest. In a separate bowl beat egg; add juice. Pour over dry ingredients and mix together. Add cranberries and nuts. Pour into pan. Sprinkle top with 1 tablespoon sugar. Bake 1 hour and 15 minutes. Cool in pan 20 minutes. Invert and allow to cool completely.

Cranberry Bread

Easy
Do ahead
Freeze

Yield: 1 loaf
Preparing: 30 minutes
Baking: 1 hour 10 minutes

2 cups sifted flour
½ teaspoon salt
1½ teaspoons baking powder
½ teaspoon baking soda
1 cup sugar
1 egg, beaten

2 tablespoons melted shortening
½ cup orange juice
2 tablespoons hot water
½ cup chopped walnuts or pecans
1 cup cranberries, cut in half
Melted butter (optional) for final coat

Preheat oven to 325°. Sift together flour, salt, baking powder, baking soda, and sugar. In a separate bowl, mix beaten egg with melted shortening, orange juice, and hot water. Combine the wet ingredients with the dry. Fold in nuts and halved cranberries. Pour into a lightly greased loaf pan (9 x 5 x 4-inch) and bake on the middle rack of a preheated 325° oven for 1 hour, or until a toothpick inserted in the middle comes out clean. Cool in the pan for 10 minutes. Remove from pan and while still warm brush with melted butter (optional). Wrap in wax paper when cool and store in the refrigerator. Allow to sit for 3 hours before slicing.

Bravo!

Charlotte's Triple Treat

Easy	Yield: 3 loaves
Do ahead	Preparing: 15 minutes
Freeze	Baking: 45 minutes

3 cups applesauce
1 cup margarine, melted
4 teaspoons baking soda
2 cups sugar
1 pound raisins

2 teaspoons cinnamon
1 teaspoon allspice
1 teaspoon nutmeg
1 teaspoon salt
4 cups flour

Preheat oven to 350°. In a large saucepan, mix applesauce and melted margarine and heat until bubbling. Remove from heat; add all other ingredients, blending well with each addition. Divide into 3 lightly greased loaf pans (9 x 5 x 3-inch) and bake for 45 minutes or until a tester comes out clean.

Super-Easy Olive-Walnut Bread

Easy	Yield: 2 free-form loaves
Do ahead	Preparing: 25 minutes
Freeze	Rising: 30 to 40 minutes
	Baking: 40 to 45 minutes

¾ cup (4 ounces or about 30)
  kalamata olives, pitted
  and chopped
1 cup (3 ounces) walnuts,
  coarsely chopped
3½ cups bread flour

2½ teaspoons salt
¼ ounce fast-rise yeast
5 tablespoons chopped parsley
3 tablespoons olive oil
13 ounces lukewarm water

Mix together olives, walnuts, flour, salt, yeast, and parsley; when thoroughly blended, make a well in the center. Put oil and water in the center and mix well to make a soft dough. Knead until smooth and elastic, for about 10 minutes, adding a little flour to your hands if the dough is too sticky. Divide dough in half and form two 7- to 8-inch rolls. Place on oiled baking sheet, well apart. Rub a little oil on top and cover loosely with plastic wrap, allowing room to rise. Allow to rise 30 to 40 minutes or until double in size. Preheat oven to 425°. Gently push sides inward so loaves are not so flat. Bake for 12 minutes, then lower temperature to 350° and continue to bake for 25 to 30 minutes until lightly browned and hollow sounding when tapped on the bottom.

Note: The only hard part of this bread, pitting the olives, may be done ahead. Store pitted and chopped olives, ready for use, in the freezer.

Zucchini Bread

Average
Do ahead
Freeze

Yield: 2 loaves
Preparing: 30 minutes
Baking: 1 hour
May be doubled

3 eggs
2 cups sugar
1 cup vegetable oil
1 tablespoon vanilla
2 cups coarsely grated zucchini
   (about 1 pound)

3 cups flour
1 tablespoon cinnamon
1 teaspoon baking soda
¼ teaspoon baking powder
¼ teaspoon salt
1 cup chopped walnuts

Preheat oven to 350°. In a large mixing bowl, beat the eggs and gradually add the sugar. Add the vegetable oil and vanilla, beating until thick and lemon-colored. Stir in the zucchini. In a separate bowl sift together the flour, cinnamon, baking soda, baking powder, and salt. Add the dry ingredients to the zucchini mixture and blend. Fold in the walnuts and pour into two 9 x 5 x 3-inch loaf pans that have been lightly greased and dusted with flour. Bake for 1 hour, or until a toothpick inserted in the middle comes out clean.

Note: To prepare the zucchini, wipe clean, trim ends, and do not peel before grating.

Coconut Bread

Easy
Do ahead
Freeze

Yield: Four small or two large loaves
Preparing: 20 minutes
Baking: 1 hour

1 cup margarine, softened
2 cups sugar
6 eggs
1 (7-ounce) package flaked coconut

1 (12-ounce) box vanilla wafers,
   crushed
1 teaspoon vanilla
1 cup chopped pecans

Preheat oven to 325°. Grease 4 small (5¾ x 3¼ x 2-inch) or 2 large (9 x 5 x 3-inch) loaf pans. Line bottoms with wax paper. Cream together margarine and sugar. Add eggs, one at a time, beating well after each addition. Fold in coconut, vanilla wafers, and nuts. Pour into prepared pans. Bake for 1 hour. (If large pans are used, bake 1 hour and 20 minutes.) Cool in pan 15 minutes before slicing.

Bravo!

Tomato Basil Boule

Average Yield: 2 small loaves
Do ahead Rising: 2 hours 45 minutes
Baking: 60 minutes

¾ teaspoon fresh yeast
4 ounces warm water
6 ounces cold water
  (approximately 60°)

2 ounces sun-dried tomatoes (soaked
  in water and chopped)
2 tablespoons chopped fresh basil
2 cups unbleached flour
1½ teaspoons salt (sea salt is best)

Dissolve yeast in warm water. Add cold water. Stir in tomato and basil. Add flour and salt, and stir with a wooden spoon until dough forms. Turn out onto a floured surface and knead until dough tightens. Allow to rise at room temperature in an oiled bowl, 1½ to 2 hours. Turn onto a lightly floured surface, divide dough in 2 equal portions, and pat each into a rectangle. Using your hands, roll dough toward you, sealing each time you turn it. When you get to the end turn the dough around and repeat the rolling-and-sealing process. When you have formed a tight roll, begin to round it by moving it from palm to palm, back and forth and around, until you have formed a smooth ball. Place on a floured cookie sheet, cover with a dry, floured towel, and allow to rise at least 45 minutes. Preheat oven to 450°. Cut boule in a flower pattern (using the top as your center, cut vertical slashes about 1½ inches long and about 3 inches apart around the sides of the boule with a razor blade). Spray with a light mist of water before placing loaves in the oven. Bake for 1 hour, until golden brown.

Note: A hollowed-out tomato basil boule makes an attractive (and delicious) serving container for your favorite salad or antipasto. The bread scooped out can be cut into cubes and dried overnight, or lightly sautéed in olive oil, for croutons.

Baker Street, Narberth, PA

Strawberry Bread

Easy   Yield: 2 loaves
Do ahead   Preparing: 15 minutes
Freeze   Baking: 1 hour

3 cups flour, sifted
2 cups sugar
1 teaspoon baking soda
1 teaspoon salt
1 teaspoon cinnamon

1 cup vegetable oil
4 eggs, lightly beaten
2 (10-ounce) packages frozen
    strawberries, puréed

Preheat oven to 350°. Lightly grease and flour 2 bread tins (9 x 5 x 3-inch). In a large bowl combine all the ingredients and mix thoroughly. Divide mixture between the 2 prepared tins and bake for 1 hour, or until tester comes out clean. Allow to cool for 10 minutes before removing from tins to a rack. Cool completely before serving.

Angel Rolls

Average   Yield: 5 to 6 dozen
Do ahead   Preparing: 20 minutes
Freeze   Baking: 15 minutes

5 cups flour
¼ cup sugar
3 teaspoons baking powder
1 teaspoon salt
1 teaspoon baking soda

1 package yeast
2 tablespoons warm water
2 cups buttermilk
½ cup solid shortening (margarine or
    butter)

Preheat oven to 400°. In a large bowl combine flour, sugar, baking powder, salt, and baking soda. Cut in the solid shortening. Dissolve yeast in 2 tablespoons warm water and add to buttermilk. Add buttermilk to flour mixture and mix well. Roll dough to ¼-inch thickness and cut with a biscuit cutter. Dip rolls in melted butter and bake on an ungreased baking sheet for 15 minutes. Cool on a rack, and store in an airtight container or freeze.

Note: Makes enough for a large gathering.

Bravo!

Cinnamon-Apple Bread

Average	Yield: 1 loaf
Do ahead	Preparing: 40 minutes
Freeze	Baking: 1 hour

2 eggs	½ cup butter
3 teaspoons cinnamon	½ teaspoon salt
1 teaspoon vanilla	2 cups flour
1 teaspoon baking soda	4 medium tart apples, peeled
1 cup sugar	and diced

Topping:
2 tablespoons butter, softened	¼ cup flour
¼ cup brown sugar	1 teaspoon cinnamon

Preheat oven to 350°. Grease a 9 x 5 x 3-inch loaf pan. In a large bowl beat eggs slightly. Add cinnamon, vanilla, soda, sugar, butter, and salt to egg mixture. Combine. Mix in flour and apples. Pour into prepared pan. Combine topping ingredients and sprinkle over top of cake. Bake 1 hour.

Easiest of Popovers

Easy	Yield: 5 or 6 popovers
Partial do ahead	Preparing: 10 minutes
	Chilling: Several hours
	Baking: 30 to 45 minutes

2 eggs	½ teaspoon salt
1 cup all-purpose flour	Oil spray
1 cup milk	Grated Parmesan cheese

Mix together the eggs, flour, milk, and salt and beat for 30 seconds to 1 minute. (It is better to under-beat than to over-beat.) Refrigerate this batter for several hours. Spray or lightly grease 6 popover pans or custard cups, and dust each one with Parmesan cheese. When ready to bake, fill the cups three-fourths full and place in a cold oven. Turn the heat to 450° and bake for 30 to 45 minutes.

Applesauce Cake

Easy   Yield: One 9 x 5 x 2-inch loaf
Do ahead   Preparing: 40 minutes
Baking: 1 hour

½ cup butter, softened
1 cup sugar
1 large egg, well beaten
1 teaspoon vanilla
2 cups flour
2 teaspoons baking soda

½ teaspoon cinnamon
¼ teaspoon ground cloves
1½ cups applesauce
2 cups coarsely chopped walnuts
1 cup dates, chopped fine

Preheat oven to 350°. Cream together butter and sugar. Add egg and vanilla. In another bowl, combine remaining ingredients; add to butter and egg mixture. Stir well by hand and pour into a well-greased, floured 9 x 5 x 3-inch bread pan. Bake for 1 hour, until center is set. Cool. Wrap in heavy-duty foil. Cake is better after standing for a few days, refrigerated.

Pauline's Banana Bread

Easy   Yield: 1 large loaf or 2 small
Do ahead   Preparing: 20 minutes
Freeze   Baking: 45 to 50 minutes

3 to 4 ripe bananas, mashed
1 cup sugar
1 egg
1½ cups flour

¼ cup melted butter
1 teaspoon baking soda
1 teaspoon salt
1 cup chopped walnuts

Preheat oven to 325°. Mix all ingredients except the walnuts in a bowl until completely blended. Add the walnuts and mix again. Pour into 2 buttered 9 x 5 x 3-inch loaf pans and bake for 45 to 50 minutes, or until a tester comes out clean. (If you want a higher loaf, pour all the batter into 1 loaf pan and bake for 1 hour.)

Bravo!

Blueberry Cake

Easy   Yield: 1 cake
Preparing: 40 minutes
Baking: 35 minutes

2 cups sifted flour
⅔ cup sugar
2 teaspoons baking powder
½ teaspoon salt
½ cup butter, softened

Topping:
½ cup light brown sugar
1 tablespoon butter

2 eggs, slightly beaten
1 teaspoon vanilla
½ to ¾ cup milk
2 cups blueberries

½ teaspoon cinnamon
¼ cup chopped pecans

Preheat oven to 375°. Sift together dry ingredients. Cut in softened butter. Add eggs, vanilla, and milk. Beat 3 minutes, then add berries. Spread evenly into an 9 x 9-inch pan. Mix topping by creaming together butter, sugar, and cinnamon. Add pecans and spread over cake. Bake for 35 minutes.

Onion-Cheese Wedges

Easy   Yield: 6 to 8 servings
Preparing: 15 minutes
Baking: 20 to 25 minutes

½ cup chopped onion
1 tablespoon margarine
1 egg, beaten
½ cup milk

1½ cups packaged biscuit mix
1 cup grated sharp American cheese
1 tablespoon melted butter
Poppy seeds

Preheat oven to 400°. Grease an 8 x 1½-inch round baking dish. Cook onion in margarine until tender but not brown. Combine egg and milk; add to biscuit mix and stir just until moistened. Add onion and half of cheese. Spread dough in prepared pan. Sprinkle top with remaining cheese and poppy seeds. Bake for 20 to 25 minutes. Cut in wedges and serve hot.

Note: Very good when served with soup or salad.

Pepperoni Bread

Average
Do ahead

Yield: 6 servings
Preparing: 1¼ hours
Baking: 40 minutes

1 loaf frozen bread dough
½ pound pepperoni, sliced

12 ounces shredded mozzarella
   cheese
1 egg yolk, whipped

Thaw bread dough. Let rise according to package instructions. Preheat oven to 350°. Grease a cookie sheet. Spread dough out on the cookie sheet to form a large rectangle. Lay pepperoni over dough; sprinkle cheese over pepperoni. Roll dough jelly-roll style; pinch together ends and seam. Place seam-side down on cookie sheet. Score top of loaf with knife at 2- to 3-inch intervals. Brush with egg. Bake 40 minutes or until golden.

Orange-Raisin Muffins

Average
Do ahead
Freeze

Yield: 40 to 50 small muffins
Preparing: 30 minutes
Baking: 12 to 15 minutes
May be doubled

1 cup sugar
¼ pound (1 stick) unsalted butter
2 eggs
1 teaspoon baking soda
1 cup buttermilk
2 cups flour

½ teaspoon salt
1 cup raisins
Zest of 1 orange
Juice of 1 orange
Sugar for dusting

Preheat oven to 400°. Lightly grease small muffin pans, or line with small muffin paper cups. Cream butter and sugar until light and fluffy. Add the eggs, one at a time, and mix well. In a separate bowl, mix baking soda with buttermilk. Sift flour and salt together, and, alternating with the buttermilk mixture, add it to the butter, sugar, and eggs, starting and finishing with the flour and salt. Mix well. In a food processor or blender, grind together the raisins and orange zest, and fold into the batter. Spoon batter into the muffin tins, filling each one three-quarters full. Bake for 12 to 15 minutes. Remove muffins from tins and while they are still warm, brush the tops with orange juice and sprinkle with a little sugar.

Bravo!

Banana Coconut Muffins

Easy	Yield: 10 to 12 muffins
Do ahead	Preparing: 20 minutes
Freeze	Baking: 20 to 25 minutes

1½ cups sifted flour
½ cup oat bran
Dash cream of tartar
1 teaspoon baking soda
2 teaspoons baking powder
½ teaspoon salt
½ cup brown sugar

6 tablespoons shortening
1 teaspoon vanilla
2 large eggs, slightly beaten
1 cup ripe bananas, mashed
¼ cup coconut, plus extra to sprinkle
   over tops of muffins

Preheat oven to 400°. In a large bowl, combine flour, oat bran, cream of tartar, soda, baking powder, and salt. Mix thoroughly. In a separate bowl, cream sugar and shortening. Whip in eggs. Add vanilla, bananas, and coconut. Stir well. Add dry ingredients to banana mixture, stirring just to moisten. Fill muffin cups, sprayed with nonstick coating, three-quarters full. Bake for 20 to 25 minutes.

Raisin Carrot Muffins

Easy	Yield: 48 miniature muffins
Do ahead	Preparing: 20 minutes
Freeze	Baking: 18 minutes

2 cups flour
1 cup sugar
2 teaspoons baking powder
½ teaspoon cinnamon
¼ teaspoon ginger
½ cup shredded carrot
½ cup raisins

½ cup chopped walnuts
1 (8-ounce) can crushed pineapple,
   undrained
2 eggs
½ cup melted butter
1 teaspoon vanilla extract

Preheat oven to 375°. With a spoon, mix together flour, sugar, baking powder, cinnamon, ginger, carrot, raisins, and walnuts. In another bowl combine pineapple, eggs, butter, and vanilla. Stir pineapple mixture into dry ingredients just until blended. Spoon into greased muffin tins and bake for 18 minutes, or until lightly browned. Turn out onto a rack to cool.

Jamaican Banana Muffins

Easy   Yield: 24 muffins
Do ahead   Preparing: 20 minutes
Freeze   Baking: 20 minutes
    May be doubled

6 ounces butter, softened	3 cups flour
1½ cups sugar	1½ teaspoons baking soda
3 eggs, lightly beaten	1½ teaspoons salt
4 to 5 ripe bananas, mashed	1 cup walnuts

Preheat oven to 350°. Grease 24 muffin cups. Cream together butter and sugar. Stir in eggs; add bananas. Sift together flour, soda, and salt. Stir into liquid ingredients until well blended. Fill muffin cups two-thirds full. Bake 20 to 25 minutes.

Lemon-Crunch Blueberry Muffins

Easy   Yield: 1 dozen muffins
    Preparing 10 to 15 minutes
    Baking: 15 to 20 minutes

1¾ cup flour	1 cup milk
⅓ cup wheat germ	¼ cup vegetable oil
⅓ cup sugar	1 egg
3 teaspoons baking powder	1 cup blueberries
½ teaspoon salt	

Topping:
    5 to 6 tablespoons sugar mixed
    with grated rind of 1 lemon

Preheat oven to 425°. Grease or paper-line 12 muffin cups. In a large bowl, combine flour, wheat germ, sugar, baking powder, and salt. In a small bowl, combine milk, oil, and egg. Beat slightly. Add liquid ingredients to flour mixture all at once. Stir until ingredients are just moistened. Fold in blueberries. Fill muffin cups two-thirds full. Sprinkle with topping. Bake 15 to 20 minutes. Serve hot from the oven!

Bravo!

Eggs Fantastic

Easy   Yield: 12 servings
Do ahead   Preparing: 40 minutes
Freeze   Baking: 45 minutes

2 tablespoons oil
1 medium onion, diced
¼ pound mushrooms, sliced
1 pound sausage meat
12 eggs
6 tablespoons sour cream
1 cup salsa

8 ounces American cheese, sliced
  or shredded
8 ounces Cheddar cheese, sliced
  or shredded
8 ounces mozzarella cheese, sliced
  or shredded

Preheat oven to 400°. Heat oil in a skillet and sauté onions until translucent, about 5 minutes. Add mushrooms and sauté until they are just soft. Transfer to a paper towel-lined bowl. In the same pan cook the sausage, separating it with the back of a wooden spoon until it loses its pink color and is thoroughly cooked. Drain sausage well on paper towels and add to the onions and mushrooms. Combine eggs and sour cream in a blender and blend for 1 minute. Pour into a lightly greased 9 x 13-inch pan and bake for 12 to 15 minutes, until it is set in the middle. Remove from the oven and spread with salsa. Add the sausage mixture and top with the cheeses. May be refrigerated or frozen at this point. To serve, preheat the oven to 300° and bake, uncovered, for 45 minutes. Allow to sit for 10 minutes before serving.

Magda Eggs

Easy   Yield: 4 servings
Preparing: 10 minutes
Baking: 2 to 3 minutes
May be doubled

8 large eggs, beaten
1 tablespoon chopped fresh parsley
1 teaspoon snipped fresh chives
½ cup grated Gruyère cheese

1 tablespoon Dijon mustard
2 tablespoons butter
Salt and pepper to taste
Croutons

QED

Mix together eggs, herbs, cheese, and mustard. Heat butter in a large nonstick frying pan. Pour egg mixture into pan and cook for 1 minute. Add salt and pepper. Stir quickly. Cook 1 minute longer, stirring, until eggs are just soft on top. Serve with croutons sprinkled on top.

Egg Casserole

Easy
Partial do ahead

Yield: 4 to 6 servings
Preparing: 15 minutes
Baking: 1 hour
May be doubled

2 cups herb croutons or stuffing
   cubes
1 cup shredded Cheddar cheese
4 eggs
½ teaspoon salt
1 teaspoon chopped onion

2 cups milk
½ teaspoon dry mustard
Dash pepper
4 slices bacon, cooked crisp
   and crumbled

Lightly grease a 2-quart casserole and cover the bottom with the croutons, then the cheese. In a blender, beat together the eggs, salt, onion, milk, mustard, and pepper. Pour over croutons. Cook the bacon until crisp; pat dry with paper towels. Crumble bacon and sprinkle it over the egg mixture. (Casserole may be refrigerated at this point.) Preheat oven to 325°. Bake casserole for 55 to 60 minutes, or until eggs are set. Bacon curls may be added as a garnish. Like a soufflé, this casserole puffs up beautifully; it also collapses quickly. Display it as soon as it comes out of the oven, and eat it as soon as possible.

Orange Crumb-Coated French Toast

Easy

Yield: 4 servings
Preparing: 30 minutes
May be doubled or tripled

5 eggs
1⅔ plus ¼ cups orange juice
   (fresh is best)
½ teaspoon salt
2½ teaspoons grated orange peel

2½ teaspoons vanilla
8 to 10 slices (approximately ¾-inch
   thick) good-quality white bread
1 cup (or more) bread crumbs
1 cup mild honey

In a bowl combine the eggs, 1⅔ cups orange juice, salt, orange peel, and vanilla. Beat well. Pour into a large, flat baking dish or pie pan. Put the bread crumbs in another flat pan. Soak each slice of bread in the egg mixture for 5 minutes, turning once. Dredge each slice in bread crumbs. Brown on a hot, lightly-oiled griddle, turning once or twice. Store cooked pieces in a warm oven while finishing the others. For a topping, combine honey with remaining ¼ cup orange juice; warm in a microwave. Do not boil. Stir to mix.
Serve French toast with the honey mixture.

Bravo!

Devonshire Toast

Easy
Partial do ahead

Yield: Variable
Preparing: 20 minutes
Soaking: 1 hour or overnight
Baking: 10 minutes

3 cups low-fat milk
4 large egg yolks, or whites,
   beaten with a fork
¼ cup Devonshire Cream liqueur
½ teaspoon cinnamon
⅛ teaspoon almond extract

¾-to-1-inch slices raisin challah bread
½ cup sliced blanched almonds
Unsalted butter or margarine
Confectioners' sugar
   or cinnamon sugar
Frozen sliced strawberries, thawed

In a large, shallow pan combine milk, egg yolks, liqueur, cinnamon, and almond extract; mix well. Soak bread slices in a single layer, turning to coat evenly. Soak for at least 1 hour; may be refrigerated overnight. Before cooking, press almonds into the batter-soaked bread. Melt butter in a sauté pan. Cook slices until golden, turning to cook both sides. To serve, sprinkle with confectioners' sugar or cinnamon sugar. Top with frozen, sliced strawberries, thawed in their juice.

Albertson's Cooking School, Wynnewood, PA

Crabmeat Toasties

Easy

Yield: 4 servings
Preparing: 10 minutes
Broiling: 3 minutes
May be doubled

8 ounces crabmeat, picked over
1 (5-ounce) jar Kraft Old English
   cheese spread
1 teaspoon dry mustard

1 tablespoon, or more, mayonnaise
4 English muffins, split
Pinch pepper

Combine cheese spread, dry mustard, and mayonnaise; blend well. Add crabmeat and mix gently. Season with pepper. Arrange muffin halves, split side up, on a baking sheet. Broil muffins for about 1 minute. When they start to color, remove from heat. Mound crabmeat mixture equally on each muffin half. Return to broiler and broil until top is lightly browned.

Note: If used as a lunch dish, serve with a tossed green salad.

Erich Kunzel

Lavash Stuffed

Easy   Yield: 8 servings
Do ahead   Preparing: 30 minutes
        Waiting: 1 hour
        May be doubled

6 lavash (obtainable from Greek food shops) each one about 12 to 18 inches in diameter
4 ounces light cream cheese softened or light mayonnaise
1 tablespoon mango chutney
¾ teaspoon curry powder
Lettuce
Sliced, smoked turkey
2 cucumbers, peeled and chopped
3 tomatoes, thinly sliced
Salt and pepper to taste

If the lavash seem hard, lightly spray with water and wrap in a damp towel while preparing the filling. Mix together, to form a smooth paste, the cream cheese, chutney, and curry powder and spread in a thin layer over the entire surface of each lavash. At one end of each lavash (to cover about ½ the surface) layer 1 leaf lettuce, cucumber, and tomato, topping all with turkey. Roll up as tightly as you can; cover and refrigerate for at least 1 hour. Shortly before serving cut the rolls into 1½-inch pieces. Serve seam side down.

French dressing is delicious served over vegetables. Add a little olive oil if the dish is to be served hot — an extra tablespoon of wine vinegar if cold. To add a bit of zip, add ½ teaspoon of oregano or dill weed.

Combine 1 tablespoon whole-grain mustard, salt and pepper, juice of 1 lemon, and 2 to 3 tablespoons butter or olive oil. Toss over cooked and drained green beans.

Bravo!

Picnic Sandwich Surprise

Average
Partial do ahead

Yield: 12 servings
Preparing: 40 minutes
Broiling: 20 minutes
Marinating: 1 hour or longer
Refrigerate: Overnight

6 red bell peppers
½ cup olive oil
¼ cup balsamic vinegar
2 small cloves garlic, minced
2 1½-pound round rye or
    pumpernickel loaves
Dijon or honey mustard
12 slices hard salami (thinly sliced)

¼ pound fresh spinach leaves,
    trimmed
12 slices provolone cheese (thinly
    sliced)
12 red onion rings (thinly sliced)
12 slices cooked white turkey
    (thinly sliced)

Char peppers over gas flame or in a broiler until blackened. Toss in a brown paper bag and let stand 10 minutes to steam. Peel, skin, and seed. Pat dry. Cut into ¾-inch strips. In a bowl combine oil, vinegar, and garlic. Add peppers; turn to coat. Marinate at room temperature for 1 hour. (May be prepared to this point 2 days ahead.) Cover tightly and refrigerate. Day before serving, drain peppers. With a sharp serrated knife cut the tops off the loaves; set aside. Remove bread from the inside of the loaves and the tops, leaving the shells of the loaves with ½ inch of bread on the sides. (Reserve removed bread for breadcrumbs or some other use.) Spread a thin layer of mustard over the inside of loaves and tops. Into each loaf layer salami, spinach, ¼ of the peppers, provolone, onions rings, and remaining peppers. Cover with turkey. Replace tops. Wrap each loaf in plastic wrap and then in foil. Refrigerate overnight. On serving day, cut each loaf into 6 wedges, held together with toothpicks.

Note: A great treat for a tailgate picnic. Goes well with a cold soup, and fresh fruit for dessert.

Soups
and Salads

Cross
Rhythm

Bravo!

The Academy of Music

The Academy of Music, a celebrated historic landmark and a focus of the cultural life of the city, is the oldest grand opera house in the United States still used for its original purpose and remains one of the busiest halls in the world, hosting myriad community functions and cultural activities. The Philadelphia Orchestra is the principal tenant of the building, which has been its home since its founding in 1900.

The Academy was designed by the Philadelphia architectural firm of Napoleon Le Brun and Gustavus Runge. Budgetary restrictions persuaded the architects to concentrate on the design of the interior, while leaving the exterior "perfectly plain and simple like a Markethouse." At a later date, the building was to be faced with marble. The opulent interior is enriched by a magnificent crystal chandelier, carved and gilded wood sculptural decorations, and painted ceiling murals. The American Academy of Music opened with a Grand Ball and Promenade Concert on January 26, 1857. Verdi's "Il trovatore" had its American premiere there in February of that year. The list of renowned artists who have performed at the Academy includes Maria Callas, Enrico Caruso, Vladimir Horowitz, Luciano Pavarotti, Anna Pavlova, Leontyne Price, Artur Rubinstein, and Pyotor Ilyich Tchaikovsky.

Numerous Presidents have visited the Academy. Ulysses S. Grant was nominated there for his second term of office in 1872. When President Grover Cleveland held his wedding dinner in the auditorium, a special wooden floor was placed over the parquet seats to allow 1,500 guests to dine and dance. The wooden floor was installed again in 1889 for the first indoor football game in Philadelphia, between the University of Pennsylvania and the Riverton Club of Princeton.

During World War II, the restaurant in the basement was converted into the Stage Door Canteen, serving refreshments and hosting stars of stage, screen, opera, concert, and radio. From June 1942 until October 1945, 2,500,000 servicemen and women were entertained there.

The Academy of Music Anniversary Concert and Ball, inaugurated in 1957, is an annual event in Philadelphia, and one of the most successful fundraising events in the country. In 1963, the Academy was designated a National Historic Landmark. Tours of the Academy are available; schedules may be obtained by contacting the Manager's Office.

Carrot and Orange Soup

Easy
Do ahead
Freeze

Yield: 6 servings
Preparing: 45 minutes
Cooling: 4 hours
May be doubled

1 large onion, peeled and sliced
1 pound carrots, peeled and sliced
3 (10¾-ounce) cans chicken broth
3 tablespoons (or less) frozen,
    concentrated orange juice

5 ounces plain yogurt
Salt and pepper to taste
Fresh peppermint, chopped, or
Fresh parsley, chopped

In a medium saucepan combine the onion, carrots, and chicken broth. Bring to a boil and simmer, covered, for 15 minutes, or until carrots are tender. Transfer to a food processor and blend until smooth. Add 2 tablespoons concentrated orange. Taste for flavor. Add more juice if necessary. Do not overwhelm; it should be subtle. Add yogurt and stir to blend. Refrigerate until cold, 4 hours or overnight. Serve cold, garnished with chopped mint or parsley.

Note: To serve hot, substitute the yogurt with light cream and serve garnished with grated orange rind and parsley.

Guiltless Creamy Carrot Soup with Fresh Herbs

Easy
Do ahead

Yield: 6 servings
Preparing: 10 minutes
Cooking: 35 to 40 minutes

⅓ cup apple juice
1 large onion, chopped
1 rib celery, chopped
2 cloves garlic, minced
6 large carrots, thinly sliced
4 cups defatted chicken stock
1 cup non-fat milk
1 tablespoon honey

¼ teaspoon freshly grated nutmeg
¼ teaspoon ground cardamom
1 teaspoon finely minced ginger root
¼ teaspoon ground cinnamon
2 tablespoons chopped parsley
2 teaspoons chopped mint
2 teaspoons chopped chives

In a large heavy saucepan bring apple juice to a simmer. Add onions, celery, garlic, and carrots. Cook 10 minutes over moderately high heat, stirring constantly. Add stock and bring to a boil. Lower heat and simmer, uncovered, until carrots are very soft (about 15 to 20 minutes). Purée in a food processor or blender, in batches. Return to pan. Add milk, honey, nutmeg, cardamom, ginger root, and cinnamon. Simmer 5 minutes. Garnish with parsley, mint, and chives. Delicious hot or cold.

Note: Best made the day before serving. For a stronger mint flavor, add the chopped mint to the final 5-minute simmer.

Bravo!

Cream of Sorrel Soup

Easy   Yield: 6 servings
Do ahead   Preparing: 20 minutes
           May be doubled or tripled

4 tablespoons butter
½ cup chopped onion
½ pound sorrel leaves, stemmed
4 tablespoons flour
Salt and white pepper

4½ cups chicken broth
2 large egg yolks
½ to 1 cup heavy cream
Freshly grated nutmeg
Chopped chives

In a heavy saucepan over low heat, sauté onion in butter. Add sorrel, increase heat to medium, and stir until wilted. Add flour; cook for 2 minutes, stirring constantly. Allow to cool slightly. In a small bowl beat egg yolks with a little of the sorrel and broth mixture, then add to saucepan. Mix. Place all in blender and process until smooth. Strain. Add cream and nutmeg. Garnish with chives.

Curried Eggplant Soup

Average   Yield: 6 servings
Do ahead   Preparing: 30 minutes

2 tablespoons olive oil
1 small (1-pound) eggplant,
    unpeeled, cubed
1 tablespoon butter
1 medium onion, peeled and chopped
½ teaspoon minced garlic
4 teaspoons flour

2 teaspoons curry powder
2 cups milk
½ teaspoon crushed, dried oregano
½ teaspoon dried rosemary
1 cup chicken broth
1 cup heavy cream
Salt and freshly ground pepper

In frying pan over high heat sauté eggplant in batches in olive oil until golden brown. Remove eggplant and reserve. Melt butter over medium heat and sauté onion and garlic until onion is translucent. Sprinkle onions with flour and curry powder and stir until well blended (about 2 minutes). Add milk and stir while mixture thickens. Add oregano, rosemary, and sautéed eggplant. Simmer, partially covered, for 20 minutes. Transfer mixture to food processor or blender, adding chicken broth little by little. Return to saucepan and bring to a boil. Add cream and serve hot, but do not boil, after addition of cream. May also be served chilled.

Harira, A Moroccan Soup

Average
Do ahead

Yield: 8 servings
Preparing: 45 minutes
Cooking: 2 hours
Soaking: 5 hours or overnight

½ **pound dried chick peas, washed and picked over**
½ **teaspoon baking soda**
4 **quarts cold water**
1 **cup olive oil**
1 **pound lamb bone (shanks, neck, or shoulder, in small pieces)**
1 **medium onion, peeled and sliced**
2 **cloves garlic, chopped**
½ **cup diced celery**

4 **tomatoes peeled and crushed or**
1 **(16-ounce) can crushed tomatoes**
2 **bay leaves**
2 **teaspoons paprika**
1 **teaspoon ginger**
½ **cup flour**
½ **pound dried lentils, washed and picked over**
½ **cup chopped fresh coriander**
Juice of 1 lemon
Salt and pepper to taste

Soak chick peas in 4 quarts of water and ½ teaspoon baking soda for 5 hours or overnight. Drain and reserve water. Set chick peas aside. Heat olive oil over medium heat in a 6-quart pot. Brown all the lamb bones gently and thoroughly. Add the onions, garlic, and celery and continue browning until vegetables are transparent but not darkened. Add the crushed tomatoes, bay leaves, paprika, and ginger. Continue cooking, stirring to prevent burning. Mix the flour in 1 cup water and add to the pot, being careful to stir constantly to prevent flour from forming lumps. Add the chick peas and their water. Add the lentils. Bring soup to a boil, reduce heat, and allow to simmer for about 2 hours, or until meat and chick peas are cooked. (Periodically check that the soup has enough water.) Just before serving, add the freshly chopped coriander and lemon juice.

Note: Harira is a vegetable/lamb soup used in Morocco during the month of August, when almost every Moroccan adult observes RAMADAN, a month-long fast for Moslems throughout the world, but more so in North Africa. Harira is the soup with which they break the fast after a 12-hour period with no eating or drinking. It is a very hearty substantial soup with ingredients that the poor can afford, ingredients that grow in abundance in Morocco. Such a soup can be a meal unto itself, depending on how much lamb is used. For this recipe, lamb bones give the soup body, flavor, and nutrition.

Bravo!

Pasta Fagioli (Bean and Pasta Soup)

Easy   *Yield: 6 servings*
Do ahead   *Preparing: 30 minutes*
Freeze   *Cooking: 1 hour 20 minutes*
   Soaking: Overnight
   May be doubled

---

2 cups dried Great Northern beans
5 cups water
½ teaspoon baking soda
2 tablespoons chopped onion
1 teaspoon chopped garlic
2 tablespoons chopped shallots
¼ cup olive oil
2 tablespoons butter
1 cup chopped, drained, canned tomatoes
2 tablespoons tomato paste
1 teaspoon Hungarian paprika
1 cup diced celery
1 cup diced carrots

1 tablespoon salt
1 teaspoon freshly ground pepper
½ teaspoon cayenne pepper (optional)
4 tablespoons chopped fresh parsley
2 tablespoons chopped fresh basil (or 1 teaspoon dried)
2 tablespoons chopped fresh thyme (or 1 teaspoon dried)
6 cups water or chicken broth
1 cup small macaroni (like pastini or very small bow ties)
3 tablespoons Parmesan, plus Parmesan for garnish

Soak beans overnight in 5 cups water and ½ teaspoon baking soda. Discard soaking liquid. Over moderate heat sauté onion, garlic, and shallots in olive oil and butter until golden. Add tomatoes and tomato paste; mix well. Add paprika, celery, carrots, salt, pepper, cayenne (optional), parsley, basil, and thyme; cover with 6 cups of water. Bring to a boil and simmer, covered, for 1 hour, or until the beans are tender. Add pasta and cook for another 20 minutes. Sprinkle with cheese and a few drops of olive oil. Serve hot. Pass Parmesan as a garnish. For a richer, creamier soup, crush some of the beans before adding the macaroni.

Note: If desired, less than ¼ cup of olive oil may be used in the initial sautéing. To prepare in a pressure cooker, use the same procedure, but cook the beans for only 30 minutes. This soup freezes well and is much better 1 or 2 days after it is made.

Minestrone

Average   Yield: 8 servings
Freeze   Preparing: 30 minutes
            Cooking: 1 hour
            May be doubled

⅓ cup olive oil
¼ cup butter or margarine
1 large onion, diced
3 medium carrots, diced
3 stalks celery, diced
2 medium potatoes, peeled and diced
1 pound green beans, cut into
   1-inch pieces
6 cups water
1 (16-ounce) can tomatoes

½ (10-ounce) bag fresh spinach,
   washed and shredded
2 medium zucchini, diced
6 beef-flavored bouillon cubes
1 teaspoon salt (optional)
1 (16- to 20-ounce) can cannellini
   beans, drained
1 (16- to 20-ounce) can kidney
   beans, drained
½ cup grated Parmesan cheese
   (optional)

In an 8-quart pot heat the oil and butter over medium heat. Add the onion, carrots, celery, potatoes, and green beans; cook, stirring occasionally, until vegetables are lightly browned (about 20 minutes). Add water, tomatoes with their liquid, spinach, zucchini, bouillon cubes, and optional salt. Over high heat bring to a boil, stirring to break up the tomatoes. Reduce heat to low, cover, and simmer for 40 minutes, or until all the vegetables are tender, stirring occasionally. Do not overcook. Stir in drained beans. Continue cooking another 15 minutes, or until soup is slightly thickened. Serve sprinkled with Parmesan cheese, if desired.

To keep a head of lettuce fresh, make a thin slice across the bottom of the stalk. Place lettuce, stalk down, in an inch of water in a bowl. Seal with plastic wrap and refrigerate.

To keep fresh tomatoes firm, store at room temperature but out of direct sunlight.

Bravo!

Tomato, Fennel, White Bean Soup

Easy   Yield: 10 to 12 servings
Do ahead   Preparing: 25 minutes
       Cooking: 35 minutes
       May be doubled

3 tablespoons olive oil
1 large white onion, chopped
2 large fennel bulbs, trimmed
   and cut into thin slices
1 (28-ounce) can tomatoes
½ teaspoon salt
½ teaspoon pepper

1 tablespoon dried thyme
2 bay leaves
8 cups chicken broth
4 cups washed, shredded,
   fresh spinach
2 cups canned white beans, drained

In a large pot heat oil over moderate heat; add onion, fennel, salt, and pepper.
Cover and cook gently until onion is soft, about 5 minutes. Drain tomatoes and
reserve the juice. Chop tomatoes and add to onions along with thyme and bay
leaf. Measure reserved tomato juice and add chicken stock to equal 9 cups.
Add to pot. Bring to a boil, cover, and simmer until fennel is very soft, about 30
minutes. Remove bay leaf. Add beans and shredded spinach; cook until
spinach has wilted, about 5 minutes. Test for seasoning.

*Note: More or fewer beans may be used depending on the desired thick-
ness. The fennel leaves may be used for added flavor.*

 *To thicken soup, add
instant potato flakes.*

Roasted Red Bell Pepper Bisque

Average
Do ahead

Yield: 4 to 6 servings
Preparing: 45 minutes
May be doubled

4 large red bell peppers, roasted	2 cups "good" chicken stock,
2 tablespoons virgin olive oil	approximately
3 tablespoons butter	Juice of ½ lemon
1 large Spanish onion, minced	2 cups half-and-half
1 carrot, peeled and minced	2 cups light cream
1 stalk celery, minced	Grill-roasted fresh corn (garnish)
2 cloves garlic, minced	Chervil leaves (garnish)
Freshly ground pepper to taste	Finely chopped fresh basil (garnish)

Remove the stem, skin, seeds, and membrane from the peppers; chop and set aside. Heat the oil and butter over moderate heat, and sauté the onion for 5 to 6 minutes, or until translucent. Do not brown. Add carrot, celery, garlic, and pepper; toss until bubbling hot and well mixed. Add enough chicken stock (2 cups, approximately) to cover, and simmer, covered, for 5 minutes. Add red peppers, cover, and simmer for another 6 minutes. Add lemon juice and remove from heat. Allow to cool to just warm. Purée in batches adding half-and-half and light cream; return to heat. Bring to a simmering heat, stirring constantly. Do not boil. Serve hot, garnished with roasted corn kernels, chervil, and basil.

To roast red peppers: Cut them in half and place, cut side down, (flattening with your hand to some extent) on a broiler pan. Broil until the skins are blackened. Keep an eye on them and remove when just blackened (about 5 minutes). Remove to a brown bag and close tightly. Will peel easily when cool.

Bravo!

Meine Gemuesesuppe — My Vegetable Soup

Average   *Yield: 8 servings*
Preparing: 45 minutes
Cooking: 30 minutes

4 tablespoons olive oil
2 onions
2 carrots
2 leeks
1 small celery root, peeled
2 stalks celery
1 red bell pepper
1 green bell pepper
1 kohlrabi (use tender leaves also)

1 quart meat broth (more or less)
A few rosettes of broccoli
A handful of green beans
2 zucchini
2 tomatoes, peeled
Some lovage
Salt and pepper to taste
Plenty of parsley

Clean and chop the vegetables into ½-inch cubes. In a large (5 quart) soup pot heat olive oil. Add onions and sauté until they are lightly browned. Add carrots, leeks, celery root, celery, peppers, and kohlrabi and cook until most liquid is reduced. Add broth and cook for 5 minutes. Add tender vegetables — beans, zucchini, broccoli, tomatoes, and lovage and simmer gently (DO NOT BOIL). Add salt and pepper to taste. Before serving add plenty of parsley.

Note: If possible use fresh vegetables — I use them from my garden.

Mrs. Wolfgang Sawallisch

Chicken Creole Soup

Easy   *Yield: 6 servings*
Preparing: 20 minutes
Cooking: 25 minutes

3 tablespoons chicken fat or
   margarine
1½ cups chopped okra
¼ cup chopped onion
¼ cup chopped green bell pepper
2½ cups peeled, chopped tomatoes

1 bay leaf
4 cups chicken stock
1 cup diced, cooked chicken
1 tablespoon chopped parsley
Salt and pepper to taste

In a large saucepan melt fat over moderate heat; add okra, onion, and pepper. Cook, stirring until soft, about 5 minutes. Add tomatoes, bay leaf, and chicken broth and bring to a boil. Lower heat and simmer, covered, for 15 minutes. Adjust seasoning. Just before serving add chicken and parsley and heat through.

Vegetable Soup with Cheese and Curry

Easy
Do ahead
Freeze

Yield: 8 servings
Preparing: 1 hour 15 minutes
Cooking: 1 hour

2 quarts cold water
1 tablespoon salt
4 cups peeled, diced potatoes
3 cups peeled, sliced carrots
3 cups sliced leeks, white part and tender green

3 tablespoons butter
3 tablespoons curry powder
4 ounces crumbled blue cheese, or to taste
Nasturtium leaves (optional garnish)

In a 4-quart saucepan bring water, salt, potatoes, carrots, and leeks to a boil. Reduce heat, partially cover, and simmer for about 1 hour until the vegetables are soft. Remove from heat and purée (with a hand-mixer, a blender, or a food processor). Add butter, curry powder, and cheese. Return to low heat and stir to blend. Do not boil. When hot, ladle into soup cups and float a nasturtium leaf on top. Serve either hot or chilled with a good white wine.

Note: If blue cheese is not to your taste, substitute a good grated Cheddar.

Vegetable/Ground Beef Soup

Easy
Do ahead

Yield: 6 servings
Preparing: 10 minutes
Simmering: 1 hour
May be doubled

5 cups water
5 beef bouillon cubes
1 pound ground beef or ground turkey
1 (16-ounce) can stewed tomatoes
½ cup chopped onion

½ cup chopped celery
1 (1-pound) bag frozen, chopped mixed vegetables
Salt and pepper to taste
Worcestershire sauce to taste

In a large pan combine all ingredients except salt, pepper, and Worcestershire sauce. Bring to a boil, reduce heat, and simmer, covered, for 1 hour. Blend in a food processor and taste for seasoning. Add salt, pepper, and Worcestershire sauce, if required. Serve hot.

Bravo!

Straciatelli Soup

Easy Yield: 4 servings
Preparing: 20 minutes

Q E D

1 quart chicken broth (homemade,
  if possible)
3 eggs

1 teaspoon fresh, puréed garlic
½ (5-ounce) bag fresh spinach,
  washed, stems removed

In a large pot bring the chicken broth to a boil. In a separate bowl whisk together the eggs and puréed garlic. Drop egg mixture into boiling broth. Whisk; remove from heat. Drop spinach into soup and serve immediately.

The Skippack Roadhouse & 4022 Rotisserie, Skippack, PA

Quick Tortellini Soup

Average Yield: 6 to 8 servings
Preparing: 20 minutes

Q E D

1½ tablespoons olive oil
1 small onion, minced
8 ounces Cremini mushrooms, sliced
2 quarts chicken stock
1 small clove garlic, minced
8 ounces store-bought, fresh,
  mushroom tortellini

2 cups shredded, cooked chicken,
  smoked turkey, or smoked turkey
  sausage
8 ounces spinach leaves, washed,
  stems removed, and shredded
2 tablespoons chopped parsley
1½ tablespoons fresh thyme leaves
Salt and pepper to taste

In a large saucepan, over moderate heat, sauté onion in olive oil until soft. Increase heat and add mushrooms. Toss until they are slightly browned. Add chicken stock and garlic and bring to a slow boil. Add tortellini and cook according to directions. Add meat of your choice; heat through. Just before serving add spinach, parsley, thyme, salt, and pepper to taste.

October Bisque

Average
Do ahead

Yield: 10 to 12 servings
Preparing: 1 hour
Cooking: 40 minutes
Freeze

6 tablespoons butter
½ cup chopped leek
½ cup chopped onion
½ cup chopped celery
2 large apples, peeled, cored, and chopped
7 cups chicken stock
4 cups peeled, diced, butternut squash (1 large)
2 tablespoons flour
1 teaspoon thyme

1 teaspoon salt
½ teaspoon dried sage
¼ teaspoon turmeric
¼ teaspoon dried rosemary
Pinch nutmeg
Pinch pepper
1 cup cider
½ cup light cream
1 cup grated Swiss cheese
Chopped parsley (garnish)

In a large saucepan, over moderate heat, melt 4 tablespoons butter; sauté leek, onion, celery, and apples until soft, about 5 minutes. Purée sautéed vegetables with ½ cup chicken stock. Return to saucepan and add remaining chicken stock. Bring to a boil and cover. Lower heat and simmer for 10 minutes. Add butternut squash and cook, covered, until squash is tender (15 to 20 minutes). With a potato masher, mash chunks of squash. In a small saucepan make a roux by melting remaining 2 tablespoons butter, stirring in flour, and cooking over low heat, stirring constantly, for 3 minutes. Whisk ½ cup of hot soup into the roux and transfer resulting mixture into the soup. Stir well. Add thyme, salt, sage, turmeric, rosemary, nutmeg, and pepper to taste. Simmer 5 minutes, stirring. Add cider and cream; heat through. Remove from heat and stir in grated cheese. Serve hot, garnished with chopped parsley.

Tuna Chowder

Easy
Do ahead

Yield: 6 servings
Preparing: 25 minutes
May be doubled

1 (13-ounce) can evaporated, skim milk
1 (12-ounce) can Mexican-style corn, undrained
1 (10¾-ounce) can mushroom soup

1 (6½-ounce) can tuna, packed in water, drained
½ cup water
1 cup low-fat, sharp cheese, cubed
1 tablespoon dry minced onions
6 drops liquid hot pepper sauce

In a large saucepan, over medium heat, combine all ingredients and cover. Cook, stirring occasionally, until cheese melts. Do not boil.
Serve hot with crackers.

Bravo!

Seafood Chowder

Easy
Do ahead

Yield: 6 to 8 servings
Preparing: 10 minutes
Cooking: 20 minutes

Q E D

1 small onion, diced
1 medium potato, peeled and diced
3 tablespoons butter
1 (10¾-ounce) can cream
  of chicken soup
1 (10¾-ounce) can cream of potato
  soup

1 (10¾-ounce) can cream
  of shrimp soup
3 (10¾-ounce) soup cans milk
2 (3-ounce) cans minced clams
2 (6-ounce) packages frozen
  tiny shrimp
½ teaspoon garlic powder

In a Dutch oven sauté onion and potato in butter. Add remaining ingredients; stir until well blended. Heat until very warm. (May be made in a crock pot.)

Randy Gardner

Margarette's Seafood Chowder

Easy
Partial do ahead

Yield: 6 to 8 servings
Preparing: 20 minutes

Q E D

1 large onion, minced
2 cloves garlic, minced
1 green (or red) bell pepper, diced
¼ cup butter
2 tablespoons olive oil
2 cups clam juice or fish stock
2 cups water
1 (16-ounce) can whole tomatoes, cut
  up, undrained
2 medium potatoes, peeled,
  and diced

½ teaspoon salt
½ teaspoon fennel
½ teaspoon thyme
Dash Tabasco sauce
Dash fresh lemon juice
1 pound medium shrimp, peeled,
  and deveined
2 filets haddock or orange roughy, cut
  into bite-size pieces
½ pound tiny scallops

Sauté the onion, garlic, and green pepper in the butter and oil until translucent. Reserve. In a large 4-quart pot heat the clam juice, water, and tomatoes to boiling. Add potatoes, salt, fennel, and thyme. Cook until potatoes are tender. Add onion mixture. May be made ahead to this point. Just before serving, bring broth to a boil and drop in fish, cooking only until shrimp turns pink and fish is opaque. Add Tabasco and lemon juice to taste. Serve immediately.

Split Pea or Lentil Soup

Average   Yield: 6 to 8 servings
Do ahead   Preparing: 1 hour
Freeze   Simmering: 2 hours

1 pound green or yellow split peas or lentils
1½ tablespoons canola oil, or any
 neutral flavored oil
1 cup chopped celery, with leaves
1 cup peeled, sliced carrots
1 medium, peeled, chopped onion
1 bay leaf
1 medium garlic clove, chopped

1 (46-ounce) can chicken broth plus
 water to equal 7 cups
½ teaspoon rubbed savory
1 small smoked ham shank
Paprika (optional)
⅛ teaspoon cayenne pepper
 (optional)
Dash vinegar (optional)

Rinse and pick over peas. Soak in water to cover and bring slowly to a boil. Simmer for 35 to 40 minutes. Drain, reserving water. In a large heavy pot over moderate heat, heat oil, and sauté celery, carrots, and onion until onion is translucent. Add chicken broth and reserved water. Add peas and ham shank. Bring to a boil, reduce heat, and simmer, covered, for 2 hours. Stir often to prevent scorching. During last ½ hour, add savory. For added flavor add paprika, ⅛ teaspoon cayenne pepper, and a dash of vinegar.

Note: By putting the covered pot in a 350° oven for the 2-hour simmer, no stirring is needed, and scorching does not occur. Lentils, if substituted for peas, require no soaking, and only 15 to 20 minutes to cook.

Blue Cheese Soup

Average   Yield: 4 to 6 servings
Do ahead   Preparing: 45 minutes
Freeze   Cooking: 40 minutes

6 tablespoons sweet butter
2 cups chopped onion
1 leek, white part only, cleaned and sliced
3 ribs celery, chopped
3 medium carrots, peeled and sliced
1 medium potato, peeled and diced

1 cup dry white wine or vermouth
3 cups rich chicken broth (preferably
 homemade)
½ pound good-quality blue cheese
6 to 8 strips bacon, cooked crisp, and
 crumbled

In a large kettle, over medium heat, melt butter and cook onions, leeks, celery, and carrots until tender, covered (about 15 minutes). Add potato, wine, and stock; bring to a boil, reduce heat, and simmer, partially covered, for another 15 to 20 minutes, until potatoes are tender. Remove soup from heat and crumble in about ¾ of the half pound of cheese, stirring until it melts. Strain soup, saving broth. Purée solids with a cup of broth in a food processor or blender. Recombine with remaining broth. Heat again to simmer. Taste for flavor and add remaining cheese, crumbled, if desired. Soup may be diluted with skim milk if too strong. Garnish with crumbled bacon.

Bravo!

Avocado and Tomato Soup

Easy Yield: 4 servings
Do ahead Preparing: 25 minutes
Chilling: Several hours

2 tablespoons olive oil
2 small onions, minced
3 to 4 medium avocados
2 cups chicken broth
½ cup heavy cream
1 to 2 tablespoons lemon juice,
  to taste

2 tomatoes, peeled and finely
  chopped
1 teaspoon salt, to taste
¼ teaspoon pepper
Sour cream or yogurt
6 slices bacon, cooked crisp,
  crumbled

In a small pan over moderate heat, cook the onions in the olive oil for about 5 minutes, until they are translucent. Peel, pit, and chop the avocados, and purée them with the chicken broth in a blender or food processor until smooth. Blend in the cooked onion and the cream. Transfer this mixture to a serving bowl and stir in the tomatoes and lemon juice. Season to taste with salt and pepper. Chill for several hours. Before serving check consistency; if too thick, add more chicken broth. Serve with a drizzle of sour cream and a sprinkle of cooked bacon.

Light Chicken Florentine Soup

Average Yield: 6 to 8 servings
Do ahead Preparing: 30 minutes
Cooking: 30 minutes

2 tablespoons butter
2 medium onions, chopped
2 tablespoons flour
1½ teaspoons curry powder
3 cups chicken broth
1 cup peeled, cubed potatoes
2 carrots, peeled and thinly sliced
½ cup chopped celery

2 tablespoons chopped, fresh parsley
½ teaspoon dried thyme
2 cups cooked chicken, cubed
2 (5-ounce) cans evaporated
  skim milk
1 (10-ounce) package frozen chopped
  spinach, thawed, and squeezed dry
Salt and pepper to taste

In a large saucepan, over medium-high heat, melt butter and sauté onions until translucent (about 5 minutes). Stir in flour and curry; cook, stirring, 2 to 3 minutes. Add broth, potatoes, carrots, celery, parsley, and thyme and bring to a boil. Reduce heat to low, cover, and simmer for 10 minutes. Add chicken, evaporated milk, and spinach. Cover and simmer until heated through, about 8 to 10 minutes. Season to taste with salt and pepper.

Low-Calorie Broccoli Soup

Easy
Do ahead
Freeze

Yield: 6 servings
Preparing: 20 minutes

Cooking spray
½ cup minced onion
1 bunch (1- to 1½-pounds) broccoli
2 (10¾-ounce) cans condensed
   chicken broth
1 tablespoon butter or margarine

Salt and pepper to taste
Sour cream (optional)
Crabmeat (optional)
Parsley (optional)
Chives (optional)

Lightly grease a small frying pan with cooking spray. Add butter; when melted, add onion and cook gently until translucent. Remove tough end of broccoli, separate flowerets, and chop the stalks. Place broccoli in a separate saucepan and barely cover with water. Boil until tender-crisp, about 7 minutes. Drain. Place broccoli and onions in a food processor and purée. Add chicken broth and purée. To serve, garnish with sour cream, crabmeat, parsley, or chives.

"Lite" Split Pea Soup with Ham

Easy
Do ahead
Freeze

Yield: 12 servings
Preparing: 15 minutes
Cooking: 2 hours

4 ounces Canadian bacon, chopped
   finely
1 medium onion, peeled and chopped
2 cups green split peas, rinsed
6 cups canned low-fat chicken broth
   combined with
6 cups water or 12 cups low-fat
   chicken broth

3 medium celery stalks, chopped
3 medium carrots, peeled and
   chopped
2 medium boiling potatoes, peeled
   and chopped
1 teaspoon celery seed
Salt and freshly ground pepper
Minced fresh parsley

In a large, heavy saucepan, over medium heat, cook the Canadian bacon until fat is rendered, stirring occasionally, about 5 minutes. Add onion; cook until translucent, stirring occasionally, about 5 minutes. Add peas and stir. Add water and broth (or broth only) and bring to a boil. Reduce heat, and simmer, covered, until peas are tender, about 1½ hours, stirring occasionally to prevent sticking. Add celery, carrots, potatoes, and celery seed; cook, covered, about 30 minutes, stirring occasionally. Season to taste with salt and pepper. Ladle into bowls and garnish with parsley.

Note: An excellent Sunday-night supper served with warm, crusty bread and a salad.

Bravo!

City Market Café's Black Bean Soup

Average   Yield: 8 to 10 servings
Do ahead   Preparing: 3 hours
               Soaking: Overnight
               May be doubled

1 pound black beans, soaked
   overnight in water to cover
¼ cup olive oil
1¼ cups diced onions
1 tablespoon grated garlic
1 ham bone
2 quarts chicken stock
½ teaspoon ground cumin
½ tablespoon oregano
1 bay leaf

1 teaspoon salt
¾ tablespoon black pepper
Pinch cayenne pepper
¼ cup chopped parsley
¼ cup diced red pepper
¼ cup sherry
1 tablespoon lemon juice
Chopped onion
Chopped hard-boiled egg

Drain beans. In a large kettle, over medium heat, sauté the onions and garlic in olive oil until onions are translucent. Add the drained beans, the ham bone, the chicken stock, the cumin, oregano, bay leaf, salt, and peppers. Bring to a boil and simmer, partially covered, until the beans are tender, stirring occasionally to prevent sticking. Skim the top occasionally to remove the oil. This process should take approximately 3 hours. During the last 30 minutes stir in red peppers, sherry, parsley, and lemon juice. Remove ham bone. Serve hot, garnished with chopped onion and chopped, hard-boiled egg.

Matthew Maher, Owner, City Market Café, Savannah, GA

Wash parsley in hot water; it not only retains its flavor better but also chops more easily.

Leek and Corn Chowder

Average	Yield: 12 servings
Do ahead	Preparing: 1 hour
Freeze	May be doubled

1 pound bacon
1 cup finely chopped leeks, white part only
1 cup finely chopped onions
1 cup finely chopped celery
½ cup finely chopped green bell pepper
½ red pepper, roasted and minced
1 cup peeled, diced baking potato
1 tablespoon salt

3 sprigs English or lemon thyme
2 bay leaves
1 teaspoon paprika
2½ tablespoons flour
3½ cups light cream
5 cups fresh corn
3 cups whole milk
Chopped fresh tomato, peeled and seeded
Chopped chives

Sauté bacon until very crisp in a large heavy pan. Remove with a slotted spoon, chop, and reserve for later use. In the remaining bacon fat, over a low-to-medium heat, sauté leeks and onions for 40 minutes, stirring frequently. Add celery, green pepper, and red pepper, and cook until celery is soft. Drain vegetables in a sieve, and transfer to a large stainless steel or non-aluminum pot. Add finely diced potato, salt, thyme, and bay leaves tied with string, paprika, and 4 cups water. Stir; bring to a boil, and simmer, covered, for 15 minutes, or until potato is tender. Mix ½ cup light cream with 2½ tablespoons flour; add to the soup. Stir and cook for 2 minutes. Add milk and the rest of the cream, the corn, and the bacon, and bring to a boil. Remove thyme and bay leaves. Serve garnished with peeled, seeded, and chopped fresh tomato and chopped chives.

Note: This is Mr. Ball's all thyme favorite soup!

Duane E. Ball, Co-Owner, The Palladium, Philadelphia, PA

Bravo!

Cold Spicy Carrot Soup

Easy   Yield: 6 servings
Do ahead   Preparing: 1 hour
Freeze   Cooling: 4 hours
              May be doubled

1 tablespoon vegetable oil	¼ teaspoon ground cumin
1½ cups chopped onion	2 cups chopped carrots
1 teaspoon chopped garlic	¼ cup peeled, chopped potato
1 teaspoon chopped fresh ginger root	4½ cups defatted chicken broth
½ teaspoon turmeric	½ cup plain low-fat yogurt
½ teaspoon curry powder	Chopped fresh parsley

In a large heavy saucepan heat oil over moderate heat. Add onion and cook, stirring, for 2 minutes; add garlic and ginger. Cook 2 minutes, stirring. Add turmeric, curry powder, and cumin, and cook, stirring, 2 minutes more. Add carrots and potato and stir. Add chicken broth and bring to a boil. Lower heat and partially cover pan; simmer for 20 minutes, or until the vegetables are tender. Remove from heat. Transfer the solids and some of the broth to a food processor and process until the mixture is almost puréed, but still retains a little texture. Pour purée into a bowl and add the broth. Stir to blend. Allow to cool. Cover and refrigerate at least 4 hours, or overnight. If the soup is too thick, thin with chicken broth. Top each portion with a generous dollop of yogurt and a sprinkling of parsley.

Potato Leek Soup

Easy   Yield: 6 servings
Do ahead   Preparing: 30 minutes
              Cooking: 45 minutes
              May be doubled

1½ cups thinly sliced, well-washed leeks, white and some green	4 cups chicken stock
1 large clove garlic, minced	2 cups peeled, diced, potatoes
3 tablespoons peeled, sliced carrots	1 cup light cream
4 tablespoons butter or margarine	Salt and pepper to taste
1 head Boston lettuce, shredded	3 tablespoons dry vermouth
	Chopped chives (optional)

In a 3-quart heavy saucepan, over medium heat, sauté leeks, onions, garlic, carrots, and lettuce in butter, until leeks are soft. Do not brown. Add chicken stock and potatoes. Bring to a boil, cover, and simmer until potatoes are tender. Purée in batches in a food processor or blender. Add cream. Adjust seasoning. Add vermouth. Reheat, but do not boil. If too thick, add more stock or cream. Garnish with optional chives.

Santa Fe Corn Chowder

Easy　　Yield: 8 to 10 servings
Do ahead　Preparing: 1 hour 15 minutes
　　　　　Standing : 30 minutes
　　　　　May be doubled or tripled

6 strips bacon, diced
1 large onion, diced
4 to 5 medium potatoes, peeled
　and diced
2 (13¾-ounce) cans chicken broth
1 (1-pound) package frozen
　yellow corn

2 (4-ounce) cans chopped green
　chilies (or more if like it hot)
1 quart half-and-half
Salt and white pepper to taste
Fresh parsley or cilantro,
　finely chopped

In a large soup kettle, over moderate heat, sauté diced bacon for 4 to 5 minutes to render fat. Add onion and sauté until onion is translucent, about 5 minutes. Add diced potatoes and chicken broth. Simmer, covered, until potato is tender, about 15 minutes. Add frozen corn and green chilies; stir. Simmer, uncovered, until corn is tender, about 5 minutes. Remove from heat and allow to cool for at least 30 minutes. Return to heat; slowly add half-and-half, stirring constantly. Bring to serving temperature over a moderate heat, stirring occasionally, about 15 minutes. Do not boil. Add salt and white pepper to taste. Garnish with finely chopped parsley or cilantro.

Note: May be served with flour tortillas that have been buttered, wrapped in foil, and heated in a 300° oven for 20 to 30 minutes. A hearty "supper soup," good for a cold winter evening.

Pea/Corn Chowder

Easy　　Yield: 3 to 4 servings
　　　　Preparing: 15 minutes

1 (10-ounce) package frozen peas
1 (10-ounce) package white baby corn
1½ cups chicken broth, more or less
1 tablespoon butter

Cream (optional)
Tabasco sauce(optional)
Onion salt (optional)

Under warm running water defrost peas and corn. In a large saucepan bring peas, corn, and chicken broth to almost boiling. Purée in a food processor and strain, if desired. Return to saucepan and heat through, adding more chicken broth if too thick. Do not overcook. Taste for seasoning and add Tabasco, onion salt, and/or cream, if desired. Enjoy hot or cold.

Mrs. H. John Heinz III

Bravo!

Mint and Green Pea Soup

Easy   Yield: 6 servings
Do ahead   Preparing: 20 minutes
              May be doubled

Q E D

1 small onion, chopped
2 tablespoons butter
2 (10-ounce) packages frozen peas
½ cup mint leaves (loosely packed)
5 cups chicken broth

Salt and pepper to taste
Juice of ½ lemon
Light cream or yogurt (optional)
6 sprigs of mint

Lightly sauté onion in butter until soft (about 5 minutes). Add peas, mint, and chicken stock. Bring to a boil and simmer, uncovered, for 3 minutes. Purée in a processor. Taste for seasoning; add salt and pepper if necessary. Just before serving add lemon juice; mix well. May be served either hot or cold with a dollop of light cream or yogurt, if desired; add a sprig of mint for garnish.

Pumpkin Soup

Easy   Yield: 10 to 12 servings
Do ahead   Preparing: 1 hour

1 long-neck pumpkin, peeled
  and sliced
2 medium onions, peeled and sliced
8 apples, peeled, cored and diced
3 tablespoons olive oil
1 tablespoon thyme
2 bay leaves
2 quarts chicken stock

1 quart heavy cream
3 tablespoons curry powder
2 teaspoons cumin
2 teaspoons cinnamon
1 teaspoon nutmeg
1 teaspoon ground cloves
Baked pumpkin seeds

Sauté onions, pumpkin, and apples in olive oil in a large pot, over moderate heat, until soft. Add the thyme, bay leaves, and chicken stock, and bring to a boil. Add the cream and bring to a boil. Remove bay leaves. In a food processor purée the soup in batches; strain through 2 layers of cheese cloth. Taste and add salt and white pepper, if necessary. Serve garnished with baked pumpkin seeds.

Note: This is particularly attractive when served in whole pumpkins.

Coventry Forge Inn, Coventryville, PA

Eggplant Soup

Average
Do ahead

Yield: 20 servings
Preparing: 1 hour
Cooking: 1 hour 30 minutes
May be halved

5 medium eggplants
1 carrot
3 large onions (1½ pounds)
10 stalks celery
1 bunch leeks
1 cup olive oil

Herb Sachet:
4 bay leaves, crumbled
4 tablespoons tarragon
4 tablespoons thyme

10 cloves garlic (½ head) peeled
2 ounces butter
4 pounds tomatoes, peeled
** and chopped**
5 quarts water

4 tablespoons basil
4 tablespoons whole black
** peppercorns**

Peel and dice the eggplants. Set aside. Peel and dice the carrots and onions. Dice the celery and place in a bowl of cold water. Remove the fiber bottoms from the leeks and any coarse or damaged outer leaves. Cut them into thin rounds and add them to the celery in the bowl of cold water to remove any dirt or sand. Heat a large, heavy-bottomed soup pot for 10 minutes over high heat. Add the olive oil and, immediately, the eggplant and garlic. Cook the eggplant, stirring frequently, until very soft. While the eggplant is cooking carefully remove the celery and leeks from the bowl of water, leaving any sand and dirt at the bottom of the bowl. In a heavy pot with a lid, heat the butter and add the carrots, onions, celery, and leeks. Stir to coat, cover, and cook over low heat until the vegetables are soft, about 15 minutes. Remove from heat. When the eggplant mixture is very soft, add tomatoes, vegetables, water, and herb sachet. Simmer soup, partially covered, for 1½ hours. Remove herb sachet. Purée soup in batches.

Note: Drained, canned tomatoes may be substituted for fresh tomatoes during winter months.

Jeffrey Miller, Caterer, Lansdowne, PA

Bravo!

Sour Cream Mushroom Soup

Average   Yield: 8 servings
Preparing: 30 minutes

Q E D

3 tablespoons butter
¼ teaspoon nutmeg
½ teaspoon dried tarragon
1 large onion, peeled and chopped
½ pound mushrooms, sliced
¼ cup flour
3½ cups beef broth

1 cup sour cream
½ cup half-and-half
½ cup whipping cream
Salt and pepper to taste
Lemon juice
Hot pepper sauce
Paprika

In a 3-quart saucepan melt butter over medium heat. Add nutmeg and tarragon, and cook for 1 minute to blend flavors. Add onion and cook until tender and translucent. Add mushrooms and cook until tender but still firm. Add flour. Cook and stir until all liquid is absorbed and there are no flour lumps. Stir in beef broth and heat just to boiling. Reduce heat, add sour cream, and stir until sour cream has no lumps. Add half-and-half and whipping cream. Season to taste with salt, pepper, lemon juice, and hot pepper sauce. Heat, stirring frequently, to serving temperature, not boiling. Garnish soup bowls with a sprinkling of paprika.

Note: This soup can still be delicious by using "more modest" ingredients.

Cream of Mushroom Soup

Easy   Yield: 6 to 8 servings
Do ahead   Preparing: 10 minutes
Freeze   Cooking: 20 minutes

Q E D

1 pound fresh mushrooms,
    with stems
4 green onions, including tops
¼ cup butter
¼ teaspoon dry mustard
¼ teaspoon black pepper
1 teaspoon salt

Dash cayenne pepper
¼ cup flour
2 cups chicken broth
2 cups milk, or half-and-half, heated
⅓ cup sherry
½ cup sour cream
Paprika

Coarsely chop (not by processor) mushrooms, stems, and onions. In a large (2-quart) heavy saucepan, over moderate heat, heat the butter and add the vegetables. Cook, stirring, for 5 minutes. Add mustard, pepper, salt, and cayenne. Stir. Add flour and blend thoroughly. Add chicken broth and milk that has been heated but not boiled. Cook, stirring constantly, until thickened. Just before serving, add the sherry and stir. Serve hot in bowls with 1 tablespoon of sour cream and a dash of paprika.

Split Pea Soup

Easy	*Yield: 6 to 8 servings*
Do ahead	*Preparing: 30 minutes*
Freeze	*Simmering: 2½ to 3 hours*

1 (1-pound) package split peas, washed	1 bay leaf
6 cups water	3 carrots, sliced
4 peeled onions	6 cups chicken stock
4 whole cloves	Salt and pepper to taste
1 ham bone (or ham shank)	¼ teaspoon sugar

Place peas in a large, heavy pot and cover with 6 cups of water. Bring to a boil and simmer for 1 hour, skimming the top occasionally. Stick 1 clove into each onion. Add onions, ham bone, bay leaf, carrots, and chicken stock; simmer for 1½ to 2 hours, adding more chicken broth if too thick. Remove and discard ham bone but save any pieces of ham that may be attached to it. Purée the soup in a food processor, in batches. Taste for seasonings and add salt and pepper, if desired. Add pieces of ham. To serve, bring carefully to a boil, stirring occasionally to prevent sticking.

Cold Cucumber Soup

Easy	*Yield: 4 servings*
Do ahead	*Preparing: 15 minutes*
Freeze	*Chilling: 3 to 4 hours*
	May be doubled

2 medium cucumbers, peeled, seeded, and chopped	3 tablespoons chopped dill plus more for garnish
½ cup walnuts	1 teaspoon salt
3 large cloves garlic, or to taste	½ teaspoon freshly ground pepper
¼ cup olive oil	½ cup low-fat sour cream or yogurt
1 cup chicken stock	Red pepper, thinly sliced (garnish)
3 tablespoons chopped fresh cilantro	Chopped dill

In a blender or food processor purée cucumbers, walnuts, garlic, olive oil, chicken broth, cilantro, parsley, salt, and pepper. Chill for 3 to 4 hours. Before serving, blend in sour cream or yogurt. Garnish each serving with sliced red pepper and a sprinkle of chopped dill.

Bravo!

Gazpacho

Easy
Do ahead

Yield: 6 servings
Preparing: 25 minutes
Chilling: 2 hours

2 large tomatoes
1 large cucumber, peeled and seeded
1 medium onion, finely chopped
1 medium green bell pepper,
  finely chopped
1 pimiento, drained

24 ounces V-8 juice
⅓ cup red wine vinegar
¼ teaspoon Tabasco sauce
1½ teaspoons salt
⅛ teaspoon ground black pepper
1¼ cups chopped chives

Drop tomatoes into boiling water for 10 seconds and remove skin. In a food processor or blender place 1 tomato, half the cucumber, half the onion, half the green pepper, and the pimiento. Add ½ cup V-8 juice. Process at high speed for 30 seconds. Mix this purée in a bowl with the remaining V-8 juice, vinegar, Tabasco, salt, and pepper. Refrigerate, covered, for 2 hours. Chop the remaining tomatoes. Mix the chives with the remaining chopped vegetables and add to soup. Serve very cold.

Jellied Clam Madrilene

Easy
Do ahead

Yield: 8 servings
Preparing: 15 minutes
Chilling: 4 hours or overnight
May be doubled or tripled

2 quarts Clamato juice
1 cup jellied consommé
½ cup medium dry sherry
4 packages gelatin

8 tablespoons jumbo lump crabmeat
Celery salt
Fresh parsley, chopped

In a large pot place the Clamato juice and the consommé. Dissolve the gelatin in the sherry and, when it is soft, add it to the pot. Bring to a boil and simmer, covered, for 6 minutes. Transfer the soup to a non-reactive, rectangular container; cool and refrigerate, covered, at least 4 hours, or overnight. To serve, draw a knife criss-cross through the jellied soup and serve the resulting glistening squares in cups or on a bed of lettuce, garnished with 1 tablespoon of crabmeat, a sprinkling of celery salt, and chopped parsley.

John Alden Philbrick, Officier Commandeur, Confrerie Des Chevaliers Du Taste Vin, Pennsylvania

Walnut Romaine Salad

Easy   *Yield: 6 to 8 servings*
Partial do ahead   *Preparing: 45 minutes*

Sugar-coated walnuts:
½ cup broken walnuts   3 tablespoons sugar

Dressing:
¼ cup walnut oil   2 tablespoons white wine vinegar
2 tablespoons honey   1 tablespoon dry white wine
½ teaspoon salt   ½ teaspoon ground ginger

Salad:
1 head romaine lettuce, torn in pieces   2 stalks celery, sliced
2 oranges, peeled and sectioned   3 green onions, sliced
1½ cups halved strawberries or
  seedless red grapes

Sugar-coated walnuts: In a medium skillet combine walnuts and sugar. Cook, stirring over low heat until sugar melts and coats walnuts. Turn out onto a sheet of waxed paper. Cool, break in pieces, and reserve.
Dressing: In a blender combine oil, honey, salt, vinegar, wine, and ginger. Blend, chill, and reserve.
Salad: In a large bowl combine lettuce, oranges, berries, celery, and onions. When ready to serve, toss salad with dressing and sugar-coated walnuts.

Spinach Salad with Hearts of Palm

Easy   *Yield: 10 servings*
Preparing: 10 minutes

3 tablespoons red wine vinegar   2 pounds fresh spinach, washed,
2 teaspoons Dijon mustard   stems trimmed
1 teaspoon sugar   1 (14-ounce) can hearts of palm,
⅓ cup olive oil   drained and sliced
Salt and pepper to taste   1½ teaspoons grated lemon peel

Whisk together vinegar, mustard, and sugar. Gradually whisk in oil. Season with salt and pepper. In a salad bowl combine spinach with hearts of palm and lemon peel. Pour dressing over spinach mixture just before serving.

Bravo!

Broccoli-Cauliflower Salad

Easy   Yield: 6 servings
Do ahead   Preparing: 30 minutes
Chilling: Overnight
May be doubled or tripled

2 cups cauliflower flowerets, in bite-
  size pieces
2 cups broccoli flowerets, in bite-size
  pieces
½ cup chopped Vidalia onion

1 cup mayonnaise
3 tablespoons white vinegar
2 tablespoons sugar
2 tablespoons sesame seeds

Combine cauliflower flowerets, broccoli flowerets, and onion. In a small bowl mix mayonnaise, vinegar, sugar, and sesame seeds. Add to vegetable mixture and refrigerate for 24 hours before serving.

Broccoli Salad

Easy   Yield: 8 servings
Do ahead   Preparing: 15 minutes
Marinating: 5 to 6 hours
May be doubled

Salad:
2 bunches broccoli (flowerets only,
  approximately 2½ pounds)
1 large red or sweet onion, finely
  chopped

Dressing:
1 cup mayonnaise
¼ cup sugar
2 tablespoons cider vinegar

½ cups raisins, soaked in hot water
  and a dash of white wine
½ cup toasted pine nuts or shaved
  almonds

Freshly ground pepper to taste
Crumbled crispy bacon, optional

Reduce broccoli flowerets to minute pieces in a food processor using on/off button (or chop finely with a very sharp knife). Drain raisins thoroughly. Mix together broccoli, onion, and raisins.
Dressing: Combine mayonnaise, sugar, cider vinegar, and ground pepper. About 5 or 6 hours before serving, toss broccoli mixture with dressing. Just before serving, mix in nuts and sprinkle on bacon, if desired.

Note: Dried cranberries may be substituted for the raisins.

Cilantro Slaw

Average Yield: 6 to 8 servings
Do Ahead Preparing: 30 minutes
  May be doubled or tripled

QED

1 head (1 pound) green cabbage
1 small onion, minced

2 tablespoons minced fresh cilantro
  (coriander leaves)
1 English cucumber (1 pound)

Lime and Garlic Dressing:
Salt and pepper
½ cup salad oil

⅓ cup fresh lime juice
2 cloves garlic, minced or pressed

Salad: In a food processor with the fine blade, or by hand, slice cabbage. In a large bowl combine cabbage, onion, and cilantro. Cut cucumber into 3-inch-long narrow sticks (like matchsticks) and add to cabbage. Salad may be covered at this point and refrigerated for 1 day.
Lime and Garlic Dressing: Whisk together oil, lime juice, and garlic. May be made up to 2 days ahead.
Assembly: Reblend the dressing and add to the cabbage mixture; mix well to coat. Taste for seasonings adding salt and pepper to taste.

Note: Serve with grilled meats or poultry. A light and refreshing salad.

Cherry Tomatoes with Vegetable Vinaigrette

Easy Yield: 4 servings
Do ahead Preparing: 15 minutes

QED

1 pint cherry tomatoes
⅔ cup parsley leaves
3 medium scallions cut into
  1-inch pieces
2 medium stalks celery cut into 1-inch
  pieces

3 tablespoons vegetable oil
4 teaspoons vinegar
¾ teaspoon dried oregano
¾ teaspoon salt
¾ teaspoon celery seed
Black pepper to taste

Put tomatoes into a 1-quart bowl; set aside. In a food processor pulse parsley 15 seconds. Add scallions and celery; pulse 10 to 12 times. Add remaining ingredients and process for 2 seconds. Pour over tomatoes and refrigerate.

Bravo!

Mixed Green Salad with Garlic Croutons and Gorgonzola

Easy   Yield: 4 to 6 servings
Preparing: 30 minutes
May be doubled

2 tablespoons red wine vinegar
1 tablespoon Dijon mustard
½ cup Gorgonzola cheese, crumbled
6 tablespoons vegetable oil
Salt and pepper to taste

10 cups loosely packed bite-size
**   pieces red-leaf lettuce, watercress,**
**   and Belgian endive**
Garlic croutons

Combine vinegar, mustard, and cheese in a bowl. Blend well. Whisk in oil, salt, and pepper. Place salad greens in a large bowl and toss well with dressing. Serve with croutons.

Gemischter Salat — Mixed Salad

Easy   Preparing: 15 minutes
Partial do ahead

My Salad Dressing: *Use a marmalade jar with a lid (10-ounce jar)*
8 teaspoons sugar
1 teaspoon salt
½ teaspoon ground white pepper
½ teaspoon garlic salt

1 teaspoon prepared mustard (Dijon)
1 tablespoon boiling water
Wine vinegar

Mix together the sugar, salt, pepper, garlic salt, and mustard. Add 1 tablespoon boiling water and mix thoroughly. Add wine vinegar until jar is ¾ full. Dressing is best when made ahead and refrigerated. Shake well before using.

Salad: *(The ingredients depend on the time of year)*
In Spring:
Tender greens
Young kohlrabi
Carrot
Cucumber
Fennel

Many Herbs:
Parsley
Dill
Chives
Watercress
Arugula

Wash all ingredients and dry them well. Place in a bowl and toss tenderly, "mit Gefühl," with a small amount of the best olive oil and a drizzle of my salad dressing.

Mrs. Wolfgang Sawallisch

Crunchy Romaine Toss

Easy   Yield: 10 to 12 servings
Preparing: 10 minutes

1 cup walnuts, chopped
1 package uncooked Ramen noodles, broken up (discard flavor packet)
4 tablespoons unsalted butter

Sweet-and-Sour Dressing:
1 cup vegetable oil
1 cup sugar
½ cup wine vinegar

1 bunch broccoli, coarsely chopped
1 head romaine lettuce, torn into pieces
4 green onions, chopped

3 tablespoons soy sauce
Salt and pepper to taste

Brown walnuts and noodles in butter. Cool on paper towels. Combine noodles, walnuts, broccoli, lettuce, and onions. Blend together all dressing ingredients. Pour sweet-and-sour dressing over mixture; toss to coat well.

Salad Sensation

Easy   Yield: 4 servings
Preparing: 10 minutes
May be doubled or tripled

1 small Red Delicious apple, chopped
Juice of ½ lemon
½ cup golden raisins
¼ cup walnut pieces
1 small head Boston lettuce, torn into bite-size pieces

1 small head red-leaf lettuce, torn into bite-size pieces
1 ripe avocado, sliced
Fresh bean sprouts

Put apple into a salad bowl. Toss with lemon juice. Add raisins and walnuts. Add lettuce and toss. Serve garnished with avocado slices and bean sprouts.

Note: Delicious with sweet-and-sour dressing (see previous recipe).

Bravo!

California Salad

Easy Yield: 8 servings
Preparing: 10 minutes

1 cantaloupe, peeled, seeded, and cut into bite-size chunks
4 tomatoes, cut into wedges
¼ pound sugar or snap peas, strings removed

1 red onion, cut into wedges or slices
2 avocados, peeled, pitted, and cut into wedges
Bottled Italian dressing

Combine all ingredients, except dressing. Just before serving, toss with dressing to taste.

Lentil Salad

Average Yield: 10 to 12 as entrée
Do ahead Preparing: 30 minutes
Chilling: 4 hours

2½ cups dried red lentils
1½ quarts chicken or vegetable stock
3 carrots, chopped

1 medium yellow onion, chopped
3 cloves garlic, minced
1 bay leaf

Dressing:
⅓ cup salad oil
⅓ cup white wine vinegar

3 garlic cloves, minced
1 cup chopped green onions

Garnish:
2 teaspoons dried thyme
¼ pound feta cheese, crumbled

1 cup walnuts
Chopped parsley

In a large saucepan, combine lentils, stock, carrots, onion, 3 minced garlic cloves, and bay leaf. Bring to a boil over moderate heat and simmer, covered, for 25 minutes.
Dressing: In a blender bowl combine oil, vinegar, 3 minced garlic cloves, onions, and thyme. Blend to mix. Pour over lentils while they are still hot. Mix well. Chill. Just before serving add feta cheese, walnuts, and parsley. Serve cold.

Wild Rice Summer Salad

Average Yield: 4 to 6 servings
Do ahead Preparing: 30 minutes
Chilling: 24 hours
May be doubled

2 shallots, chopped	1 hard-boiled egg, chopped
1 tablespoon chopped parsley	1 tablespoon whipped cream
1 tablespoon Dijon mustard	3 tomatoes, quartered
1 clove garlic, crushed	½ large red onion, sliced in rings
3 tablespoons red wine vinegar	1 cup wild rice, cooked according to
6 tablespoons olive oil	directions on the box

In a bowl combine shallots, parsley, mustard, garlic, and vinegar. Mix well. Season to taste with salt and pepper. Add oil, stirring constantly. Add egg and mix. Gently incorporate whipped cream. Place rice and vegetables in a large bowl. Mix to combine and season again with salt and pepper. Add vinaigrette mixture and refrigerate 24 hours. Serve at room temperature.

"Bessie G." Oriental Salad

Average Yield: 6 servings
Preparing: 30 minutes

1 tablespoon mayonnaise	1 cup sliced ripe olives
1 tablespoon vegetable oil	1 medium green pepper cut
2 tablespoons lemon juice	into 1-inch pieces
⅓ cup soy sauce	1 cup sliced green onions
4 cups salad greens	¾ cup chopped celery
1 (8-ounce) can water chestnuts,	2 to 3 cups cooked chicken, cubed
sliced and drained	4 slices bacon, cooked and crumbled
1 (14-ounce) can bean sprouts, rinsed	
and drained	

Combine mayonnaise, lemon juice, vegetable oil, and soy sauce; set aside. Combine vegetables and chicken in a large salad bowl; mix well. Just before serving, pour dressing over the salad. Mix thoroughly. Sprinkle bacon over salad and toss again.

QED

Bravo!

Salad Niçoise

Average   *Yield: 8 as entrée*
Preparing: 1 hour

2 pounds green beans, cooked crisp
2 green peppers, sliced
2 cups celery, chopped
1 pint cherry tomatoes, sliced
5 medium red potatoes, cooked
  and sliced
3 (7-ounce) cans white tuna, drained

Dressing:
2 teaspoons Dijon mustard
2 tablespoons red wine vinegar
1½ teaspoons salt
1 to 2 cloves garlic, chopped

1 (2-ounce) can anchovies, drained
  and chopped
10 black olives, sliced
2 small red onions, sliced
2 tablespoons fresh basil, chopped
⅓ cup parsley, chopped
¼ cup scallions, sliced thin
6 hard-boiled eggs, sliced

6 tablespoons vegetable oil
6 tablespoons olive oil
¼ teaspoon ground black pepper
1 teaspoon dried thyme

In a large, flat bowl arrange symmetrically beans, peppers, celery, tomatoes, and potatoes. Flake tuna; add to bowl. Add anchovies; scatter olives, scallions, onions, basil, parsley, and eggs over top. In a jar, combine mustard, vinegar, salt, garlic, oils, pepper, and thyme. Shake well. Pour over salad or serve in a small pitcher.

To keep fresh basil leaves for winter-time use, roll together 3 leaves, place each bundle in a section of an ice cube tray, add water, and freeze. Remove from tray, and store in the freezer in an airtight container. Try the same trick with fresh parsley and dill.

Don't dry tarragon or dill; pat them dry and freeze them in small plastic bags.

Crabmeat Salad

Easy
Do ahead

Yield: 8 servings
Preparing: 30 minutes
Chilling: 30 minutes

12 ounces crabmeat, picked over
1 pound spiral pasta
1 tablespoon salt
8 ounces snow peas, cleaned,
blanched 15 seconds, patted dry

Dressing:
1 clove garlic
1 large egg
¼ cup wine vinegar
½ teaspoon salt
¼ teaspoon pepper
Pinch sugar

1 head broccoli flowerets, blanched 1
minute, patted dry
1 pint cherry tomatoes, halved if
large, seeded
1 cup sliced water chestnuts

2 tablespoons parsley, minced
2 tablespoons fresh dill, minced
¼ teaspoon pepper
1 teaspoon dried basil, crushed
1 cup vegetable oil

Set aside cleaned crabmeat. In a large pot bring to a boil enough water to cook pasta. Add oil and salt; cook according to package directions; drain. Dressing: In a food processor fitted with a steel blade, mince garlic. Add all remaining ingredients, except oil. With motor running, slowly add oil through feed tube until dressing thickens. If serving immediately, toss a little dressing with warm pasta. Set aside. To serve, toss pasta with crabmeat and some dressing. Add vegetables. Toss with more dressing to taste. Chill 30 minutes.

Albertson's Cooking School, Wynnewood, PA

Ichiban Noodle Salad

Easy

Yield: 12 servings
Preparing: 30 minutes

4 packs Ichiban Japanese noodles
2 bunches green onions, sliced

Ginger Dressing:
2 tablespoons ginger root, peeled and
chopped
2½ tablespoons lemon juice
2½ tablespoons rice wine vinegar
1½ tablespoons soy sauce

2 cups carrots, julienned

¾ teaspoon Dijon mustard
¼ cup corn oil
2½ tablespoons sesame oil
1 tablespoon sugar

In a large pot cook noodles in boiling salted water until al dente. Drain. Chill well. Toss with green onions and carrots; mix well. Combine all ingredients for dressing. Pour enough over noodles to coat. Season with salt and pepper.

David C. Iacobucci, Executive Chef, Culinary Concepts, Caterer, Philadelphia, PA

Bravo!

Korean Meat Salad

Average   Yield: 8 servings
Do ahead   Preparing: 30 minutes
            Chilling: 24 hours

3 pounds top sirloin, eye round, or
   any other cut, lean and good quality
5 dried Chinese mushrooms
1 (4½-ounce) can sliced mushrooms
2 tablespoons peanut oil
3 tablespoons soy sauce
1 tablespoon vinegar from
   bottled capers
1 tablespoon white vinegar

3 cloves garlic, crushed
2 red onions, finely chopped
1 yellow onion, sliced into rings
6 scallions, sliced, green part included
1 tablespoon finely chopped shallot
2 tablespoons finely chopped parsley
3 tablespoons capers
2 tablespoons sesame oil

Trim meat of all fat and cut into thin strips, ¼-inch x 2-inch. Place dried mushrooms in a bowl with lukewarm water to cover and allow to stand for at least
15 minutes. Heat peanut oil in a large skillet and sauté beef just until it loses its
color. Transfer meat to a large mixing bowl, leaving juices in the skillet. Add to
the skillet the liquid from the can of mushrooms, soy sauce, both vinegars;
bring to a boil. Remove Chinese mushrooms from soak, discard stems, and
slice the caps. In a bowl large enough to hold all the ingredients combine
garlic, onions, scallions, shallots, parsley, capers, and both kinds of mushrooms (Chinese and canned). Pour the boiling liquid in the skillet over the
mixture and allow to stand until it is cool. Add the cooked beef and stir in the
sesame oil. Mix well. Cover and refrigerate for at least 24 hours.
Serve at room temperature.

Caesar Salad with Avocado

Easy   Yield: 4 to 6 servings
       Preparing: 20 minutes

½ cup good olive oil
1 large garlic clove, minced
3 tablespoons lemon juice
1 tablespoon Worcestershire sauce
1 tablespoon Dijon mustard
3 tablespoons sour cream
1 tablespoon anchovy paste

1 head romaine lettuce, torn
   into pieces
Parmesan cheese, grated
Croutons
1 large avocado, cut into
   bite-size pieces

Mix together oil, garlic, lemon juice, Worcestershire sauce, mustard, sour
cream, and anchovy paste. Place lettuce in a large bowl; add cheese and
croutons to taste. Toss with prepared dressing. Add avocados,
toss gently, and serve.

Lemon-Ginger Chicken Salad

Easy
Do ahead

Yield: 4 servings for lunch
2 servings for dinner
Preparing: 15 minutes
Chilling: 2 hours

½ cup mayonnaise	¼ teaspoon salt
¼ cup plain yogurt	Dash cayenne pepper
1 teaspoon grated lemon rind	2 cups cooked, cubed chicken
1 tablespoon fresh lemon juice	1 cup green grapes
1 teaspoon ground ginger	1 cup sliced celery

In a large bowl combine mayonnaise, yogurt, lemon rind, lemon juice, ginger, salt, and cayenne; mix well. Add chicken, grapes, and celery; stir gently. Cover and refrigerate at least 2 hours to allow flavors to blend.

Apple and Fennel Salad

Easy
Partial do ahead

Yield: 4 servings
Preparing: 15 minutes

1 teaspoon fennel seeds	2 fennel bulbs, white only,
1 clove garlic, minced	finely sliced
¼ teaspoon salt	1 large, red, tart, apple, cored
1½ teaspoons cider vinegar	and sliced
1½ teaspoons Dijon mustard	Lettuce leaves
2 tablespoons olive oil	

Blend or process fennel seeds until coarsely ground. Add garlic, salt, vinegar, mustard, and olive oil and mix well. This may be done well ahead of time. Place a lettuce leaf on each plate. Toss apple and fennel with the dressing and arrange on the lettuce. Garnish with chopped fennel green.

Bravo!

Chicken Salad Teriyaki

Easy   Yield: 8 to 10 servings
Do ahead   Preparing: 45 minutes

5 whole chicken breasts, split
3 cups chicken broth
2 large carrots, peeled
1 large green pepper, seeded
    and cored
1 large red pepper, seeded and cored

24 snow peas, strings removed
1 bunch scallions
½ can (6 ounces) water chestnuts
½ cup oyster sauce
¼ cup soy sauce
½ cup sesame oil

In a large pot bring chicken broth to a boil. Add chicken breasts, cover, and simmer for 20 minutes. Do not boil. Remove from heat; when cool enough to handle, remove skin and bone and cut into even slices about ¼-inch thick. Save chicken broth to use another time. Cut carrots, green and red peppers, and snow peas into julienne strips 1-inch long. Slice scallions on the diagonal. Julienne water chestnuts. In a blender, at high speed, mix oyster sauce with soy sauce. With speed on low, gradually add sesame oil. In a large bowl thoroughly combine the chicken and vegetables. Add enough dressing just to coat. Cover and refrigerate. Before serving, toss and add more dressing if necessary.

Caesar & Cleopatra Salad

Easy   Yield: 4 to 6 servings
Preparing: 20 minutes

1 clove garlic, mashed
1 (2-ounce) can anchovies
½ teaspoon Dijon mustard
1 teaspoon Worcestershire sauce
⅓ cup olive oil
⅙ cup wine vinegar

Croutons: (optional)
5 slices white or wheat bread
1 clove garlic

Freshly ground pepper
1 egg
1 head romaine lettuce, outer leaves
    removed
⅓ cup grated Romano cheese

Olive oil

Drain the anchovies on paper towels and mince. Combine minced anchovies, mashed garlic, mustard, and Worcestershire sauce. Add olive oil, vinegar, and freshly ground pepper. Blend well. Add egg. Blend well. Tear lettuce into bite-size pieces and place in salad bowl just before serving. Toss with dressing to coat. Add grated cheese and optional croutons. Toss lightly. Serve.
Croutons: Pour olive oil into frying pan to a depth of ¼ inch. Cut bread into ½-inch cubes. Heat oil until 1 bread cube browns in 30 seconds. Brown the whole garlic clove in the oil and discard the garlic. Add the bread cubes and brown. Drain well on paper towels.

Cleo Laine

Field Salad with Walnut Toasted Goat Cheese

Average Yield: 6 servings
Partial do ahead Preparing: 30 minutes
Baking: 4 to 5 minutes
Chilling: 1 to 2 hours

⅓ cup fresh soft bread crumbs
⅓ cup ground walnuts
1 5½-ounce log mild goat cheese
1½ tablespoons walnut oil

Dressing:
½ cup olive oil
4 tablespoons red wine vinegar
1 tablespoon Dijon mustard
½ teaspoon sugar

½ pound mixed salad greens - Boston
lettuce, watercress, curly red-leaf
lettuce, oak-leaf lettuce, etc.

¼ teaspoon salt
¼ teaspoon freshly ground pepper
Minced parsley or tarragon

Combine bread crumbs and ground walnuts in a low-sided dish. Cut the cheese into 6 even slices. Dip each slice into walnut oil and then into the crumb/nut mixture. Press crumbs onto all surfaces of each cheese slice, put in 1 layer on a plate, and refrigerate for 15 to 30 minutes. Wash salad greens and spin dry. Refrigerate in a plastic bag with a paper towel to absorb extra moisture. Dressing: Combine ingredients in a covered glass jar and shake well. Chill until 10 minutes before serving. Preheat oven to 350°. Place cheese slices on a cookie sheet and bake for only 4 to 5 minutes. (If heated too long, they will lose their shape.) Toss the greens with the dressing in a bowl. Place a portion of greens on each serving plate with a slice of baked cheese on top.
Serve immediately.

Spinach Salad with Strawberries

Easy Yield: 6 servings
Partial do ahead Preparing: 20 minutes

Dressing:
½ cup sugar
2 tablespoons sesame seeds, toasted
1½ teaspoons minced onion
¼ teaspoon Worcestershire sauce

¼ teaspoon paprika
¼ cup wine vinegar
½ cup olive oil

Salad:
4 cups torn spinach leaves, washed,
   dried, and stemmed
1 cup halved strawberries

⅓ cup coarsely chopped macadamia
   nuts
1 kiwi, peeled and thinly sliced

Combine dressing ingredients in a jar, cover, and shake well. (Dressing may be prepared ahead of time.) In a large salad bowl combine spinach, strawberries, and kiwi; toss with enough dressing to coat. Just before serving top with nuts.

Bravo!

Mixed Greens and Roasted Mushroom Salad

Easy
Partial do ahead

Yield: 8 servings
Preparing: 20 minutes
Baking: 15 minutes

5 tablespoons balsamic vinegar or
   ¼ cup red wine vinegar
1 tablespoon Dijon mustard
½ teaspoon dried thyme, crumbled
⅔ cup olive oil
¾ pound mushrooms, quartered
Pinch sugar
1 head radicchio, leaves torn into
   bite-size pieces

1 head Belgian endive, cut into
   1-inch wide pieces
1 head curly endive, romaine or Bibb
   lettuce, torn into bite-size pieces
½ small red onion, thinly sliced
¼ cup chopped fresh chives, chopped
   in 1-inch long pieces

Preheat oven to 400°. In a small bowl whisk together vinegar, mustard, and thyme. Gradually whisk in oil. Season to taste with salt and pepper. (May be made a day ahead, covered, and stored at room temperature.) Place mushrooms on a baking tray. Drizzle mushrooms with ¼ cup dressing and toss to coat. Bake until crisp on edges (about 15 minutes). Cool. In a large bowl, shortly before serving, combine mushrooms, lettuces, onion, and chives. Add enough dressing to coat; toss well. Divide salad among plates and serve.

Note: Mushrooms may be served on top of dressed greens if desired.

Nico's Greek Salad

Easy
Do ahead

Yield: 6 servings
Preparing: 10 minutes

2 tomatoes, quartered
1 cucumber, sliced
1 Vidalia onion, sliced
½ pound Kalamata olives
   (not canned)

6 ounces feta cheese, crumbled
½ green bell pepper, sliced (optional)
¼ teaspoon oregano
Salt and pepper to taste
¼ cup (or more) virgin olive oil

Combine all ingredients and mix well. Refrigerate until ready to serve. Toss before serving.

Salad of Baby Squid with White Beans and Arugula

Complicated   Yield: 4 servings
              Preparing: 1 hour

Beans:
½ pound fresh white beans, shelled
1 onion, cut in half
1 clove garlic, peeled

1 bouquet garni (see note)
1 cup water
1 teaspoon salt

Dressing:
8 sun-dried tomatoes, chopped
6 black olives, pitted and halved
4 scallions, peeled and chopped
1 tablespoon chopped basil

3 tablespoons sherry wine vinegar
8 tablespoons olive oil
Salt and pepper to taste

Squid:
12 baby squid, tube only,
   cleaned and halved
1 tablespoon olive oil

4 tablespoons sherry wine vinegar
Salt and pepper to taste
2 handfuls arugula

Beans: Place the beans in a pot with the onion, garlic, bouquet garni, and water (not the salt). Bring to a boil and simmer for 20 minutes. Add salt and continue cooking for 10 minutes, or until beans are tender. Drain and discard onion, garlic, and bouquet garni.

Dressing: Combine all dressing ingredients and stir into the beans. Mix well.

Squid: Scar the squid with the tip of a knife and season lightly with salt and pepper. In a non-stick frying pan heat the oil over high heat. When smoking, add squid and sauté 30 seconds on each side. Remove the pan from the heat and add the vinegar. Keep hot.

To Serve: On the center of a plate arrange 2 or 3 tablespoons of beans. Place arugula on top of beans. Arrange squid around the beans, and pour juice over the squid.

Note: Bouquet garni: 2 parsley sprigs, ⅓ bay leaf, and 1 fresh sprig (or ⅛ teaspoon dried) thyme tied in cheesecloth.

Four Seasons Hotel, Philadelphia, PA

Bravo!

Black Bean Salad

Easy
Do ahead

Yield: 6 servings
Preparing: 1 hour
Soaking: 6 to 8 hours
Chilling: 1 hour

1 pound black beans
1 large red bell pepper
1 large yellow bell pepper
1 jalapeño pepper
1 small red onion
½ cup canola oil

¼ cup red wine vinegar
1 tablespoon ground cumin
1 large clove garlic, crushed
Salt and pepper to taste
½ cup chopped cilantro

Soak beans in water to cover for 6 to 8 hours or overnight. Drain. In a 2-quart saucepan place the soaked beans and 4 cups of water. Bring to a boil, cover, reduce heat, and simmer for 1 hour, or until beans are tender. Drain. Seed and dice the bell peppers and the jalapeño, using gloves to chop the jalapeño. Peel and dice the onion. Mix the chopped vegetables with the beans. Combine the oil, vinegar, cumin, and garlic; dress the bean mixture, tossing gently to keep the beans whole. Refrigerate until 1 hour before serving.
Fold in the chopped cilantro.

Roberta Powlis, The Cheese Co., Narberth, PA

Add a little chopped tart apple to tuna salad. It's delicious.

Entrees

Main Themes

Bravo!

The Fabulous Philadelphians

The Philadelphia Orchestra, since its founding in 1900, has performed in the Academy of Music, a celebrated historic landmark building. The Orchestra plays as many as 180 concerts a year, of which almost 100 are by subscription. The Opening Night concert, a Halloween program, the annual Academy of Music Anniversary Concert, and performances of the Messiah are among the many non-subscription concerts attended by large and admiring audiences.

During the summer months, concerts by the Orchestra are held at the Mann Music Center in Philadelphia's Fairmount Park and at the Saratoga Performing Arts Center in Saratoga Springs, New York. The extended summer program brings music to thousands of listeners beyond those who regularly attend concerts during the Orchestra's subscription season.

The Orchestra tours extensively in the United States, as well as in Europe, Latin America, and Asia. In fact, the Orchestra often has been heralded as Philadelphia's most successful ambassador since Benjamin Franklin.

Currently, the Orchestra records for the Angel / EMI, Deutsche Grammophon, London / Decca, and Sony Classical labels. As the Orchestra's 1999-2000 centennial season approaches, its mission as a world-class orchestra performing the broadest spectrum of repertoire has not changed.

Poulet à la Moutarde

Easy   *Yield: 4 to 6 servings*
         Preparing: 20 minutes
         Cooking: 35 minutes

1 3-pound chicken, cut into
  serving pieces
Salt and pepper to taste
2 tablespoons butter
12 baby carrots, trimmed
½ pound small fresh mushrooms
2 tablespoons finely chopped shallots
2 tablespoons flour

½ cup white wine
1 cup chicken broth
1 bay leaf
3 sprigs fresh thyme (or ½ teaspoon
  dried)
2 tablespoons Dijon or Düsseldorf
  mustard

Sprinkle chicken on all sides with salt and pepper. Over moderately high heat melt butter in a large skillet and add the chicken, skin side down. Cook until golden brown, about 5 minutes. Turn and cook another 5 minutes. Pour off any excess fat and scatter carrots, mushrooms, and shallots between the chicken parts. Cook for 5 minutes. Sprinkle with flour, stirring to distribute the flour evenly. Add the wine and stir. Add the chicken broth, bay leaf, and thyme. Cover, lower heat, and cook gently for 20 minutes. Remove from heat and swirl in the mustard. Serve immediately with buttered noodles or rice.

Chicken Breasts with Lemon

Easy   *Yield: 4 servings*
         Preparing: 30 minutes
         May be doubled

Q E D

1½ pounds boneless, skinless
  chicken breasts
Flour for dredging
2 tablespoons olive oil

Salt and pepper to taste
2 lemons
Water
Chopped parsley to garnish

With a very sharp knife cut chicken into thin scallops approximately ¼ inch thick (except for the filet, which remains whole). Dredge in flour and shake off excess. In a large, non-stick frying pan heat oil over medium heat and sauté chicken pieces in one layer approximately 2 minutes on each side until cooked through. Do not overcrowd the pan. Remove chicken to a warmed dish; add salt and pepper. Repeat until all chicken is cooked. Keep warm. Remove zest from lemon and chop zest into small pieces. Squeeze juice from lemons; put juice into a measuring cup and add water to measure ¾ cup liquid. Pour into frying pan, add zest, and stir over medium heat. Return chicken to pan; continue heating while sauce thickens slightly and coats the chicken. Place on a serving dish and sprinkle with chopped parsley.

Note: Can substitute ¾ cup dry Marsala wine for lemon juice and add sautéed mushrooms to sauce.

97

Bravo!

Chicken Pot Pie

Average
Do ahead

Yield: 6 to 8 servings
Preparing: 20 minutes
Cooking: 30 minutes
Baking: 50 minutes

1 3- to 4-pound chicken
2 cups chicken broth
12 small white onions
2 carrots, thinly sliced
1 garlic clove, crushed
½ cup chopped fresh parsley
3 tablespoons butter

3 tablespoons flour
1 cup half-and-half cream
  (may use milk)
Salt and pepper to taste
¼ teaspoon Tabasco sauce
1 recipe pie crust
1 egg

In a large pot poach chicken until tender. Allow to cool in broth. Reserve broth; chill it and remove grease. Cook vegetables in the chicken broth just until tender (about 10 minutes); add parsley and garlic. Drain; reserve liquid. In a saucepan melt butter. Add flour and cook for 2 minutes, stirring. Add 1 cup of cooking liquid from vegetables, the half-and-half, salt, pepper, and Tabasco. Set aside. Remove chicken from bones and cut into chunks. Place chicken pieces in the bottom of a 1½-quart baking dish. Arrange vegetables over chicken and cover with sauce. Cool while preparing the crust. Roll pastry ¼-inch thick, large enough to fit the top of the dish with a 1½-inch overlap. Crimp edges with fork to seal. Make a vent in the center top to allow steam to escape. Brush well with a beaten egg mixed with water. Bake in a preheated 450° oven for 15 minutes. Reduce heat to 350° and continue baking for 35 minutes or until crust is nicely browned.

Chicken Pot Pie - Part II - Pie Crust

Easy
Do ahead

Yield: 2 8- or 9-inch crusts
Preparing: 10 minutes
Chilling: 10 minutes
May be doubled or tripled

1½ cups sifted flour
½ teaspoon salt

½ cup shortening
4 to 5 tablespoons ice water

Into a bowl lightly measure flour; add salt. Cut in shortening until mixture resembles the size of small peas. Sprinkle water over mixture, 1 tablespoon at a time, mixing gently with a fork until the dough is moistened. Gather dough into a ball, and wrap in wax paper. Chill for 10 minutes before rolling.

Mustard Chicken

Easy   Yield: 6 servings
Preparing: 15 minutes
Cooking: 25 minutes

3 boneless chicken breasts, split
  and cleaned
½ cup Dijon mustard
Salt and pepper to taste
2 tablespoons oil

1 small onion, finely chopped
½ cup dry white wine
Several sprigs rosemary
⅓ cup crème fraîche
2 tablespoons chopped parsley

Cover chicken with mustard, add salt and pepper to taste. Heat oil in a large skillet over medium heat. Sauté onions for 2 minutes. Sear chicken pieces, turning frequently, until chicken is browned. Remove chicken from pan. Deglaze pan with white wine. Reduce heat and return chicken to pan with rosemary. Cover pan and cook gently until chicken is cooked through (about 15 minutes). Remove chicken from pan and transfer to a warm platter. Stir crème fraîche and parsley into sauce and pour over chicken. Serve on a bed of hot, sliced, new potatoes.

Bud Bruno, Greenfield Grocer, Ardmore, PA

Chicken Crescent Squares

Easy   Yield: 4 servings
Partial do ahead   Preparing: 20 minutes
Baking: 25 minutes
May be doubled

1 (3-ounce) package light cream
  cheese, softened
3 tablespoons melted butter
2 cups cooked, cubed, chicken breast
¼ teaspoon salt
¼ teaspoon pepper

2 tablespoons chopped chives
1 teaspoon chopped pimiento
1 (8-ounce) can crescent rolls
¾ cup seasoned bread crumbs,
  crushed

Preheat oven to 350°. In a bowl blend cream cheese and 1½ tablespoons melted butter. Add the chicken, salt, pepper, chives, and pimiento. Mix well. Separate the crescent rolls into 4 rectangles; firmly press perforations to seal. Pull and flatten slightly into a square shape. Spoon ½ cup chicken mixture into center of each. Pull corners to top center and twist slightly. Seal edges. Brush tops with remaining butter, dip in crushed crumbs, and bake on an ungreased cookie sheet for 20 to 25 minutes.

Note: May be served with a light chicken gravy.

Bravo!

Chicken (or Veal) Paprika

Easy   Yield: 6 servings
Preparing: 1 hour
May be doubled

3 tablespoons vegetable oil
1 large onion, finely chopped
1½ tablespoons sweet paprika
1 clove garlic, finely chopped
⅛ teaspoon nutmeg
¼ teaspoon saffron
1 large tomato, diced

1 (2- to 3-pound) frying chicken cut
  into eighths
1 large green pepper cut into 1-inch
  wide strips
1 (8-ounce) container sour cream
Salt and pepper to taste

In a large, non-stick frying pan heat oil. When hot, add onions; sauté approximately 5 minutes. Do not brown. Stir. Add paprika, garlic, nutmeg, and saffron. Mix well. If mixture is too dry, add 1½ teaspoons water. Stir 1 minute; add tomato and pepper and stir well. Lay chicken pieces over mixture in pan. Cover and cook slowly (do not boil) for 30 minutes. Remove chicken from pan, leaving sauce. To sauce add sour cream. Mix well; do not boil. Add chicken to pan to warm. Serve immediately.

Jerk Chicken

Easy   Yield: 4 servings
Partial do ahead   Preparing: 10 minutes
Marinating: 3 hours
Grilling: 10 to 12 minutes

4 (6-ounce) skinless, boneless,
  chicken breasts
¼ cup diced onion
2 cloves garlic, minced
1 teaspoon thyme
¼ teaspoon allspice
¼ cup diced, roasted red peppers
1 bunch chopped scallions

1 minced jalapeño pepper (seeds
  removed)
Zest of 1 lemon
Juice of 2 lemons
1 teaspoon cracked black pepper
¼ teaspoon nutmeg
Salt to taste

Place chicken in a Ziploc bag. Combine all other marinade ingredients and add to chicken. Close bag and refrigerate for 3 hours, turning occasionally. Grill chicken over direct heat, turning frequently, for 10 to 12 minutes or until cooked through.

Queen of Hearts, Paoli, PA

Tarragon Chicken with Shiitake Mushrooms

Average
Partial do ahead

Yield: 4 servings
Preparing: 30 minutes
Cooking: 15 minutes

Chicken:
- 1 pound skinless, boneless chicken breast, sliced
- 2 egg whites
- 2 tablespoons cornstarch
- ¼ teaspoon white pepper
- 1 tablespoon vegetable oil
- ¾ tablespoon olive oil

- 1 teaspoon minced fresh ginger root
- 1 teaspoon minced garlic
- 10 to 12 shallots, peeled, quartered
- ⅓ pound snowpeas, strings removed, cut
- ⅓ pound fresh shiitake mushrooms
- 10 to 12 sprigs fresh tarragon

Sauce:
- 4 tablespoons rich chicken stock
- 2 tablespoons soy sauce
- 1 tablespoon sugar
- ½ tablespoon tomato ketchup
- ½ tablespoon white vinegar
- ½ tablespoon oyster sauce
- 1 teaspoon minced garlic
- 1 teaspoon minced fresh ginger root

- 1 teaspoon hot pepper sauce
- 1 teaspoon fresh tarragon leaves
- Pinch black pepper
- Pinch white pepper
- ½ teaspoon sesame oil
- Pinch five-spice powder
- 2 tablespoons cornstarch mixed with ¼ cup water

In a large bowl combine sliced chicken, egg whites, cornstarch, white pepper, and 1 tablespoon vegetable oil. (Some cookbooks refer to this as velveting the chicken.) Set aside in the refrigerator. Mix together all the sauce ingredients. Set aside. In a large pan of simmering water poach the velvet chicken until barely cooked (about 10 minutes). Remove from poaching liquid and set aside. Heat wok. Add ¾ tablespoon olive oil and heat. Add ginger, garlic, and shallots, and stir-fry for a few seconds. Add poached chicken, snowpeas, mushrooms, and tarragon. Stir-fry quickly until crisp tender, adding a little water if needed to prevent sticking. Add sauce mixture and heat through. Using the cornstarch/water mixture, thicken the sauce using only enough to create a light sauce. Discard any excess cornstarch/water mixture. Mix well and remove to serving platter. Garnish with fresh tarragon and carved vegetables.

Yangming, Bryn Mawr, PA

When buying fresh ginger root, look for knobs that are very hard and firm in appearance, not shriveled. To keep it fresh in the refrigerator, store in a plastic bag lined with a paper towel.

Bravo!

Chicken Ukraine

Easy Yield: 4 servings
Preparing: 30 minutes
Baking: 30 minutes
May be doubled

⅔ cup margarine
½ cup dry bread crumbs
2 tablespoons grated Parmesan cheese
1 teaspoon basil
1 teaspoon oregano
2 teaspoons dried onion flakes

¼ teaspoon salt
2 chicken breasts boned, skinned, and halved
¼ cup dry white wine or apple juice
¼ cup chopped green onion
¼ cup chopped parsley

Preheat oven to 350°. Melt margarine in a saucepan. On a piece of wax paper combine bread crumbs, Parmesan cheese, basil, oregano, onion flakes, salt, and pepper. Dip chicken into melted margarine, then roll in crumb mixture to coat. Place in an ungreased baking dish. Bake, uncovered, for 30 minutes or until chicken is cooked through. While chicken is baking, add wine, green onions, and parsley to remaining margarine. Pour this sauce over the cooked chicken and return to oven for 5 minutes to heat the sauce.
Serve with sauce spooned over the chicken.

Main Dish Potato Boats

Easy
Partial do ahead

Yield: 4 servings
Preparing: 30 minutes
Baking: 80 minutes
May be doubled

4 (14-ounce) baking potatoes
¼ pound cooked turkey, cubed
¼ pound baked ham, cubed
¼ pound sharp cheddar cheese, cubed

¼ pound Provolone cheese, cubed
1 sweet pepper (green, yellow, or red), chopped
1 medium onion, chopped
¼ to ½ stick butter

Preheat oven to 400°. Scrub potatoes, prick with a fork and bake in preheated oven for 1 hour. While the potatoes are baking combine all other ingredients except the butter. When potatoes are done, allow them to cool enough to handle. Reduce the oven temperature to 375°. Cut each one in half lengthwise and remove ¼ of the pulp; save for another use. Closely fit potato halves into a 7 x 11-inch baking dish. Spread some butter over each half and mound the meat/cheese mixture, packing in as much as possible. (May be may ahead to this point.) Bake, uncovered, for 15 to 20 minutes, or until heated through.

Chicken Presto

Easy   *Yield: 2 servings*
Preparing: 20 minutes
Cooking: 10 minutes
May be doubled or tripled

2 boneless chicken breasts	**1 (10¾-ounce) can cream of**
1 onion, diced	**mushroom soup**
1 cup chopped black olives	**2 tablespoons olive oil**
1 tablespoon crushed garlic	**½ teaspoon curry powder**
1 tablespoon ginger	**½ teaspoon paprika**

Pound chicken to an even thickness. Slice into 2 x 1-inch pieces. In a large skillet place 1 tablespoon olive oil to cover surface. Heat to medium high. Combine garlic with ginger; add to skillet along with the onion. Sauté lightly for 5 minutes. Add olives; sauté another 3 minutes. Move ingredients to one side; place remaining tablespoon of olive oil on the open side of skillet. Add chicken pieces. Sprinkle with curry and paprika. Simmer until 1 side is done. Flip chicken and repeat. When chicken is almost cooked, add the soup. Do not add water. Mix all ingredients together. Cover and simmer for 5 minutes. Serve on a bed of rice; garnish with orange slices.

"The name of this recipe is derived from the fact that this dish should take no longer than 30 minutes to prepare and cook. The result is actually quite sensational but should not be judged by its appearance. Therefore, it is suggested that it be prepared for the cook and mate and/or guests that are true friends."

Peter Nero

To garnish chicken, Cornish hens, or pheasant, drain a can of Alberta peach halves. Arrange them in a flat pan, put a dollop of red currant jelly and a bit of butter into the peach half, sprinkle with curry powder, and broil until the mixture melts.

For an undefinable tang, place a small peeled tangerine into the cavity of a pheasant or Cornish hen before cooking.

103

Bravo!

Western Style Chicken

Easy	Yield: Corresponds to number of chicken pieces used
Do ahead	Preparing: 10 minutes
	Baking: 45 minutes

Bisquick flour	**Chicken pieces, skin on and bone in**
Salt and pepper to taste	**Butter**
Milk	**Paprika**

Preheat oven to 350°. Put Bisquick, salt, and pepper into a paper bag. Dip chicken pieces in milk and place in bag, one at a time; shake to coat well. Place chicken pieces onto a greased baking pan, or one lined with foil. Dot each with butter and sprinkle with paprika. Bake, uncovered, for 45 minutes.

Note: This recipe works for any amount of chicken and reheats well. This comes from a radio-TV chef from Dallas. "It has never let me down. It's Southern-fried chicken without the grease!"

Wayne Conner

Cajun Barbecued Chicken Breasts

Easy	Yield: 6 servings
	Preparing: 30 minutes
	Marinating: 4 hours
	Grilling: 10 minutes
	May be doubled

6 large boneless, skinless chicken breasts	**1 large yellow pepper, cut into ½-inch cubes**
2 cups canola oil	**1 large red pepper, cut into ½-inch cubes**
4 tablespoons or less Cajun seasonings	**Prepared chutney sauce**
1 large green pepper, cut into ½-inch cubes	

Pound chicken breasts to make them tender. Mix oil with the Cajun seasonings (use more or less seasoning to your taste). Marinate the chicken in this mixture for up to 4 hours. Preheat barbeque grill and barbeque chicken until juices run clear when chicken is pierced with a fork. They will blacken slightly with grill flare-up in the beginning. This is desirable. The grilling takes about 10 minutes (5 on each side) depending on the heat of the grill and thickness of the breasts. Meanwhile, stir-fry the peppers. Remove the chicken from the grill to a warm platter. Brush the chicken with chutney (about 1 teaspoon per breast) and top the platter with the stir-fried peppers.

Note: A very colorful and pretty dish for summer entertaining.

Chicken with Capers

Easy Yield: 4 servings
Preparing: 20 minutes
Cooking: 10 minutes

4 boneless, skinless chicken breasts
Flour for dredging
Salt, pepper, and garlic powder
  to taste
2 tablespoons butter

1 tablespoon olive oil
1 tablespoon chopped parsley
2 tablespoons drained capers
1 tablespoon lemon juice
¼ cup dry white wine

Cut the chicken into long ½-inch wide strips and dredge lightly in flour. In a frying pan over moderate heat melt the butter and oil until the foam subsides. Sauté the chicken in batches (do not overcrowd the pan) until it is lightly golden, about 3 to 5 minutes per batch. While chicken is cooking, season it with salt, pepper, and garlic powder to taste. Do not overcook. Return chicken to pan and add parsley, capers, lemon juice, and white wine. Stir constantly to deglaze the pan, about 1 minute. Lower the heat, cover the pan, and cook 1 minute longer.

Note: This dish is excellent served with pasta, salad, and Italian bread.

Herb Chicken

Easy Yield: 6 servings
Preparing: 20 minutes
Baking: 2 to 2½ hours

1 4- to 5-pound roasting chicken
4 tablespoons butter
1 clove garlic, pressed
1 teaspoon dried tarragon
1 teaspoon dried rosemary
1 teaspoon dried thyme

1 small onion, quartered
1 stalk celery, including leaves, cut
  into 3-inch strips
1 carrot, peeled, cut into 3-inch strips
½ cup dry white wine
Salt and pepper to taste

Cream together butter, garlic, tarragon, rosemary, and thyme. Rub butter mixture over the outside of chicken. Add salt and pepper to taste. Place onion, celery, and carrot into cavity of chicken. Truss. Bake chicken in a roasting pan for 2 hours at 350°, basting several times during cooking with white wine and pan juices. Remove chicken from pan; deglaze pan and serve juices on the side.

Bravo!

Chicken with Walnuts

Easy Yield: 4 servings
Preparing: 20 minutes
Cooking: 5 minutes

QED

3 tablespoons soy sauce
3 teaspoons cornstarch
2 teaspoons diced ginger root
2 tablespoons dry sherry
½ teaspoon red pepper flakes
2 tablespoons oil

1 pound snow peas, strings removed
1 bunch scallions, cut into ½-inch
  diagonal pieces
1 cup walnut halves or pieces
1⅓ pounds boneless, skinless chicken
  breasts in 1-inch cubes

Combine in a bowl the soy sauce, cornstarch, ginger root, sherry, and red pepper flakes. In hot oil stir fry the snow peas, scallions, and walnuts. Remove with a slotted spoon. Stir fry the chicken in two batches, each batch for 2 minutes. Return all chicken to the pan and stir in soy mixture. Add vegetables and walnuts. Cover and cook for 1 minute. Serve with rice and cut-up fresh fruit.

Sesame Chicken

Easy Yield: 4 servings
Partial do ahead Preparing: 10 minutes
Marinating: Overnight
Baking: 45 minutes
May be doubled

¼ cup soy sauce
2 tablespoons sesame oil
1 teaspoon toasted sesame seeds
1 tablespoon sugar
⅓ cup chopped onion

4 tablespoons chopped green onions
⅓ teaspoon minced garlic
¼ teaspoon black pepper
⅓ teaspoon chopped ginger root
2 pounds cut up chicken, bone-in

Combine all ingredients except the chicken and mix thoroughly. Clean and wipe dry the chicken parts. In a non-reactive container thoroughly mix chicken and marinade. Cover and refrigerate overnight. Preheat oven to 375°. Place chicken in flat baking pans and pour the marinade over. Bake for 45 minutes, turning occasionally.

Note: This marinade is also good for beef and turkey.

Chicken and Carrot Curry

Average
Do ahead

Yield: 4 servings
Preparing: 45 minutes

2 whole boneless, skinless
   chicken breasts
6 large carrots
1 tablespoon orange juice
½ teaspoon salt, plus 1 teaspoon
2 medium onions
2 tablespoons olive oil
1 tablespoon butter or margarine

1½ teaspoons turmeric
2½ teaspoons mustard seed
½ teaspoon cumin seed
¼ teaspoon cayenne pepper
¼ teaspoon ground cumin
1 teaspoon curry powder
1½ tablespoons cornstarch

Cut chicken breasts in half and place on a broiler pan; broil on low for 10 minutes each side, or until lightly browned and cooked through. Remove from oven and slice thinly, across the grain. While the chicken is cooking, peel and slice the carrots diagonally. Place in a saucepan with 2 cups water, ½ teaspoon salt, and orange juice. Bring to a boil, cover, and cook for 5 minutes. Turn off heat and let carrots sit until needed. Slice onions from top to bottom and then into thin wedges to make slivers. In a large skillet heat oil and butter over low heat. Add turmeric, mustard seed, cumin seed, cayenne, ground cumin, and curry powder and warm gently for 2 to 3 minutes. Do not burn. Add chicken pieces and stir to coat with spices. Add onions and sauté briefly (about 2 to 3 minutes). Add cooked carrots and their liquid. Add water, if necessary, (up to 1 cup) to nearly cover all ingredients. Cover and simmer 5 to 10 minutes. Dissolve cornstarch in 2 tablespoons water and stir into mixture until blended. Continue to simmer until thick and rich (about 10 to 15 minutes). If necessary adjust consistency with more cornstarch or more water. Taste for seasoning and adjust if desired. Serve with white or brown rice.

Note: Reheats well the next day. Particularly good in the winter but light enough to serve year round.

Bravo!

Australian Chicken

Average Yield: 10 servings
Preparing: 20 minutes
Baking: 20 to 25 minutes

Meat from 2 cooked chickens
3 tablespoons butter
2 sweet red peppers, chopped
2 green peppers, chopped
1 large onion, chopped
2½ cups chopped mushrooms

Salt and pepper
3 cups heavy cream
3 tablespoons prepared mustard
3 tablespoons Worcestershire sauce
Paprika

Remove only the meat from the 2 chickens, saving the skin and bones to make stock at a later time. Place the chicken in chunks in a large 3- to 4-quart casserole, lightly greased. Sauté the peppers, onions, and mushrooms in butter, in a large frying pan over moderately high heat, until they are just tender. Add vegetables to chicken. Preheat oven to 350°. In a large bowl combine cream with mustard and Worcestershire; whip until the cream is quite stiff. Spoon cream over vegetables, spreading gently with a knife. Sprinkle with paprika. Bake for 20 to 25 minutes, or until the sauce has melted and the top is slightly brown. Serve with rice, a green salad, and French bread.

David Zinman

Capon with Wild Rice Stuffing

Average Yield: 6 servings
Preparing: 20 minutes
Roasting: 2½ hours

1 pound mushrooms, chopped,
  sautéed
2 ounces raisins
1 apple, peeled and diced
1 tablespoon mousse foie gras
1 cup chestnuts, peeled and chopped

2 cups cooked wild rice
1 egg yolk
1 tablespoon chopped fresh thyme
½ cup dried apricot, chopped
1 capon
1 cup chicken stock

Preheat oven to 450°. Mix all ingredients and stuff the capon. Sew the cavity closed. Roast for 30 minutes on bed of giblets. Reduce temperature to 350° and roast for 15 minutes per pound, basting often. When cooked, remove capon, deglaze pan with chicken stock, and reduce to make a light juice. Serve with capon.

Le Bec-Fin, Philadelphia, PA

Maureen Forrester's Company Chicken Casserole

Easy | Yield: 6 servings
Partial do ahead | Preparing: 30 minutes
Baking: 1¾ hours

4 pounds chicken pieces, thighs, legs, and breasts
1 cup flour
1 tablespoon ground ginger
1 teaspoon salt
6 slices bacon
1 medium onion, chopped

1 (10-ounce) can beef broth
1 (10-ounce) can mushroom soup
1 (8-ounce) jar applesauce
2 tablespoons coconut
2 tablespoons lemon juice
2 tablespoons ketchup

Preheat oven to 275°. Dredge the chicken pieces in the mixture of flour, ginger, and salt; place in an open, shallow casserole (not more than 4-inch deep). Fry bacon until crisp. Sauté onion in the bacon fat. Set aside the bacon and onion. In a large bowl combine beef broth with mushroom soup and applesauce; mix well. Add curry powder, coconut, lemon juice, and ketchup. Add crumbled bacon and onion. Pour this mixture over the chicken. (May be made ahead to this point and stored, covered, in the refrigerator for 24 hours.) Cover casserole and bake for 1 hour. Remove cover and bake for an additional 45 minutes. Serve over white rice.

Note: Add a green salad and you have a terrific party casserole.

Maureen Forrester

Pecan Chicken

Easy | Yield: 4 servings
Partial do ahead | Preparing: 10 minutes
Baking: 15 minutes

4 large, skinless, boneless chicken breast halves
½ cup buttermilk

¼ cup Dijon mustard
Salt and pepper to taste
2 cups finely ground pecans

Pound chicken breasts between two pieces of wax paper until they are half their original thickness. Combine buttermilk and mustard. Season with salt and pepper to taste. Place the chicken breasts in the buttermilk mixture to coat thoroughly. Cover and refrigerate until ready to cook. (May be left overnight, if desired.) When ready to cook, preheat oven to 375°. Wipe excess buttermilk from each piece of chicken and roll in ground pecans. Place on an ungreased cookie sheet and bake for 12 to 15 minutes. Serve with Orange Rice (page 190).

Bravo!

Chicken Genghis Khan

Average Yield: 4 servings
Preparing: 20 minutes
Cooking: 20 minutes
May be doubled

3 tablespoons butter
1 tablespoon olive oil
½ cup chopped onion
2 large garlic cloves, chopped
¼ teaspoon freshly ground
   black pepper
Several dashes cayenne pepper
¼ teaspoon ground ginger
¼ teaspoon coriander
¼ teaspoon cumin
Good pinch saffron
2 dashes Tabasco sauce

¾ cup chicken broth
½ cup dry white wine
Juice of half a large lemon
1 pound boneless, skinless chicken
   breast, cut into large,
   bite-size pieces
¼ cup raisins
¾ cup green grapes
⅓ cup sliced green olives
2 tablespoons pine nuts
2 teaspoons cornstarch, dissolved
   in
   ¼ cup water

In a large frying pan, gently sauté onion and garlic in butter and oil until soft but not brown. Add all the spices and stir well. Add chicken stock, lemon juice, and white wine. Add the chicken and stir to coat all pieces of meat. Bring to a boil and immediately turn heat down to a low simmer. Cover and simmer gently for 5 minutes. Add raisins and cook 5 minutes, covered. Add grapes and cook 5 minutes, covered. Add olives and pine nuts and cook 2 minutes, uncovered, until heated through. Add the cornstarch/water mixture to thicken the sauce, stirring constantly. Serve over white rice seasoned with a little ground ginger and grated lemon rind.

Note: This dish goes well with a fresh fruit salad and a good dry white wine.

William Smith, Associate Conductor of The Philadelphia Orchestra 1952-1993

Chicken with Orange and Lemon for 100 People

Easy	*Yield: 100 servings*
Do ahead	*Preparing: 30 minutes*
Freeze	*Baking: 90 minutes*
	May be halved or quartered

8 cups orange juice
2 cups lemon juice
4 cups light brown sugar
6 tablespoons cornstarch
4 tablespoons dry mustard

½ cup olive oil or canola oil
2 teaspoons ground nutmeg
30 pounds skinless, boneless
   chicken breasts
8 sliced oranges

Preheat oven to 375°. In a heavy saucepan mix orange and lemon juices (fresh is best), sugar, cornstarch, mustard, oil, and nutmeg. Bring to a boil; reduce heat and simmer for 10 minutes. Clean and dry chicken and place in pan in a single layer. Pour sauce over the chicken and cover with slices of orange. Bake, uncovered, for 1½ hours.

Note: If reducing the quantity of the recipe, cut down the baking time appropriately (3 pounds of chicken should be done in 30 minutes). Do not overcook.

Turkey Loaf

Easy	*Yield: 4 servings*
Do ahead	*Preparing: 15 minutes*
Freeze	*Baking: 45 minutes*
	May be doubled

1 pound ground turkey
1 medium onion, finely chopped
1 cup bread crumbs
   ("homemade kind")
1 egg, lightly beaten
½ cup toasted pine nuts

12 sun-dried tomatoes in oil, drained
   and chopped
⅓ cup skim milk
2 teaspoons dried rosemary,
   crumbled
2 teaspoons oregano
Salt and pepper to taste

Preheat oven to 375°. Mix all ingredients together and put into a lightly greased 8½ x 4½-inch loaf pan. Bake, uncovered, for 45 minutes.

Bravo!

Turkey Country Pâté

Easy	*Yield: 3 1-pound loaves*
Do ahead	*Preparing: 15 minutes*
Freeze	*Baking: 60 minutes*

1 pound hot turkey sausage
2 pounds ground turkey
1 cup fresh bread crumbs, preferably whole wheat
Milk to moisten

3 eggs
1½ envelopes dry onion soup mix
4 tablespoons Worcestershire sauce
½ cup chopped fresh parsley

Preheat oven to 350°. In a large bowl mix together all the ingredients and divide into 3 (8-inch or 9-inch) loaf pans. Bake for 1 hour. Serve hot, room temperature, or cold.

Note: This is good both hot and cold. It makes excellent sandwiches, an attractive first course, a lunch with a salad, or an appetizer with melba toast.

Turkey Breast with Lemon/Caper Sauce

Average	*Yield: 8 servings*
Partial do ahead	*Preparing: 30 minutes*
	Marinating: 4 hours or overnight
	Roasting: 90 minutes

Marinade:
1 cup parsley leaves
5 large garlic cloves
1½ cups fresh lemon juice (about 6 lemons)
1 cup olive oil
4 teaspoons dried rosemary, crumbled

1½ teaspoons salt
Freshly ground pepper to taste
1 5- to 6-pound turkey breast (bone in)
¼ cup drained capers

Marinade: In a food processor, with the machine running, place the parsley and garlic; process. Add lemon juice, oil, rosemary, and 1 teaspoon salt and freshly ground pepper to taste. Process 3 seconds to blend. Put turkey in large plastic bag and pour marinade over. Seal and marinate in the refrigerator overnight (or at room temperature for 4 hours), turning occasionally. Remove turkey from refrigerator and allow to stand, at room temperature, for 1 hour before cooking. Preheat oven to 400°. Take turkey from bag and reserve marinade. Season turkey with remaining ½ teaspoon salt and freshly ground pepper to taste. Place in roasting pan and cook, uncovered, for 30 minutes. Baste with marinade, reserving ⅔ cup for sauce. Continue cooking, basting occasionally, for 1 hour, or until meat thermometer registers 175° when inserted in the thickest part. Allow breast to stand at room temperature. Boil reserved marinade to reduce it slightly. Remove from heat and add capers. Carve turkey into thin slices, and spoon a little sauce over all.
Pass remaining sauce separately.

Poached Marinated Turkey Breast

Average
Do ahead

Yield: 6 to 8 servings
Preparing: 15 minutes
Simmering: 1 hour 15 minutes
Cooling: 30 minutes

1 5½- to 6-pound turkey breast, with skin and bone
1 large onion, chopped
3 carrots, peeled and chopped
2 bay leaves

1 teaspoon whole black peppercorns
¼ cup plus 2 tablespoons white vinegar
1 tablespoon salt

Marinade:
6 tablespoons fresh lemon juice
3 tablespoons balsamic vinegar
1 cup olive oil
Zest of 2 large lemons, in strips
⅔ cup golden raisins

4 tablespoons drained capers
2 tablespoons chopped parsley
2 tablespoons chopped fresh mint
Toasted pine nuts

In a large pot place turkey breast and cover it by 1 inch with cold water. Remove turkey. To the water left in the pot add the onion, carrots, bay leaves, peppercorns, white vinegar, and salt. Bring to a boil. Return turkey to the pot and simmer, covered, for 1 hour and 15 minutes. Do not boil (the meat will toughen); maintain a bare simmer. Remove pot from heat and allow to cool for 30 minutes, uncovered. Discard liquid and solids. Remove skin and bone from the turkey, keeping the meat in 2 large pieces, if possible. While the turkey is poaching, make the marinade.

Marinade: Soak raisins in boiling water to cover for 5 minutes; drain and set aside. In a small bowl whisk together the lemon juice and balsamic vinegar. Add the oil in a stream, whisking until the sauce is emulsified. Add the zest, drained raisins, and capers. Place breast in a bowl and pour marinade over it. Cover and marinate for at least 4 hours or overnight in the refrigerator, turning occasionally. Before serving, allow turkey to stand at room temperature for 30 minutes. Transfer meat to a carving board and slice on the diagonal in ¼-inch slices. Arrange slices on a platter. Stir parsley and mint into the marinade and pour over the turkey slices. Garnish with toasted pine nuts.

Bravo!

Orange Game Hens

Easy	*Yield: 4 servings*
Partial do ahead	*Preparing: 5 to 10 minutes*
	Marinating: 6 to 12 hours
	Grilling/Roasting: 30 to 40 minutes
	May be doubled

4 fresh or frozen Cornish game hens	**1 teaspoon fresh thyme, chopped**
4 oranges, juice and grated rind	**1 large clove garlic, minced**
1 cup dry vermouth	**¼ cup olive oil**
2 tablespoons fresh rosemary, chopped	**⅛ teaspoon freshly ground pepper**

Rinse and dry game hens and place in a non-reactive bowl. Mix together the orange juice and rind, the vermouth, rosemary, thyme, olive oil, and pepper. Pour over the hens, cover, and refrigerate for at least 6 hours or up to 12 hours, basting occasionally. If desired, stuff hens (recipe follows) and either grill over medium hot coals for about 30 minutes, basting frequently, or roast, uncovered in a preheated 350° oven for 40 minutes, basting frequently. For a sauce, degrease and reduce marinade slightly. Garnish with fresh rosemary sprigs and orange slices.

Note: Cooking varies according to the size of the game hens and how old they are. Watch them carefully, therefore, so as not to overcook.

Stuffing for Orange Game Hens

Easy	*Yield: 4½ to 5 cups*
	Preparing: 15 minutes
	Baking: 30 minutes

½ large onion, finely chopped	**3 cups cooked basmati rice**
½ (7-ounce) can water chestnuts, chopped	**(1 cup uncooked)**
	1 clove garlic, minced
½ cup mango chutney	**½ teaspoon dried crushed rosemary**
¼ cup chopped red or green pepper	**Large pinch mustard powder**
	Salt and pepper to taste

Mix all the ingredients together, and stuff game hens just before cooking, or heat, covered, in a 350° oven for 30 minutes, to serve separately.

Roasted Rock Cornish Hens

Easy   Yield: 6 servings
Partial do ahead   Preparing: 15 minutes
     Marinating: 2 hours
     Roasting: 25 minutes
     May be doubled

3 Cornish hens, split, backbone removed
¼ cup plus 2 tablespoons fresh lemon juice
¼ cup plus 2 tablespoons olive oil
2½ teaspoons minced fresh thyme
1½ teaspoons dried rosemary

3 cloves garlic, minced
1 bay leaf
Salt and pepper to taste
3 tablespoons butter substitute, melted
Watercress or parsley for garnish

In a non-reactive bowl combine lemon juice, olive oil, thyme, rosemary, garlic, and bay leaf; add salt and pepper to taste. Pour this marinade over the split hens and coat all sides thoroughly. Cover and refrigerate for 2 hours. Remove hens from marinade and pat dry with paper towels. About 30 minutes before cooking preheat oven to 500°. Arrange hens, skin side up, in a single layer in a baking dish. Brush with melted butter substitute and sprinkle with salt and pepper. Roast for 20 to 25 minutes. Transfer to a platter garnished with watercress or parsley. Serve warm or at room temperature.

Broiled Rock Cornish Game Hens with Herbed Butter

Easy   Yield: 4 servings
     Preparing: 15 minutes
     Broiling: 25 minutes

4 game hens, about 1¼ pounds each
¼ cup olive oil

Salt and freshly ground pepper

Sauce:
5 tablespoons butter
1 tablespoon Worcestershire sauce
2 tablespoons fresh tarragon, minced

2 tablespoons fresh parsley, minced
1 tablespoon fresh thyme leaves
2½ tablespoons fresh lemon juice

Preheat broiler. Using kitchen scissors, split game hens down the back and place on a rack in a broiling pan. With your palms, press down hard on the breast bone to flatten (or use a mallet). Brush chicken all over with olive oil and season with salt and pepper. Arrange hens, skin side down, on rack and broil close to heat 5 minutes. Turn and broil a further 5 minutes. Close the oven door, turn heat down to 350°, and continue to cook for 15 minutes. To test if the meat is fully cooked, pierce in the thickest section; juices should run clear. While the chicken is baking make the sauce. Melt the butter over a low heat and add herbs. Mix well and leave on low heat, to enhance flavor, until ready to serve.

115

Bravo!

Oriental Duckling

Average
Partial do ahead

Yield: 2 servings
Preparing: 1 hour
Baking: 2 hours
Cooling: 30 minutes
Cooking: 15 minutes
May be doubled or tripled

1 duckling
2 tablespoons paprika
2 tablespoons black pepper
2 tablespoons granulated garlic
1 onion, chopped
1 orange, peeled
2 tablespoons butter
1 tablespoon toasted sesame oil
1 cup julienned leeks
1 carrot

1 parsnip
1 daikon radish, julienned
1 red bell pepper, julienned
1 teaspoon minced fresh ginger root
1 teaspoon crushed garlic
3 tablespoons tamari soy sauce
1 tablespoon sherry
1½ cups fresh orange juice
1 cup snow peas

This recipe uses a twice-cooked method for the duckling. Duck is baked ahead so you can finish the same day or hold it and finish the dish even 2 days later. Step I: Remove excess fat from cavity of duckling. Cut off neck skin and discard. Mix the paprika, black pepper, and garlic to make a seasoning mix. Sprinkle 1 tablespoon of this mix in the cavity of the duck together with half the onion and half the orange, squeezing the juice first and then the remaining flesh. Preheat oven to 425°. Place the duckling in a roasting pan sprayed with vegetable spray. Sprinkle 1 tablespoon of the seasoning mix and scatter the remaining onion and orange. Cover tightly with foil and bake for approximately 2 hours or until the leg joint is very loose. Remove from oven and allow to cool, covered, for 30 minutes. Remove leg and thigh and breast. (The remaining duck parts may be used to make stock.)
Step II: In a large sauté pan heat 2 tablespoons butter with 1 tablespoon toasted sesame oil; over high heat sauté the julienned leeks, carrot, parsnip, radish, and pepper with the ginger root and garlic until the "aroma fills the nose." Reduce heat to medium and add duck parts, cooking for 2 or 3 minutes on each side. Cover; lower heat to a bare simmer. Simmer for 7 minutes. Add 1 cup snow peas. Replace lid and remove pan from heat; in 15 seconds the snow peas will be cooked. Serve immediately over rice or angel-hair pasta.

Gracie's 21st Century Café, Pine Forge, PA

Duck Cassoulet

Average
Do ahead

Yield: 10 servings
Soaking: Overnight
Preparing: 1 hour
Baking: 3 hours
May be doubled or tripled

2 pounds dry white navy beans
2 large carrots
3 cloves of garlic
2 to 3 large sprigs thyme
3 to 4 large bay leaves
10 large duck legs with skin
1½ pounds gourmet garlic sausage

2 teaspoons of oil
2 medium onions, cut into eighths
1 tablespoon tomato paste
1 cup bread crumbs
French bread
Chopped parsley

Soak beans (just covered) in warm water overnight. Cook softened beans in the same water with carrots, garlic, thyme, and bay leaves in an 8-quart pot for 1 hour over a medium flame. Add salt and pepper to taste. In a large skillet or pan braise duck and sausage in 2 teaspoons of oil until golden brown all over. Add onions and tomato paste. Cook for a few minutes. Add the bean mixture to the duck mixture. Cover with foil and bake for 2 hours in a 375° oven. Transfer to an oven-to-table casserole dish. Cover with bread crumbs mixed with melted butter and broil until golden brown. Garnish with toasted French bread croutons dipped in cassoulet juice then chopped parsley.

Jacques R. Vitré Catering

Marinated Flank Steak

Easy
Partial do ahead

Yield: 4 servings
Preparing: 10 minutes
Marinating: 2 hours
Broiling: 10 minutes
May be doubled

¾ cup prepared Italian dressing
¾ cup soy sauce
2½ tablespoons brown sugar

½ teaspoon ground ginger
2 pounds flank steak

Thoroughly combine first four ingredients to make marinade. Lightly score flank steak on each side; place in a shallow glass pan. Pour marinade over steak and turn to coat both sides. Cover and marinate at room temperature for 2 hours or in the refrigerator overnight. Turn meat in marinade from time to time. In a preheated broiler, about 4 inches from the heat, broil steak 5 minutes on each side or until sufficiently cooked. To serve, slice on the diagonal.

Bravo!

Jill's Beguiling Brisket

Easy Yield: 6 servings
Preparing: 5 minutes
Baking: 20 minutes per pound

1 3- to 4-pound brisket (any cut)   **1 (1-ounce) package onion soup mix**
¼ pound fresh mushrooms, sliced

Preheat oven to 375°. Place brisket in the center of a large piece of foil. Sprinkle sliced mushrooms over the top. Pour contents of onion soup mix over the mushrooms. Close the foil around the brisket so that it is well sealed, but leave enough room for meat to expand. Bake 20 minutes per pound of brisket. The meat will make its own gravy. Unwrap carefully, reserving gravy. Slice meat at an angle. Serve with gravy. Additional gravy may be made by adding a little boiling water to the existing gravy, or by using fresh stock and adding more mushrooms. Delicious served with potato pancakes.

Jill Pasternak, WFLN-FM 95.7, Philadelphia, PA

Tenderloin of Beef Deluxe

Easy Yield: 8 servings
Preparing: 10 minutes
Roasting: 45 minutes

1 3-pound whole beef tenderloin,   **1 teaspoon Dijon mustard**
** room temperature**   **Dash freshly ground pepper**
4 tablespoons butter   **¾ cup dry sherry**
¼ cup chopped scallion   **Chopped parsley**
2 tablespoons soy sauce

Preheat oven to 400°. Soften 2 tablespoons butter and spread on tenderloin. Place on a rack in a shallow roasting pan and bake, uncovered, for 20 minutes. Meanwhile, sauté onions in remaining 2 tablespoons butter until soft. Add soy sauce, mustard, pepper, and sherry; heat just until boiling. After beef has baked for 20 minutes baste it with the sauce and continue baking for another 20 to 25 minutes, for medium-rare, basting frequently. Remove from oven and allow to rest for 10 minutes. Carve in 1-inch slices, arrange slices overlapping on a platter, and garnish with parsley. Serve with its own sauce on the side.

Note: For best results the meat should sit at room temperature for 2 to 3 hours before roasting.

Barbecued Filet of Beef

Easy Yield: ½ pound per person
Preparing: 5 minutes
Broiling: 34 minutes

1 filet of beef (any size)	**1 (6-ounce) jar stoneground or Dijon mustard**

Prepare the filet by removing all excess fat and the tail. (Reserve for another use.) Cover all sides of the beef with mustard. Turn grill to high for about 10 minutes.Grill filet on high for 10 minutes. Turn and cook for another 10 minutes. Turn grill to medium. Turn beef and cook for 7 minutes; turn beef again and cook for another 7 minutes. This will make it medium-rare. For less rare, after the grill is reduced to medium, cook meat for 10 minutes per side.

Tenderloin of Beef with 5 Peppercorns

Easy Yield: 8 servings
Preparing: 20 minutes
Roasting: 45 to 55 minutes

1 3½- to 4-pound beef tenderloin, trimmed of fat	**3 tablespoons coarsely ground 5-peppercorn blend**
3 tablespoons Dijon mustard	**8 fresh large sage leaves**
1½ tablespoons green peppercorns (packed in water, drained)	**2 tablespoons butter, softened**
	Salt to taste
	4 bay leaves

Preheat oven to 425°. Using a sharp knife, make a cut lengthwise down the center of the tenderloin through two-thirds of the thickness. Spread meat open and flatten slightly with meat pounder. Spread mustard in a thin layer over the opened beef and sprinkle with green peppercorns, pressing them lightly into the meat with your fingers. Sprinkle with 1 tablespoon of 5-peppercorn blend. Place sage leaves in a row down the center. Put the meat back into its original shape and with string, tie it closed in several places. Rub the outside with softened butter and press remaining peppercorn blend onto the outside surface. Sprinkle with salt to taste. Place meat, seam-side down, in a shallow roasting pan and slip the bay leaves under the strings on top. Roast the meat, uncovered, for 45 to 55 minutes for rare. Allow to stand for 10 minutes. Remove strings and bay leaves and carve into 1-inch slices. Serve with the pan juices spooned over the slices.

Bravo!

Filet of Beef Stuffed with Bell Peppers, Spinach, and Goat Cheese

Complicated Yield: 8 servings
Partial do ahead Preparing: 1 hour
  Roasting: 1 hour

4 medium red bell peppers
1¼ pound fresh spinach, stemmed
8 ounces goat cheese, crumbled
½ teaspoon dried rosemary, crumbled
½ teaspoon dried thyme
¼ teaspoon freshly ground pepper

1 3-pound filet of beef (center plus tail)
½ pound bacon slices
3 tablespoons olive oil
Fresh chives

Up to 1 day Ahead: Char peppers, until blackened on all sides, over an open flame or in the broiler. Enclose in a paper bag and allow to stand for 10 minutes. Peel and seed. Rinse and pat dry. Cut into quarters. Refrigerate until ready to use. Set aside 10 large spinach leaves and refrigerate. Blanch remaining leaves in a large pot of boiling water just until wilted, about 2 minutes. Drain and refresh under cold water. Wrap spinach in a towel and squeeze dry. Coarsely chop spinach and transfer to a large bowl. Add the goat cheese, rosemary, thyme, and pepper. Mix thoroughly. Set cheese mixture on a large piece of wax paper and roll into a 12-inch long log. Wrap and refrigerate until firm.

Day of Serving: Cut beef lengthwise down the center, cutting two-thirds through. Open flat and pound to a thickness of ¾ inch. Season with salt and pepper. Arrange 10 reserved spinach leaves over cut side of beef leaving a 1-inch border. Cover with peppers, skin side up. Place cheese/spinach log on long side of beef and roll it all into a tight cylinder, tucking tail piece under. Tie at 1-inch intervals. (May be refrigerated for up to 6 hours at this point.)

2 hours Before Serving: Preheat oven to 375°. Blanch bacon in large pot of boiling water for 10 minutes. Drain and pat dry. Heat oil in large roasting pan over medium-high heat. Add beef and brown on all sides (about 10 minutes). Place bacon over the beef on roasting rack and roast for about 1 hour or until thermometer registers 125° for rare. Allow to cool for 15 minutes. Remove and discard bacon. Slice meat into 1-inch slices and arrange on a platter. Garnish with chives.

Grilled Beef Kebabs Caribbean Style

Easy
Do ahead

Yield: 4 servings
Preparing: 15 minutes
Marinating: 1 to 2 days
Grilling: 7 to 8 minutes
May be doubled

Marinade:

1½ teaspoons freshly grated ginger
  root
1 teaspoon crushed hot red
  pepper flakes
1 large garlic clove, crushed

¼ cup grated coconut (unsweetened)
½ cup unsweetened coconut milk
½ cup amber rum
¼ cup corn oil

Meat:

1½ pounds sirloin steak, cut into
  1½-inch cubes
1 bunch scallions, cut into
  1½-inch lengths

Oranges cut into segments, rind on,
  seeds out

Combine all ingredients for the marinade and mix well. Marinate the beef for at least 24 hours, or up to 2 days, in a covered non-reactive container, in the refrigerator, stirring occasionally. Thread meat on skewers, alternating with scallions and orange pieces. Grill, turning and basting with the marinade for 7 to 8 minutes or until required degree of rareness is achieved. Serve with rice and fresh fruit salad.

Note: Unsweetened coconut milk and grated coconut may be obtained at health-food stores.

Cook celery or carrots in consommé and serve cold with Roquefort dressing.

121

Bravo!

Stuffed Flank Steak with Red Wine Sauce

Easy | Yield: 4 servings
| Preparing: 40 minutes
| Marinating: 30 minutes
| Baking: 35 minutes

1 flank steak
⅓ cup soy sauce
⅔ cup dry red wine
½ cup thinly sliced green onions

2 cups packaged herbed stuffing mix
¼ pound fresh mushrooms, sliced
1 tablespoon unsalted butter
Chopped parsley to garnish

Score steak across the grain in several places on both sides with top of sharp knife. Lay flat in a shallow baking pan. Combine soy sauce, wine, and green onions; pour over meat and marinate 30 minutes. Prepare stuffing mix according to package directions. Drain marinade into a saucepan. Reserve. Spread stuffing on meat, roll lengthwise, and close securely along length at both ends with skewers. Bake approximately 35 minutes at 400° (meat should be medium), brushing 3 or 4 times with marinade. Meanwhile, sauté mushrooms in butter and heat marinade just to boiling. Remove cooked meat to warm platter, top with mushrooms, and pour warm marinade over all. Sprinkle with chopped parsley. Slice thinly on the diagonal.

Involtini alla Siciliana

Average | Yield: 4 servings
Do ahead | Preparing: 30 minutes
| Broiling: 20 minutes
| May be doubled

8 thinly sliced bottom round
   beef cutlets
½ cup grated pecorino
   Romano cheese
4 sprigs parsley, chopped
½ teaspoon dried, or 1 tablespoon
   freshly chopped basil
½ cup plain bread crumbs

Salt and pepper to taste
¼ cup milk, approximately
½ cup butter or margarine
¼ cup olive oil
1 cup plain bread crumbs
8 bay leaves
8 chunks of onion

Lay out beef cutlets. Combine cheese, parsley, basil, and ½ cup bread crumbs. Spread one side of each cutlet lightly with butter or margarine. Spread cheese mixture over cutlets and roll them up. Roll in oil and then in bread crumbs to coat. To assemble: Place 4 involtini on each of 2 8-inch meat-skewers, alternating the meat roll-ups with bay leaves and onion chunks. Repeat with remaining involtini, bay leaves and onion. Pierce each piece of meat with 2 more skewers to make a secure broiling arrangement. Can be made ahead to this point. Preheat broiler and broil meat about 4 inches from heat for 10 minutes on each side.

Steak and Onion Pie with Egg Pastry

Average
Partial do ahead

Yield: 6 servings
Preparing: 1 hour
Baking: 25 minutes
May be doubled

1 cup sliced onions
¼ cup shortening
1 pound sirloin steak, cut into
  ½-inch cubes
¼ cup flour
2 teaspoons salt
⅛ teaspoon pepper

½ teaspoon paprika
Dash ground ginger
Dash allspice
2½ cups boiling water
2 cups raw potatoes cut into
  ½-inch cubes

Melt shortening in a large heavy skillet and cook onions slowly until yellow. Remove and set aside. Mix together flour, salt, pepper, and spices and roll meat in mixture to coat. Brown quickly in hot shortening. Add boiling water to skillet, cover, and simmer 10 to 15 minutes. Add potatoes and cook 10 minutes longer. Pour contents of skillet into a buttered 8-inch casserole. Lay reserved onions over the top. Fit with egg pastry; seal edges.
Bake at 450° for 25 minutes.

Egg Pastry:
1 cup flour
½ teaspoon salt

⅓ cup shortening
1 egg, slightly beaten

Mix together flour and salt; cut in shortening. Blend in egg. Roll dough to ½-inch thickness. Fit over pie. Seal edges, and slit top.

Bravo!

Gracie's Beef Stew Provençal

Average   *Yield: 4 servings*
Preparing: 20 minutes
Baking: 2 hours

2½ pounds beef stew meat,
    cut into cubes
Flour for dredging
2 cups sliced onions
2 cups sliced mushrooms
2 cups tomatoes, peeled, seeded,
    and juiced
1 cup vermouth
¼ cup gin

2 bay leaves
1 teaspoon dried basil
1 teaspoon dried oregano
1 teaspoon dried thyme
2 large cloves garlic, mashed
3 tablespoons Dijon mustard
⅓ cup olive oil
½ cup chopped parsley
2 tablespoons drained capers

Preheat oven to 350°. Dredge stew meat in flour and place in the bottom of a large casserole. Place the onions, mushrooms, and tomatoes on top of the meat. Add the vermouth and gin, the bay leaves, basil, oregano, and thyme. Add salt and pepper to taste. Cover and bake for 2 hours. Meanwhile, make an "enrichment" by combining mashed garlic, mustard, olive oil, parsley, and capers. When meat is tender, add enrichment and blend thoroughly. Taste for seasoning. Remove bay leaves. Serve hot with noodles and green beans.

Sir Georg Solti's "Goulash"

Easy   *Yield: 6 servings*
Do ahead   *Preparing: 20 minutes*
Cooking: 2 hours
May be doubled

2 ounces lard
½ pound onions, peeled and diced
2½ pounds braising steak, cut into ½-
    inch cubes
2 cloves garlic, chopped
Pinch caraway seeds
Salt to taste

2 tablespoons finest quality paprika
8 cups beef stock
½ pound tomatoes, peeled and diced
2 green peppers, cut into rings
1 pound potatoes peeled, cut into
    ½-inch cubes

In a heavy-bottom saucepan heat lard. Sauté onions lightly in lard; add beef, and sauté for 10 minutes. Remove pan from heat; add garlic, caraway seeds, salt, and paprika. Add beef stock and return to heat. Cover and simmer for 1½ hours. Add tomatoes, and peppers to pan; cover and simmer for 30 minutes, adding additional stock, if needed, to maintain a soup-like consistency. Add potatoes and cook until tender (about 10 minutes). Serve with little dumplings.

Sir Georg Solti

124

Polenta with Beef and Sausage

Easy　　*Yield: 8 servings*
Do ahead　　*Preparing: 15 minutes*
　　　　Cooking: 1 hour
　　　　May be doubled

Stew:
3 tablespoons olive oil
¼ cup butter
½ pound onion, diced
2 cloves garlic, minced
1½ pounds lean stewing beef, cut into ½-inch cubes
1 pound Italian sausage, hot or sweet, casings removed
½ pound mushrooms, sliced

2 tablespoons finely chopped celery
2 tablespoons finely chopped carrot
1 (35-ounce) can plum tomatoes, drained and chopped
Nutmeg to taste
1 bay leaf
4 sprigs parsley, finely chopped
½ cup dry white wine

Polenta:
1 cup yellow cornmeal
1 cup cold water
4 cups boiling water

2 to 3 tablespoons butter
¾ cup grated Parmesan cheese
Salt to taste

Stew: Heat butter and olive oil; add onions and garlic and cook over medium heat for 5 minutes. Add beef and sausage and cook, stirring, for 5 minutes. Add the remaining stew ingredients one by one, stirring with each addition. Simmer, uncovered, for 40 minutes, stirring occasionally, until beef is tender. Taste for seasoning; add salt and pepper if necessary.
Polenta: Combine cornmeal with cold water. In a 2-quart pan bring 4 cups of water to a boil. Add cornmeal mixture and simmer, stirring frequently, for 15 or 20 minutes. Add 2 to 3 tablespoons of butter; taste for seasoning. Add salt to taste. Pour polenta onto a flat board and sprinkle cheese on top; cut into 8 pieces. Serve stew with a piece of polenta on the side.

The Parson's Lamb Shanks

Easy　　*Yield: 4 servings*
Do ahead　　*Preparing: 10 minutes*
　　　　Baking: 3 hours

4 lamb shanks
Crushed garlic or garlic powder to taste

1 envelope dried onion soup mix
⅔ cup water
⅓ cup sherry

Place a very long double layer of heavy aluminum foil in a roasting pan. Place lamb shanks on top of foil; sprinkle with garlic and onion soup mix. Pour water and sherry around the sides of shanks. Bring foil up over lamb and crimp edges to make it air-tight. Bake at 350° for 3 hours. Serve with rice or mashed potatoes.

Bravo!

Balsamic Broiled Lamb Chops

Easy *Yield: 2 servings*
Preparing: 5 minutes
Marinating: 30 to 45 minutes
Broiling: To desired degree of doneness

2 cloves garlic, minced
4 tablespoons balsamic vinegar
1½ teaspoons dried rosemary,
　crushed

1 teaspoon Dijon mustard
½ teaspoon pepper
Salt to taste
4 lamb chops

In a pie plate combine all ingredients except chops. Add lamb chops; coat to marinate for 30 to 45 minutes. Broil or grill, basting with marinade, until desired doneness is achieved.

Marinated Lamb Chops

Easy *Yield: 4 servings*
Preparing: 15 minutes
Marinating: 1 hour
Grilling: 10 minutes
May be doubled

⅓ teaspoon ground ginger
¼ teaspoon ground allspice
1 teaspoon curry powder
1 cup tomato sauce

3 tablespoons cider vinegar
3 garlic cloves, mashed
8 loin lamb chops
Salt and pepper to taste

Place first 6 ingredients in a small saucepan and bring slowly to a boil. Simmer for 10 minutes. Place lamb chops in a deep, non-reactive dish; pour marinade over the chops making sure that each is thoroughly coated. Marinate at room temperature for 1 hour. Place chops on a hot grill and cook for 5 minutes, basting with the marinade. Turn the chops and cook 5 minutes more, basting occasionally. This amount of time will produce a rare meat. If more well-done is desired, cook longer on each side.

Lamb with Walnuts

Average	Yield: 8 to 10 servings
Do ahead	Preparing: 1 hour
Freeze	Baking: 1¾ hours
	Cooling: 24 hours

---

4 pounds boneless leg of lamb, all fat removed, in 1½-inch cubes
1 tablespoon flour
4 tablespoons olive oil
1 large clove garlic, finely chopped
2 large onions, sliced
1½ cups pineapple juice
4 strips lemon zest
¼ cup tomato purée
3 tablespoons malt vinegar
2 tablespoons soy sauce
1½ tablespoons brown sugar
½ teaspoon curry powder
¾ cup chopped walnuts

Preheat oven to 350°. Dredge lamb cubes in flour. Over moderately high heat brown the lamb in 2 tablespoons of oil, working in batches. Do not overcrowd the pan. As the meat browns, remove it with a slotted spoon to a large, heavy casserole. With the remaining 2 tablespoons of oil sauté the onions and garlic until golden, about 5 minutes. Add all the ingredients, except the walnuts, stir well, and simmer for 5 minutes. Pour this sauce over the meat. Cover and bake for 50 minutes. Allow to cool and refrigerate, covered, for 24 hours. Before reheating, remove any accumulated fat and add the walnuts. Place, covered, in a preheated 350° oven for 45 minutes or until heated through and bubbly. Serve with rice and an avocado/spinach salad.

Note: A 6-pound leg of lamb with the bone yields about 4 pounds of boneless. This dish can be made for a crowd and frozen in batches of 4 pounds each.

Bravo!

Roasted Rack of Lamb with Fresh Plum Mint Sauce

Average Yield: 4 servings
Preparing: 5 minutes
Roasting: 35 to 40 minutes
May be doubled

1 8-ribbed rack of lamb ("Frenched" by butcher)
2 tablespoons (approximately) Dijon mustard
½ cup fresh bread crumbs
1 tablespoon olive oil

4 plums, pitted and diced
2 shallots, diced
¾ cup cassis
2 tablespoons chopped fresh mint
Brown sugar to taste
Freshly ground black pepper

Preheat oven to 400°. Brush lamb with mustard and sprinkle with bread crumbs. Roast for 35 to 40 minutes for medium doneness. Remove lamb to a warm serving platter and keep warm while preparing sauce. In a small frying pan heat oil; sauté plums and shallots briefly. Deglaze the roasting pan with cassis. In a small saucepan combine the cassis with the plums and shallots. Add mint, brown sugar to taste, and freshly ground pepper. To serve, place sauce under the lamb.

Richard Hamilton, Marshallton Inn, West Chester, PA

Encore Indonesian Lamb Casserole

Average Yield: 6 servings
Do ahead Preparing: 30 minutes
Baking: 30 to 45 minutes

1 tablespoon olive oil
1 tablespoon butter
1 large onion, chopped
3 cloves garlic, pressed
1 tablespoon flour
1¼ cups vegetable cocktail juice
½ cup creamy peanut butter

3 tablespoons lemon juice
2 tablespoons brown sugar
3 tablespoons soy sauce
4 cups cubed, cooked lamb
1 (10-ounce) bag frozen peas and carrots, partially thawed
Parsley for garnish

Preheat oven to 350°. In a frying pan large enough to hold all the ingredients, sauté the onion and garlic in the oil and butter until the onion is limp (about 5 minutes). Add the flour and mix well; gradually add the juice, stirring until combined. Add all the remaining ingredients except the parsley. Stir well. Pour this mixture into a lightly greased 2½-quart casserole and cover. Bake for 30 to 45 minutes until bubbly and hot. Garnish with chopped parsley.
Serve with noodles.

Note: Cooked chicken or pork may be substituted for the lamb.

Lamb Tart

Easy
Partial do ahead

Yield: 8 servings
Preparing: 30 minutes
Chilling: Overnight
Baking: 45 minutes

Pie Crust:
8 ounces cream cheese, at room temperature

8 ounces butter, at room temperature
2 cups flour

Filling:
1 tablespoon butter
1 cup chopped onion
½ cup dried mushrooms (soaked for several hours and wrung out)
8 ounces hot sausage meat
1 clove garlic, minced

1 pound ground lamb
½ cup chopped pistachios
2 eggs
¾ cup buttermilk
Salt, pepper, and nutmeg, to taste

Pie Crust: Cream together cheese and butter; add flour. Mix well and form into a ball. Wrap ball airtight and chill overnight. Cut dough in half and roll each half between 2 pieces of wax paper to make 2 10-inch crusts. (Tightly wrap and freeze 1 for later use.)

Filling: Preheat oven to 375°. Melt butter in a pan large enough to hold all remaining ingredients. Sauté onion for 5 minutes, add mushrooms, and cook for 2 minutes. Add sausage and minced garlic; cook 5 minutes longer, stirring. Add lamb and pistachios, and taste for seasoning. Add salt, pepper, and nutmeg, to taste. Remove from heat to cool slightly. Beat together eggs and buttermilk and add to the meat mixture. Pour into the unbaked pie shell and bake for 15 minutes. Lower heat to 350° and continue baking for 30 to 35 minutes, or until set (when a knife inserted in the center comes out clean). May be served hot, warm, or chilled.

If chilled, serve with mayonnaise mixed with hot, prepared mustard, to taste.

Gary Graffman

Bravo!

Hell Fire Stew

Easy
Do ahead

Yield: 6 servings
Preparing: 30 minutes
Cooking: 2 hours 10 minutes

2 tablespoons vegetable oil
1½ pounds boneless leg of lamb, in 1-inch cubes
2 (13½-ounce) cans chicken broth
⅓ cup barley
1½ cups chopped onion
1 cup chopped carrot
1 (14-ounce) can whole tomatoes and juice

1¼ teaspoons freshly ground black pepper
1 tablespoon dried thyme
1½ teaspoons dried basil
3 medium boiling potatoes, peeled and diced
1 large green pepper, diced
1 cup frozen, cut, green beans
1 cup frozen peas
2 tablespoons chopped Italian parsley

In large (2½-quart) heavy pot heat oil over medium heat. Add half the lamb cubes and brown them on all sides. Remove them to a holding plate with a slotted spoon and keep warm. Repeat with the remaining lamb and return the first batch to the pot with their juices. Add the chicken broth and bring to a boil. Add the barley and simmer slowly for 1 hour, stirring occasionally to prevent the barley from sticking and burning. Add the onions, carrots, tomatoes, ground pepper, thyme, and basil. Break up the tomatoes into smaller pieces and continue slowly simmering, covered, stirring occasionally for 30 more minutes. Add the potatoes and green pepper; simmer for 15 minutes. (If the stew is too thick, add more chicken broth.) Add frozen beans and peas; simmer for 15 minutes. Check that potatoes are thoroughly cooked by testing with a fork. Taste for seasoning and add salt and pepper if necessary. Garnish with chopped parsley and serve with a crusty bread and a tossed green salad.

Note: The barley is used to thicken the stew. If desired, it could be replaced with a mixture of 2 tablespoons of flour stirred into 3 tablespoons water, which can be added toward the end of the cooking process.

The Rabbit, Courtesy of Philip Randolph, Philadelphia, PA

Mixed Grill Brochette of Duck and Lamb with Red Leek Béarnaise Sauce

Average Yield: 4 servings
Preparing: 30 minutes
Grilling: 10 minutes

Béarnaise:
2 small leeks
2 cups zinfandel wine
1 cup red wine or tarragon vinegar
4 egg yolks

1 cup heavy cream
Salt and pepper to taste
2 tablespoons fresh tarragon

Brochettes:
2 large boneless duck breasts
1½ pounds leg of lamb, without fat

2 tablespoons olive oil or duck fat
Freshly cracked pepper

Sauce: Split the leeks lengthwise and wash carefully. Chop only the white part and place in a saucepan with wine and vinegar. Reduce rapidly until it is a glaze. Set aside. Heat the heavy cream until little bubbles appear at the sides of the pot (do not boil). Place egg yolks in the small, steel bowl of a double boiler and whisk in the hot cream. Add a splash of water and set the bowl over boiling water; whisk continuously until the mixture has thickened to a hollandaise texture. Continue whisking while adding the leek glaze and the chopped tarragon. Taste for seasoning and add salt and pepper if necessary. Set aside in a warm place, covered with plastic wrap.

Brochettes: Cut the duck and lamb into 1½-inch squares and brush them with olive oil or duck fat. Put the meat on skewers alternating lamb with duck until the skewer is full. Roll the brochettes in oil, and pepper generously. Grill to taste. To serve, put some of the sauce onto warmed plates, pull out the skewer, and arrange the meat on top of the sauce, adding more sauce to the top if desired. Serve at once.

Reunion Inn & Grill, Camden, ME

Freeze béarnaise sauce in an orange-juice can. Remove from the can, slice, and store in small plastic bags. When ready to use, remove the slices, defrost, but do not reheat. Place a round of sauce on top of a hot filet mignon or steak.

Bravo!

Pork Tenderloin

Easy
Partial do ahead

Yield: 8 servings
Preparing: 5 minutes
Marinating: Overnight
Grilling: 25 to 30 minutes

⅓ **cup sherry**
⅓ **cup oil**
⅓ **cup soy sauce**

½ **teaspoon ground ginger**
½ **teaspoon garlic powder**
1 **2-pound pork tenderloin**

Mix together the sherry, oil, soy sauce, ground ginger, and garlic powder. Put pork in a Ziploc plastic bag and add marinade. Refrigerate overnight, turning periodically. Grill, indoors or out, for 25 to 30 minutes, turning frequently and basting with the marinade. Pork should be pink inside. Slice and serve.

Pork Tenders with Bourbon Apple Dijon Marinade

Easy
Partial do ahead

Yield: 4 to 6 servings
Preparing: 10 minutes
Marinating: 4 to 12 hours
Cooking: 15 minutes

3 **pork tenderloins**

Marinade:
1½ **cups apple juice concentrate**
½ **cup Dijon mustard**
2 **scallions, diced**
2 **tablespoons chopped parsley**
2 **cloves garlic, minced**

⅛ **cup oil**
½ **cup bourbon**
½ **tablespoon cracked black pepper**
1 **teaspoon salt**

Place tenderloins, all fat removed, in a Ziploc bag. Combine all ingredients for the marinade and pour over pork. Close bag tightly and refrigerate 4 to 12 hours, basting with marinade and turning occasionally. Grill over medium heat, turning occasionally, to brown (approximately 10 minutes). Cook over indirect heat, covered, for an additional 5 to 7 minutes. Check internal temperature and cook to 150°. Allow meat to stand for 5 minutes before carving. In a small saucepan over low heat reduce leftover marinade to a syrup consistency. Slice meat into medallions and brush with sauce before serving.

Queen of Hearts, Paoli, PA

Roasted Pork Loin Stuffed with Pistachios

Average	Yield: 6 servings
Partial do ahead	Preparing: 45 minutes
	Marinating: 3 hours
	Roasting: 2 hours

⅓ cup shelled pistachios
⅓ cup golden raisins
⅓ cup finely chopped parsley
2 garlic cloves, finely chopped
1 3-pound pork loin, boned and rolled

½ teaspoon salt
Freshly ground pepper
⅓ cup butter
⅓ cup apple jelly
⅓ cup dry sherry

In a small bowl combine the pistachios with the raisins, parsley, and garlic. Lard the pork throughout by making holes, first with the point of a sharp knife, then enlarging them with the handle of a wooden spoon; stuff the holes with the nut/raisin mixture. Cover and allow to sit for at least 3 hours in the refrigerator. Bring to room temperature (1 hour) before roasting. Preheat oven to 325°. Lightly season the roast with salt and pepper and place in a roasting pan, on the middle rack of oven. Roast, uncovered, for 1½ hours. Gently melt the butter, apple jelly, and sherry in a small saucepan. During the next ½ hour of roasting, baste frequently until all the mixture is used (2 hours total). Remove the pork to a warm platter and cover loosely with aluminum foil. Pour the accumulated juices into a small serving bowl and remove any fat. Deglaze the cooking pan with a little water and add to the sauce. This gravy will be dark, rich brown in color. To serve, cut the pork into even slices and place on top of a spoonful of gravy to expose the marbled effect of the nuts and raisins.

Note: The cooked roast should sit for 15 minutes before being carved.

Easy Pork Chops

Easy	Yield: 4 servings
	Preparing: 5 minutes
	Baking: 1 hour

8 boneless pork loin chops, center-cut
6 tablespoons chili sauce
6 tablespoons lemon juice
1 teaspoon dry mustard

2 teaspoons Worcestershire sauce
⅛ teaspoon curry powder
¼ teaspoon paprika
½ cup water

Preheat oven to 325°. Place chops in a 2-quart casserole. Combine all other ingredients and mix well. Pour sauce over the chops and bake, covered, for 1 hour. Good served with rice or noodles.

133

Bravo!

Cambridge Chase Chops

Easy *Yield: 4 servings*
Preparing: 10 minutes
Cooking: 40 to 45 minutes

4 pork chops, ½-inch thick
1 tablespoon oil

1 clove garlic, minced

Sauce:
2 teaspoons oil
4 tablespoons dry sherry
**   or chicken broth**
4 tablespoons soy sauce

2 tablespoons brown sugar
¼ teaspoon crushed red pepper
2 teaspoons cornstarch
2 tablespoons water

Trim any fat from chops. Heat oil in a skillet; brown chops on both sides. Remove chops from pan; add a little more oil if necessary. Sauté garlic for 1 minute, watching carefully not to burn it. In a bowl combine oil, sherry, soy, sugar, and pepper. Place chops in skillet, pour sauce over them, and cover tightly. Simmer 30 to 35 minutes, turning once. Remove chops to platter. Dissolve cornstarch in water and add to skillet. Cook until thickened. Serve with chops.

Note: If too dry, add more sherry or broth.

Cayenne Garlic Pork Loin

Easy *Yield: 4 to 6 servings*
Partial do ahead *Preparing: 10 to 15 minutes*
Marinating: 1 to 4 hours
Roasting: 50 to 80 minutes
May be doubled

Marinade:
4 to 5 cloves garlic, pressed
**   or finely chopped**
½ cup olive oil
⅓ cup cayenne pepper sauce
Meat:
1 2-pound pork loin

½ tablespoon sesame oil
2 tablespoons soy sauce
⅛ teaspoon ground ginger

Combine marinade ingredients (even more cayenne pepper sauce for the bold!) and, in a non-reactive container, pour it over the pork. Cover and refrigerate, turning occasionally, for at least 1 hour, but preferably 4 hours. Preheat oven to 350° and roast pork, uncovered, for 50 to 80 minutes until the internal temperature reaches 180°. Do not overcook. For the brave, the marinade may be served as a sauce on the side. This dish makes a lovely addition to a cold, summer buffet.

Note: Pork may be cooked on the grill.

Pork Tenderloin with Mustard

Easy Yield: 4 servings
Preparing: 10 minutes
Cooking: 15 minutes
May be doubled

1½ pounds pork tenderloin	¼ cup dry vermouth
2 teaspoons dried thyme	½ cup cold milk
2 tablespoons olive oil (or less)	1 tablespoon instant flour
Salt and pepper to taste	2 tablespoons coarse Dijon mustard

Remove all fat from pork and cut into ¼-inch rounds. In a large heavy-duty frying pan, heat 1 teaspoon thyme with 1 tablespoon oil until moderately hot. Add half of the pork in 1 layer and cook about 3 minutes on each side, until juices are no longer pink. Sprinkle with salt and pepper to taste and, with a slotted spoon, transfer to a warm dish. Repeat with the remaining pork, adding more oil only if necessary. Transfer to the warm dish. Pour the vermouth into the pan and bring to a boil, scraping up any pork residues. Boil for 2 minutes to remove the alcohol. Combine the milk with the instant flour and, stirring briskly, add the mixture to the vermouth. It will thicken very quickly. Stir until thoroughly blended and add the mustard. Return the meat to the sauce and coat all pieces evenly. Serve with rice and a green vegetable.

Note: Leftovers may be puréed into a delicious pâté. For a richer sauce, ½ cup of light cream may be substituted for the milk/flour mixture.

Pork Roast

Easy Yield: 6 servings
Preparing: 30 minutes
Roasting: 90 minutes

1 3-pound loin of pork (boneless)	1 cup fine prepared stuffing mix
1 Granny Smith apple, diced	½ teaspoon dried rosemary or thyme
3 large celery stalks, diced	Salt and pepper
¾ cup raisins	1 cup applesauce, or more

Preheat oven to 350°. Have butcher make a pocket in the middle of the roast. Stuff with the apple mixed with celery, raisins, and stuffing mix. Sprinkle the top with a little salt and freshly cracked pepper, thyme, or rosemary. Spread applesauce over the top. Roast for 1½ hours. Add more applesauce if meat appears to be drying out.

Chopped Veal in Cream Sauce

Easy   *Yield: 6 servings*
Preparing: 15 minutes
Cooking: 20 minutes

1 (10-ounce) package frozen peas, defrosted
1 (16-ounce) can tomatoes
1 ounce butter
2 ounces butter
1 medium onion, chopped

1½ pounds chopped veal
Salt and pepper to taste
¾ pound mushrooms, sliced and sautéed
1½ cups dry white wine
1 cup heavy cream

Melt 1 ounce butter in a frying pan, add peas and tomatoes plus half the juice from the can. Stir gently so as not to break the tomatoes. Set aside and keep warm. In a large frying pan heat 2 ounces butter and sauté the onion until it starts to turn brown (about 7 minutes). Add the veal and, over high heat, sauté, turning meat continuously until it loses all pink color. Add the mushrooms, salt, and pepper. Add wine; simmer for 2 to 3 minutes. Add heavy cream, stir well, and serve immediately with peas and tomatoes.

Vladimir Ashkenazy

Veal Piccata

Easy   *Yield: 4 servings*
Preparing: 10 minutes
Cooking: 20 minutes

2 pounds boneless veal medallions, flattened slightly
1 teaspoon salt
½ teaspoon ground pepper
3 tablespoons flour
¾ teaspoon oregano
3 tablespoons olive oil

1 large onion, finely chopped
2 garlic cloves, crushed
1½ cups beef broth
¼ cup fresh lemon juice
Lemon slices
¼ cup minced parsley
2 tablespoons drained capers

Rub the veal with a mixture of the salt, pepper, flour, and oregano. Over medium heat in a large skillet, sauté the onion and garlic until it is soft but not brown, about 5 minutes. Remove with a slotted spoon. In the same pan, over slightly higher heat, brown the veal on both sides. Return the onion and garlic to the pan. Add the broth, bring to a boil, cover, reduce heat, and simmer for 10 to 15 minutes, or until meat is tender. Do not overcook. Stir in lemon juice and coat veal with sauce. Arrange on a warm platter and garnish with lemon slices, parsley, and capers.

Transylvania (Sauerkraut) Stew

Average Yield: 6 servings
Do ahead Preparing: 20 minutes
Cooking: 90 minutes
May be doubled or tripled

2 tablespoons olive oil
2 large onions, roughly chopped
2 tablespoons paprika
2 pounds lean pork or veal, cubed
2 pounds sauerkraut

½ to 1 cup white wine or water
1 teaspoon thyme or marjoram
   (optional)
Salt to taste
½ to 1 cup sour cream

In a Dutch oven heat the oil; sauté the onions and the paprika for about 5 minutes. Add the pork or veal and sauté for another 5 minutes. Squeeze sauerkraut and discard the juice. Add the squeezed sauerkraut to the meat and mix. Add optional thyme or marjoram. Add enough wine to keep the stew from burning and bring to a near boil. Reduce the heat and simmer gently, covered, for 1½ hours, or until the meat is tender. During this time check the moisture, occasionally adding more wine to prevent burning but being careful not to make the stew soupy. Taste for seasoning and add salt if necessary. Before serving, mix in some sour cream.

Kalbsroellchen Napoleon — Veal Rolls Napoleon

Easy Yield: 4 servings
Preparing: 15 minutes
Cooking: 10 minutes

1 6-ounce veal medallion per person
Salt and pepper to taste
Mushrooms, finely diced
Onion, finely diced
Cooked ham, finely diced

Parsley, chopped
Vegetable shortening
White wine or beef broth
Crème fraîche, to taste

Lightly pound the veal until thin, and season with salt and pepper. Make a mixture of the mushrooms, onions, ham, and parsley, spread it over the veal, and roll. Tie with cotton string or stainless steel skewers. Brown roll in short-ening until lightly golden brown, add wine or broth and braise gently until tender. Remove meat from pan and finish the sauce by adding crème fraîche and any extra filling that may be left over. Sprinkle with freshly chopped parsley. Serve with rice.

Note: The editor suggests for 4 people the following quantities for the filling may be used: ½ cup chopped mushrooms, ½ cup chopped onion, ¼ cup chopped ham, ½ cup chopped parsley. It is also recommended that the mushrooms, onions, and ham be sautéed in a little oil until the onions are tender before they are spread on the veal.

Mrs. Wolfgang Sawallisch

Bravo!

Filet of Veal

Easy Yield: 3 servings
Preparing: 5 minutes
Cooking: 20 minutes
May be doubled

Q E D

Filet of veal, about 1 pound	Olive oil
Salt and cracked pepper	Mushroom or tomato sauce
Thyme	Watercress for garnish

Preheat oven to 325°. Pat the meat dry with a towel. Sprinkle with salt and freshly cracked pepper and a small amount of thyme. In a hot oven-proof pan, sear all sides of the meat in a small amount of oil. Transfer the pan with the meat to the oven and cook, uncovered, for 10 to 15 minutes. Do not overcook. Serve with a mushroom or tomato sauce. Garnish with watercress. Good served with "baby" vegetables - patty pan squash, haricot verts, and baby carrots.

Note: This is an expensive cut of meat, but there is no waste. It makes an elegant serving size per person.

Côtes de Veau aux Fines Herbes

Average Yield: 6 servings
Preparing: 10 minutes
Cooking: 30 minutes

1 cup chopped mushrooms	1 cup dry vermouth
6 tablespoons butter	2 tablespoons chopped fresh tarragon
2 pounds veal for cutlets	1 teaspoon dried rosemary
Salt and pepper to taste	1 tablespoon chopped chives
⅓ cup flour	¼ cup chopped fresh parsley for
6 slices Swiss cheese	garnish

In a medium-hot frying pan melt 1 tablespoon butter and briefly sauté mushrooms. Set aside for later use. Flatten veal to ¼-inch thickness and cut into 6 uniform pieces. Season with salt and pepper and dredge in flour. In a hot frying pan melt 3 tablespoons butter; brown veal on both sides, then cover pan, reduce heat, and cook gently until tender, about 15 minutes. Remove cover and place 1 slice of cheese over each piece of meat; cook for 2 minutes, or until cheese melts. Remove to a heated platter while preparing the sauce. Pour the vermouth into the frying pan and scrape up any accumulated juices. Simmer for 2 minutes. Stir in sautéed mushrooms, remaining butter, tarragon, rosemary, and chives. Pour sauce over cutlets and sprinkle with chopped parsley.

Note: Sliced turkey breast may be substituted for the veal.

Foie de Veau au Marais

Average Yield: 3 to 4 servings
Partial do ahead Preparing: 1 hour
Cooking: 10 minutes

3 large onions, finely chopped	1 pound calves liver, thinly sliced
3 tablespoons butter	2 tablespoons flour
2 tablespoons olive oil	½ cup balsamic vinegar
1 tablespoon sugar	

In a large skillet over low heat slowly caramelize the onions by sautéing them in 1 tablespoon butter, 1 tablespoon oil, and 1 tablespoon sugar. This should take about 1 hour stirring frequently. The onions should not brown; they should turn golden as they caramelize. Remove to a bowl and keep warm. Lightly coat the liver with flour. Melt 1 tablespoon butter and 1 tablespoon oil over high heat and sauté liver, one layer at a time, 2 minutes per side. Remove to a warm plate. Add 1 tablespoon butter to the skillet and stir in the vinegar, scraping down all particles. Stir until sauce resembles a fine glaze (1 to 2 minutes). Divide liver onto plates, cover each portion with caramelized onions and a drizzle of glaze.

Jeffrey Brillhart

Sole with Tarragon Cream Sauce

Easy Yield: 4 servings
Partial do ahead Preparing: 30 minutes
Cooking: 10 minutes
May be doubled

2 tablespoons butter	2 tablespoons fresh tarragon,
⅓ cup dry vermouth	coarsely chopped
¼ teaspoon ground black pepper	4 filets of sole, or any light, white fish
¼ teaspoon dry mustard	¼ cup heavy cream

Melt butter in a frying pan large enough to hold all the fish without crowding. Add vermouth, pepper, and mustard; swirl pan. Bring to a boil. Add tarragon and immediately lower heat, reducing sauce to a bare simmer for 10 minutes. Turn off heat and let sit for 30 minutes. (Can be made ahead at this point and left for up to 2 hours.) Wash and dry carefully fish filets. Heat sauce gently over a low heat. Add the fish in 1 layer and poach until fish is white, spooning sauce over the filets as they cook. Carefully remove filets to a warm platter. Turn the heat to high and add heavy cream, swirling it around the pan. Stir constantly with a wooden spoon until thick, about 2 minutes. Place fish on serving plates and spoon some sauce over each.

Tuck one small tarragon plant into your flower garden. You'll have all you could possibly use.

Bravo!

Sautéed Shad Roe

Easy   *Yield: 2 servings*
           Preparing: 5 minutes
           Cooking: 10 minutes

Q E D

2 sets shad roe
Salt and pepper to taste
4 tablespoons clarified butter
1 medium onion, thinly sliced

1 teaspoon fresh lemon juice
4 tablespoons chopped parsley
¼ teaspoon rosemary

Wash, dry, and season roe with salt and pepper. Over medium heat melt butter in a heavy skillet and sauté onion for 30 seconds. Push onion aside; add roe, lemon juice, parsley, and rosemary. Sauté until quite brown on both sides (about 10 minutes), turning carefully with spatulas to avoid breaking. If onions begin to burn, remove them to a hot plate.

Note: To clarify butter, melt, then strain through layers of cheesecloth. Dispose of the residue.

Catfish Consummate

Easy   *Yield: 2 servings*
           Preparing: 5 minutes
           Grilling: 10 minutes

Q E D

2 catfish filets
1 clove garlic, pressed
2 tablespoons light soy sauce
½ to ¾ teaspoon crumbled fish-
** flavored bouillon**

Freshly ground pepper
1 tablespoon corn or canola oil
2 tablespoons lemon juice
Lemon slices

Combine garlic, soy sauce, bouillon, pepper, oil, and lemon juice. Brush on fish. Let stand in a glass container a few minutes, turning at least once. Grill 5 minutes per side in a lightly oiled fish cooker. Serve with lemon slices.

Note: Can be baked in 350° oven for 20 minutes.

The Pier's Baked Red Snapper

Average | Yield: 6 servings
Preparing: 30 minutes
Baking: 35 minutes

1 whole red snapper (about 5 pounds)
1 medium onion, chopped
1 large green pepper, chopped
1 clove garlic, minced
2 tablespoons butter

2 cups bread crumbs
3 beaten eggs
1 tablespoon fresh dill, minced
1 tablespoon butter

Basting Mixture:
1 tablespoon butter
1 tablespoon lemon juice

1 cup white wine or vermouth

Preheat oven to 400°. Sauté onion, green pepper, and garlic in 3 tablespoons butter. Add crumbs, eggs, dill, and butter. Toss well; stuff fish loosely. Secure fish with skewers. Lay fish on oiled baking pan. Pour basting mixture over fish. Bake for 35 minutes. Baste often during cooking.

The Pier, Pascagoula, MS

Grilled Tuna with Lime Butter or Tomato Purée

Easy | Yield: 4 servings
Partial do ahead | Preparing: 10 to 40 minutes
Grilling: 2 to 5 minutes

Lime Butter:
2 limes, zest and juice only
1 (1-inch) cube fresh ginger root, minced

4 ounces butter at room temperature
Salt and pepper to taste

Tomato Purée:
6 plum tomatoes
2 cloves garlic

1 cup fresh basil leaves, julienned
Salt and pepper to taste

4 5-ounce tuna steaks

Oil for tuna

The sauces may be made ahead and stored in the refrigerator for 1 week.
Lime Butter: In a food processor purée the zest, juice, and ginger. Cream butter and gradually add lime/ginger mixture until it is absorbed. Add salt and pepper to taste.
Tomato Purée: Blanch the tomatoes for 10 seconds in boiling water. Peel, seed, and dice tomatoes; place in a small saucepan. Crush garlic and add to tomatoes. Simmer for 30 minutes, stirring occasionally, until mixture thickens. Add basil, salt, and pepper to taste.
Tuna: Lightly rub tuna steaks with oil. Grill over high heat for 2 to 5 minutes on each side, depending on thickness. Serve with either sauce.

Note: These sauces are also excellent with grilled chicken breasts.

Bravo!

Fish Chowder

Average   *Yield: 6 to 8 servings*
              Preparing: 90 minutes

2 large onions, chopped
½ cup olive oil
1 green bell pepper, chopped
1 red bell pepper, chopped
1 (28-ounce) can whole plum
   tomatoes

1 (6-ounce) can tomato paste
1 cup red wine
1½ cups water
1 tablespoon sugar
¾ teaspoon salt
2 pounds white fish

Sauté onions in olive oil until clear. Add peppers and sauté. Add remaining ingredients, except fish, and simmer for 30 to 40 minutes. Add half the fish in large chunks and simmer 20 minutes longer. Add remaining fish in chunks and simmer 5 minutes longer. Serve hot with crusty bread.

Fish in Parchment

Average   *Yield: 4 servings*
              Marinating: 25 minutes
              Preparing: 20 minutes
              Cooking: 25 minutes

White wine
8 pieces filet of sole, 2- to
   2½-pounds total
2 (10-ounce) bags fresh spinach
2 (12-ounce) boxes fresh mushrooms
1 pound mild cheddar cheese

4 15-inch squares of parchment
½ cup bread crumbs
1 teaspoon paprika
Butter
Salt and pepper to taste

In a shallow dish, marinate fish in white wine, no longer than 25 minutes. Preheat oven to 375°. Wash spinach; remove stems, and towel dry. Wash and slice mushrooms. Grate cheese. Divide ingredients evenly among 4 15-inch squares of parchment, layering all the spinach, one third of cheese, half the fish, salt and pepper, one third of cheese, half the mushrooms, bread crumbs, remainder of fish, salt and pepper, remainder of mushrooms, paprika, and dots of butter. Wrap parchment so that package is completely closed. Melt some butter (about 2 tablespoons) and brush outside of package so it does not burn. Cook on a lightly greased jelly-roll pan for 25 minutes. Unwrap so that spinach is on the bottom of packet.

Fabulous Swordfish for Two

Easy   Yield: 2 servings
Preparing: 5 minutes
Marinating: 30 minutes
Grilling: 6 to 8 minutes
May be doubled

---

12 ounces swordfish
2 tablespoons Dijon or coarse-grained
  mustard
2 tablespoons fresh lime juice
½ cup olive oil

2 shallots, chopped fine
2 tablespoons fresh rosemary
  (or 1½ teaspoons dried)
Pepper

Marinade: Combine mustard and lime juice in a small bowl. Gradually whisk in oil. Add shallots, rosemary, and a generous amount of pepper. Lay swordfish flat in a non-reactive container of about the same size as the fish and cover with marinade. Allow to sit for 30 minutes at room temperature or in the refrigerator for up to 3 hours.

Method: Broil or grill until done (about 3 to 4 minutes per side, depending on the thickness).

Note: This marinade is delicious as a general fish marinade. Try it with halibut, tuna, or orange roughy. As a general rule, grill fish for a total cooking time of 10 minutes per inch.

Grilled Swordfish Steaks

Easy   Yield: 4 servings
Preparing: 10 minutes
Marinating: 2 hours
Grilling: 8 to 10 minutes

Marinade:
½ cup vegetable oil
3 tablespoons soy sauce
2 tablespoons medium-dry sherry

4 (6-ounce) swordfish steaks,
  ¾-inch thick

1½ teaspoons freshly grated
  ginger root
1 teaspoon grated orange rind
Freshly ground pepper

Parsley
Lemon juice

Combine all marinade ingredients. Place swordfish in a casserole and cover with marinade. Turn fish to coat. Cover and chill for at least 2 hours, turning occasionally. Grill fish over hot coals, basting with marinade, for 4 to 5 minutes per side.

Bravo!

Swordfish with Cajun Butter

Average   Yield: 4 servings
            Preparing: 20 to 25 minutes
            Broiling: 8 to 10 minutes

Q E D

4 swordfish steaks

Cajun Butter:
Lemon juice, to taste
Salt and pepper, to taste
¼ teaspoon black pepper
½ teaspoon white pepper
¼ teaspoon sage

1 tablespoon olive oil

1 teaspoon chopped jalapeño pepper
2 garlic cloves, peeled and puréed
½ pound unsalted butter, softened
Pinch cayenne pepper
Juice of ½ lemon

Brush both sides of fish with olive oil. Grill 5 minutes to the inch per side. Just before serving, place a large slice of Cajun butter on each steak. Sprinkle with lemon juice. Let butter melt before serving.
Cajun Butter: Combine spices, jalapeño pepper, and garlic. Add softened butter; mix well. Season with salt and lemon juice and mix well. Shape into a log and freeze. Use as needed.

Orange Roughy with Fresh Dill

Easy   Yield: 2 servings
          Preparing:10 minutes
          Broiling: 5 minutes
          May be doubled or tripled

Q E D

12 ounces orange roughy filets
1 lime, juice and pulp
2 tablespoons fresh dill
1 clove garlic, minced

1 teaspoon Dijon mustard
½ ripe mango, peeled and diced
Pinch ground cardamom
1 teaspoon sugar

Preheat the broiler. Lightly grease the broiling pan and preheat it. Wash and dry orange roughy and place in pan. In a jar shake lime juice pulp, garlic, dill, and mustard. Spoon over fish. Broil 3 to 4 inches from the heat for 5 minutes, or until fish flakes. While fish is cooking combine mango, cardamom, and sugar to serve with the fish.

Cook fish 8 to 12 minutes per inch of
thickness, regardless of cooking method
(bake, broil, grill, pan-fry, or poach).

Faster Flounder

Easy · Yield: 6 servings
Preparing: 10 minutes
Broiling: 12 to 15 minutes

Q E D

2 pounds flounder filets
2 tablespoons grated onion
1½ teaspoons salt
⅛ teaspoon pepper

2 large tomatoes, cut in small pieces
¼ cup melted butter
1½ cups Swiss cheese, cubed

Place filets in one layer on a well-greased baking platter. Sprinkle with onion, salt, and pepper. Cover with tomatoes. Pour butter over tomatoes. Broil about 4 inches from heat for 10 to 12 minutes, or until fish flakes easily when tested with a fork. Remove from heat and sprinkle with cheese. Broil 2 to 3 minutes longer, or until cheese melts.

Poached Salmon with Dill Sauce

Easy
Do ahead

Yield: 4 servings
Preparing: 30 minutes
Baking: 20 minutes

Poaching Broth:
4 cups water
2 cups white wine vinegar
½ cup chopped onion
¼ teaspoon salt
¼ teaspoon sugar

¼ teaspoon freshly ground black
 pepper
1 bay leaf
1½ pounds salmon

Sauce:
½ cup plain non-fat yogurt
¼ cup snipped fresh dill, plus sprigs
 for garnish

½ teaspoon Dijon mustard
Dash hot pepper sauce
Dash Worcestershire sauce

Poaching broth: Combine water, vinegar, onion, salt, pepper, and bay leaf in a medium-sized saucepan. Bring to a boil, cover, and boil for 25 minutes over moderately high heat. Preheat oven to 325°. Pour some of the hot poaching broth into a casserole large enough to hold the salmon in 1 layer. Add the salmon and pour in the remaining broth. Bake, uncovered, for 20 minutes. Remove casserole from oven, cover, and allow fish to cool in the liquid. Refrigerate until serving time.
Sauce: Combine yogurt, dill snips, mustard, hot pepper sauce, and Worcestershire in a small bowl. Cover and refrigerate until serving time. Before serving, carefully take the salmon out of the broth and remove skin and any bones. Divide onto serving plates and garnish with a sprig of dill and a spoonful of sauce.

Note: Low-fat sour cream may be substituted for the yogurt.

Bravo!

Cold Poached Salmon with Cucumber Sauce

Average
Do ahead

Yield: 4 to 6 servings
Preparing: 20 minutes
Cooking: 15 minutes
Cooling: Overnight or several hours

4 to 6 salmon steaks (or filets)
4 cups boiling water
3 chicken bouillon cubes
2 tablespoons white vinegar
1 medium onion, sliced

1 bay leaf
1 teaspoon salt
Dash pepper
1 teaspoon dill weed

Cucumber Sauce:
1 cup shredded cucumber (do not drain)
½ cup sour cream
¼ cup mayonnaise
1 tablespoon chopped fresh parsley

1 tablespoon grated onion
2 teaspoons vinegar or lemon juice
1 tablespoon, or more, dill weed or minced fresh dill
Salt and pepper to taste

In a large skillet, combine boiling water, bouillon cubes, vinegar, bay leaf, salt, and pepper. Bring to a boil and simmer for 5 minutes. Add salmon, cover, and simmer for 8 minutes. Remove with slotted spoon; cool. Wrap and refrigerate. Sauce: Combine all ingredients and chill. Serve salmon on lettuce leaves or watercress; garnish with lemon wedges and fresh dill.
Serve sauce on the side.

Poached Salmon

Easy

Yield: 8 servings
Preparing: 15 minutes
Marinating: 30 minutes
Baking: 15 minutes

¼ cup peanut oil
3 tablespoons white wine
½ cup soy sauce
4 teaspoons honey

1 clove garlic, minced
Juice of 1 lemon
¼ teaspoon ginger
4 pounds filet of salmon

Preheat oven to 350°. Combine all ingredients except fish. Place salmon in baking dish. Pour sauce over all. Marinate only ½ hour. Poach in oven, covered, for 15 minutes.

Mussels or Seafood Marinara

Average Yield: 6 to 8 servings
Preparing: 1 hour
May be doubled or tripled

4 large tomatoes, peeled, or
  2 (8-ounce) cans whole Italian
  tomatoes
1 cup chicken broth
2 tablespoons olive oil
1 large onion, chopped
1 bunch scallions, chopped
4 cloves garlic, minced

¼ cup Italian parsley, chopped
¼ cup fresh basil leaves, chopped
½ cup white wine
2 to 3 pounds mussels, cleaned
Oregano to taste
Salt and pepper to taste
Crushed red pepper to taste

Crush tomatoes in large skillet, add chicken broth, and cook on low heat until thickened. In a separate skillet, cook onion, scallion, and garlic in olive oil until translucent. To tomatoes and chicken broth add parsley, basil, oregano, salt, pepper, and red pepper to taste. Add sautéed onions and garlic. Simmer 45 minutes. Add white wine and mussels. Steam until open (about 5 minutes). Serve over hot pasta, such as angel-hair or linguine.

Note: Clams and/or shrimp may also be added.

Outer Banks Baked Scallops

Easy Yield: 4 servings
Preparing: 20 minutes
Baking: 15 minutes for bay scallops
25 to 30 minutes for sea scallops
May be doubled or tripled

2 pounds scallops, bay or sea
¼ pound fresh mushrooms
4 sprigs parsley, finely chopped
1 cup bread crumbs
1 teaspoon white pepper

1 teaspoon salt
¼ cup butter, melted
1 tablespoon fresh lemon juice
½ cup dry sherry

Preheat oven to 400°. Wash and drain scallops. Wash and dry mushrooms; chop coarsely. Mix together mushrooms, parsley, crumbs, pepper, and salt. Spread scallops in a 9-inch square baking dish. Sprinkle with bread-crumb mixture. Pour melted butter, lemon juice, and sherry over all. Bake 15 minutes (bay scallops) or 25 to 30 minutes (sea scallops).

Bravo!

Stuffed Calamari with Shrimp and Scallops

Complicated   Yield: 4 servings
Preparing: 2 hours
Cooking: 50 minutes

8 squid (calamari), 6- to 7-inches long, cleaned
½ pound scallops, cleaned
½ pound shrimp, cleaned
1½ cups ricotta cheese
1 cup chopped Italian parsley
¼ teaspoon salt

½ teaspoon black pepper
½ tablespoon oregano
½ teaspoon paprika
2 to 3 cloves garlic, pressed
4 cups tomato sauce
2 cups olive oil

Wash and rinse squid, making sure sacs are clean. Cut shrimp into small pieces and combine with scallops. Sauté over medium heat, approximately 3 minutes, in 2 tablespoons of olive oil. Combine cheese, parsley, salt, pepper, oregano, and garlic. Mix well. Fold in scallops and shrimp. Stuff squid sacs with mixture, being careful not to overstuff. Close sacs with a round heavy toothpick. In an 8-quart pot bring 4 quarts of water and remaining olive oil to a boil. Add squid and cook slowly, uncovered, 25 minutes. Keep squid covered with water, and keep water at a slow boil. Remove from pot. Preheat oven to 325°. Place squid in a baking dish just large enough to accommodate it. Cover with tomato sauce and bake for 25 minutes.

Easy Shrimp Casserole

Easy   Yield: 6 to 8 servings
Preparing: 15 minutes
Baking: 35 minutes
May be doubled

1 cup mayonnaise
½ cup chili sauce
½ cup chopped green pepper

½ cup chopped onion
½ cup chopped celery
1½ pounds cooked, cleaned shrimp

Preheat oven to 350°. Combine mayonnaise and chili sauce. Add remaining ingredients. Bake in a covered casserole for 35 minutes. Do not overcook. Serve with lemon rice. (See page 191)

Note: Horseradish or fresh dill may be added, if desired.

 Precook scallops or oysters for 1 to 2 minutes if they are to be served in a cream sauce. The sauce will not thin out.

Shrimp Risotto

Average   Yield: *6 to 8 servings*
Preparing: *40 minutes*
Cooking: *20 minutes*

1 large onion, finely chopped
4 cloves garlic, minced
2 carrots, finely chopped
2 celery stalks, finely chopped
1 tablespoon olive oil
1 tablespoon butter
1 pound arborio rice
1¼ pounds medium shrimp,
   peeled and deveined

2 (10-ounce) packages frozen
   artichoke hearts, defrosted
1 (48-ounce) can chicken broth,
   heated to boiling
12 sprigs parsley, chopped
3 tablespoons Parmesan cheese
Salt and pepper to taste

Over medium heat in a large skillet, very slowly sauté onion, garlic, carrots, and celery in melted olive oil and butter. Do not allow to brown. Add rice and sauté slowly until rice is opaque. Add shrimp and cook until pink. Add artichoke hearts and boiling chicken broth; cover and simmer for approximately 20 minutes or until rice is tender. Add parsley and taste for seasoning. Add salt and pepper if necessary. Serve with a sprinkling of Parmesan cheese.

Bravo!

Shrimp Stir-Fry

Easy   *Yield: 4 servings*
Preparing: 10 minutes
Cooking: 20 minutes

Q E D

¼ cup vegetable oil
1 cup celery, sliced
1 cup green pepper, sliced
⅓ cup onion, sliced
2 tablespoons flour
1½ cups tomato juice

¼ to ½ cup brown sugar
½ teaspoon salt
1 tablespoon lemon peel
¼ cup fresh lemon juice
1½ pounds peeled, uncooked shrimp

Heat oil. Sauté celery, pepper, and onion until limp (about 10 minutes). Stir in flour and slowly add tomato juice. Stir until thickened. Add brown sugar, salt, lemon peel, and lemon juice. Stir until blended; cook 5 minutes. Add shrimp. Cook just until they turn pink. Serve over rice.

Fresh Fish Stew with Orange and Fennel

Easy   *Yield: 2 servings*
Preparing: 20 minutes
Cooking: 15 minutes

1 large onion, thinly sliced
1 teaspoon minced garlic
2 tablespoons olive oil
¾ cup dry white wine
1 (14-ounce) can crushed tomatoes
3 tablespoons tomato paste
Grated peel of 1 orange

1 teaspoon fennel seeds
1 teaspoon dried thyme
1 small bay leaf
12 ounces fish (monk, grouper, snapper, or swordfish) cut into 1- to 2-inch chunks
12 ounces tiny new potatoes

Sauté onion and garlic in olive oil in a non-stick skillet until soft. Add white wine, tomatoes, tomato paste, orange peel, fennel seeds, thyme, and bay leaf. Cover and cook 10 minutes. Add fish; cook 2 to 3 minutes. Serve over boiled potatoes.
Potatoes: Scrub but do not peel. Place in pot. Cover with cold water. Cook until done (about 20 minutes). Drain. Place potatoes on dinner plates. Quarter or halve. Top with fish stew.

Seafood Casserole

Average
Partial do ahead

Yield: 10 servings
Preparing: 35 minutes
Baking: 20 minutes

Sauce:
¾ cup butter
9 tablespoons flour
1 teaspoon salt
Pepper to taste
2 cups milk, scalded

1 cup dry white wine
3 egg yolks, lightly beaten
1 cup grated Swiss cheese
1 cup heavy cream

2 pounds shrimp, cooked
2 pounds scallops, poached

1½ pounds lobster meat, cooked

Melt butter in heavy saucepan. Add flour; stir and cook until mixture is smooth and light brown. Add salt, pepper, and hot milk. Stir until smooth and thickened. Add wine, egg yolks, cheese, and cream. Stir and cook until smooth. Preheat oven to 350°. Place seafood in a buttered au gratin dish. Pour sauce over all; top with buttered crumbs. Bake just until heated through (about 20 minutes).

Oyster Casserole

Average
Do ahead

Yield: 6 servings
Preparing: 15 minutes
Baking: 25 minutes

3 dozen oysters, with liquid reserved
1 cup saltine crumbs
Fines herbes or thyme
Salt and pepper to taste
Dash cayenne

1 (10¾-ounce) can cream
  of celery soup
¼ to ½ cup milk
Butter
3 to 4 slices bacon, cooked crisp and
  crumbled

Preheat oven to 375°. Butter a 9 x 13-inch casserole. Put half the oysters in dish; sprinkle with crumbs, fines herbes, salt, pepper, and cayenne. Mix soup, milk, and reserved liquid from oysters. Pour half over oysters. Dot with butter and half of the bacon. Repeat. Bake for 25 minutes, or until mixture is bubbly.

Bravo!

Eastern Shore Crabcakes

Easy | Yield: 6 servings (14 3-ounce crabcakes)
Partial do ahead | Preparing: 15 minutes
Freeze | Cooking: 10 minutes

2 pounds lump crabmeat, picked over
½ cup diced onion
⅓ cup mayonnaise
⅛ cup Tabasco sauce
⅛ cup Worcestershire sauce

¼ cup Dijon mustard
½ cup fresh chopped parsley
1 whole egg
½ cup flour

Combine all ingredients except flour. Mix well, sprinkling in flour while stirring. Shape into 14 crabcakes. Heat oil in a large skillet and panfry over medium-high heat until golden brown.

United States Hotel Bar & Grille, Manayunk, PA

Shellfish Paella

Average | Yield: 4 servings
Partial do ahead | Preparing: 45 minutes
| Cooking: 30 minutes

1 cup arborio rice
1 tablespoon olive oil
½ cup chopped onions
1 clove garlic, minced
½ pound hot Italian sausage,
**   casing removed**
2 large plum tomatoes, peeled and
**   chopped**

2 tablespoons chopped, fresh basil
1 teaspoon saffron threads
½ cup dry white wine
6 ounces clam juice
1 pound clams
½ pound scrubbed mussels
½ pound peeled, deveined shrimp
1 (10-ounce) box frozen peas

Cook rice according to directions on the box. Set aside and keep warm. In a large frying pan heat the oil and sauté, over medium-high heat, the onions, garlic, and sausage, breaking the sausage with the back of a wooden spoon. Cook until the sausage loses its pink color. Add the tomatoes, basil, saffron, white wine, and clam juice. Bring to a boil and add the clams and mussels. Cover and cook until the shells open (5 to 10 minutes). Add the shrimp and cook only until they become opaque. Remove the shellfish and set aside. Continue cooking the sauce to reduce it, simmering for an additional 10 to 15 minutes. Add peas. When ready to serve, toss in cooked shellfish just to reheat it. Arrange the cooked rice on a warm platter and pour the sauce over it. Serve at once.

"Oyster Bar" at Marshallton Inn, West Chester, PA

White Chili

Average
Partial do ahead

Yield: 6 to 8 servings
Preparing: 30 minutes
Soaking: Overnight
Cooking: 90 minutes

2½ to 3 pounds chicken breast with skin and bone	½ teaspoon cinnamon
6 cups chicken broth	1 pound small white beans, soaked overnight
2 tablespoons olive oil	Tabasco sauce
2 medium onions, chopped (2 cups)	3 to 4 cups grated Monterey Jack cheese
8 large cloves garlic, chopped	Sour cream
3 to 4 red or green chilies, finely chopped	Tomato salsa
1 tablespoon ground cumin	Lime wedges
1 tablespoon dried oregano	

In a large pot combine chicken and broth. Bring to a simmer and poach, uncovered, for 18 to 20 minutes. Allow chicken to cool in the broth for 15 minutes. Remove from broth; skin and bone breasts and cut into cubes. Set aside. Reserve the broth. In the same large pot warm the oil and sauté the onion for 8 to 10 minutes. Stir in garlic and sauté for 30 seconds. Add chilies, cumin, oregano, cinnamon, drained beans, and reserved broth. Cook, covered, at a brisk simmer for 1½ hours, or until beans are tender. (May be made ahead to this point.) Stir in cubed chicken. Taste and season with Tabasco and salt if necessary. Just before serving, stir in half of the grated cheese. Serve with sour cream, salsa, remaining grated cheese, and lime wedges.

Mix together equal amounts of mayonnaise and stone-ground mustard, spread thickly over fresh fish filets, and bake at 350° 10 minutes per inch of thickness. Serve with lemon wedges.

Bravo!

Indian Curry

Average	*Yield: 3 servings*
Do ahead	*Preparing: 20 minutes*
Freeze	*Cooking: 20 minutes*
	May be doubled

1 tablespoon oil or butter
½ medium onion, chopped
½ medium carrot, peeled and sliced thinly
½ tablespoon curry powder
1 tablespoon flour
¾ cup canned tomatoes, drained
1 bouillon cube

¾ cup boiling water
½ small apple, peeled and chopped
½ tablespoon pickle relish
2 tablespoons raw or defrosted grated coconut (optional)
1½ cups diced cooked meat (beef, lamb, chicken, veal, lobster, or shrimp)

Melt butter in a large frying pan over medium heat. Add onion and carrot and sauté until onion is yellowed. Add curry powder and stir. Add flour, tomatoes, and bouillon cube dissolved in boiling water. Stir well. Add apple, pickle relish, and optional coconut. Mix well. Add meat. Lower heat, cover, and simmer for 20 minutes. Flavor benefits from sitting an hour or more. Serve with rice.

Note: This is an excellent way of using leftovers.

To thicken sauces without heavy cream, mix 1 tablespoon of instant flour with 1 cup of cold skim milk. Add to the sauce.

Vegetables Medleys

Bravo!

The Orchestra in the Community

Members of The Philadelphia Orchestra share their musical talents as active members of their communities. Many of them teach privately or serve on the faculties of several fine music schools including The Curtis Institute of Music, The Settlement Music School, the University of the Arts, Temple University Music School, and the University of Pennsylvania.

Among the Orchestra members are several talented conductors who often participate at teaching institutions or lead community orchestras of volunteer musicians. Others enjoy success as composers and have their works performed in the city and beyond. The musicians of the Orchestra, especially the principal players, are virtuoso artists who are often featured as soloists at various programs in the area. Countless chamber groups, duos, trios, quartets, and quintets are formed among orchestra personnel. These groups frequently lend their talents to a number of charitable causes benefiting the homeless, people with AIDS, victims of domestic violence, the annual Philadelphia Orchestra/WFLN Radiothon, and other worthy projects.

There would seem to be no limit to what Philadelphia Orchestra members will do. For a concert on Halloween, they all came in costume. How serious can the program be when the concertmaster and the associate concertmaster are Batman and Robin? In addition, it may not be widely known that The Philadelphia Orchestra fields one of the best softball teams in the city, the Firebirds. Avid baseball fans, the entire Orchestra donned concert tails and baseball caps to play the National Anthem on a drizzly field before the fourth game of the 1993 World Series between the Toronto Blue Jays and the Philadelphia Phillies.

Mendocino Black Bean Chili

Average   *Yield: 8 to 10 servings*
Preparing: 20 minutes
Cooking: 1¾ hour plus 20 minutes

4 cups black beans (or black turtle beans), picked over
3 cups canned crushed whole tomatoes
2 large yellow onions, finely chopped
1½ cups finely chopped green bell peppers
½ cup olive oil

2 tablespoons cumin seed
2 tablespoons oregano
1 teaspoon cayenne pepper
1½ tablespoons paprika
½ cup finely chopped jalapeño chilies (may be canned)
2 cloves garlic, minced (optional)
1 teaspoon salt

Garnish:
½ pound Monterey Jack or Cheddar cheese, grated
½ cup finely chopped green onions

⅔ cup sour cream
8 or 10 sprigs of cilantro (or more)

Carefully pick over the beans, and rinse well. Place in a large pot and cover with water to several inches above top of beans. Cover and bring to a boil. Reduce heat and cook for 1¾ hours, or until tender. Add water if beans are no longer covered. When beans are cooked, strain them and reserve 1 cup of the liquid; return the 1 cup liquid to the beans. While the beans are cooking, place the cumin seed and oregano in a small pan. Bake them in a 325° oven for 10 minutes. Do not burn. Sauté onions, green peppers, and garlic in oil, with cumin seed, oregano, cayenne pepper, paprika, and salt for 10 minutes or until onions are soft. Add tomatoes and chilies. Add all to beans and mix thoroughly. To serve, place 1 ounce grated cheese then 1¼ cups hot chili in a heated bowl. Top with a spoonful of sour cream and sprinkle with green onions. Garnish with a sprig of cilantro.

Café Beaujolais, Mendocino, CA

Bravo!

Green Beans with Basil Vinaigrette

Easy   *Yield: 6 to 8 servings*
Partial do ahead   *Preparing: 10 minutes*
Cooking: 10 minutes

Q E D

Vinaigrette:
1 clove garlic, sliced
12 to 15 leaves fresh basil, chopped
Salt and pepper to taste

4 to 6 scallions, trimmed, thinly sliced

¼ cup white wine vinegar
¼ cup olive oil plus ¼ cup walnut oil
(or ½ cup olive oil)

2 pounds green beans, trimmed

Vinaigrette: In a bowl combine garlic, basil, salt, and pepper. Add vinegar. In a cup combine oils and whisk into basil mixture. In a saucepan steam beans until tender (about 10 minutes). Remove from pot. Add scallions to beans. Toss with vinaigrette just before serving.

Crunchy Broccoli Dijon

Easy   *Yield: 4 servings*
Preparing: 10 minutes
Cooking: 10 minutes
May be doubled or tripled

Q E D

2 bunches broccoli, cut into flowerets
½ red pepper, diced
½ red onion, diced
1 tablespoon olive oil

1 clove garlic, minced
Soy sauce to taste
1½ teaspoons Dijon mustard

Heat garlic in oil over high heat. Add onion; stir fry for 1 minute. Add pepper; stir fry 1 minute longer. Add broccoli and stir fry several minutes until broccoli turns bright green. Add soy and mustard. Mix well and serve.

When cooking Brussels sprouts, add a rib or 2 of celery. Your kitchen will smell clean.

Broccoli with Broiled Topping

Easy
Partial do ahead

Yield: 4 to 6 servings
Preparing: 15 minutes
Broiling: 3 minutes
May be doubled

1½ to 2 pounds fresh broccoli
½ cup mayonnaise
¼ cup freshly grated Parmesan
  cheese

2 teaspoons lemon juice
2 tablespoons finely chopped
  fresh parsley
2 egg whites

Trim outer skin off broccoli and separate the bunches into thin spears. Rinse well. Steam, until tender, over boiling water (about 7 minutes). Arrange broccoli in 1 layer in a shallow oven-to-table dish. Combine mayonnaise, Parmesan cheese, lemon juice, and parsley. Beat egg whites until stiff but still moist. Fold egg whites into mayonnaise mixture. Spread over cooked broccoli. (May be made ahead to this point.) Preheat broiler, and broil 8 to 10 inches below heat until topping is browned and broccoli is heated through (about 3 minutes). Watch carefully to prevent burning. Serve immediately.

Note: Cauliflower, green beans, or frozen broccoli may be substituted.

Brussels Sprouts with Mustard

Easy
Partial do ahead

Yield: 8 servings
Preparing: 5 minutes
Cooking: 15 minutes
May be doubled or tripled

2½ pounds Brussels sprouts, trimmed
  and crosscut in the base
¼ cup butter

2 tablespoons mustard seed
¼ cup coarse grained Dijon mustard

In a large pot bring salted water to a boil. Add the sprouts and boil briskly for about 10 minutes or until a knife just pierces the base. Drain immediately, and, if not continuing to cook, immerse the sprouts in cold water to stop further cooking and preserve the fresh green color. This can be done several hours in advance. Set aside until needed. Shortly before serving, melt the butter in a large frying pan and add the mustard seed and prepared mustard. Stir to mix thoroughly. When pan is quite hot add the precooked sprouts. Sauté to heat them through and coat them with the mustard. Serve hot.

Bravo!

Carrot Mousse

Easy	*Yield: 10 servings*
Do ahead	*Preparing: 10 minutes*
	Cooking: 20 minutes
	Drying: 30 minutes

**3 pounds large carrots, peeled
  and sliced**
2½ cups heavy cream

4 tablespoons butter
2 ounces honey
Salt and pepper to taste

Cook the carrots in boiling, salted water until tender (about 15 minutes). Drain and place on a sheet pan in a 200° oven for 30 minutes to dry. Place carrots in a food processor. Heat the cream, but do not boil. Process the carrots and add the hot cream, butter, and honey while the machine is running. Taste for seasoning and add salt and pepper. Pass the carrot mousse through a food mill and reheat to serve.

Le Bec-Fin, Philadelphia, PA

Puréed Carrots

Easy	*Yield: 6 servings*
Do ahead	*Preparing: 20 minutes*
	Cooking: 10 minutes

2 pounds carrots, peeled and sliced
1 teaspoon sugar
1 teaspoon salt

2 tablespoons butter
2 tablespoons heavy cream
2 tablespoons sweet sherry

Combine carrots, sugar, and salt in a medium saucepan. Add water to cover and bring to a boil. Cover and simmer for 10 minutes or until carrots are tender. Drain off excess liquid. Transfer to a blender or food processor and process with 2 tablespoons butter. Add cream and sherry; blend. Taste for seasoning and add salt and pepper if desired.

Note: May be made ahead and reheated in the microwave before serving.

Frozen vegetables taste fresher when removed from the package, placed in a plastic bag, and microwaved.

Carrot Soufflé

Average   Yield: 6 servings
Preparing: 30 minutes
Baking: 25 minutes

3 tablespoons butter	1 cup milk
3 tablespoons flour	2 cups cooked, mashed carrots
¼ teaspoon salt	3 eggs, separated
¼ teaspoon pepper	Bread crumbs

Preheat oven to 350°. In a large saucepan, melt butter. Add flour, salt, pepper and mix. Gradually add milk and bring to a boil, stirring constantly. Simmer for 3 minutes. Add carrots and well-beaten egg yolks. Stir to mix well. Remove from heat and fold in stiffly beaten egg whites. Turn into a buttered 9 x 9-inch baking dish; cover with crumbs. Bake for 25 minutes.

Carrots and Parsnips

Easy   Yield: 8 servings
Do ahead   Preparing: 30 minutes
Cooking: 10 minutes

1 pound carrots, chopped	1 ripe pear, chopped
1 pound parsnips, chopped	2 tablespoons parsley, chopped

Steam carrots and parsnips until tender (about 10 minutes). Reserve liquid. Transfer carrots and parsnips to a food processor. Add pears. Purée until smooth, adding just enough reserved liquid to facilitate blending. Reheat just before serving.

Mustard-Glazed Carrots

Easy   Yield: 6 servings
Preparing: 15 minutes
Cooking: 15 minutes
May be doubled

2 pounds carrots, peeled	2 tablespoons brown sugar
3 tablespoons Dijon mustard	Chopped parsley
3 tablespoons butter	

Cut carrots diagonally into ¼-inch slices. Boil in water, covered, 5 to 10 minutes, until tender-crisp. Drain well. Stir in mustard, butter, and brown sugar, stirring over medium heat until carrots are glazed (1 to 2 minutes). Sprinkle with parsley and serve.

Bravo!

Tomatoes Florentine

Easy   Yield: 6 to 8 servings
Preparing: 20 minutes
Baking: 15 to 20 minutes

2 packages (10 ounces) frozen
  chopped spinach
4½ tablespoons butter
¼ cup minced scallions
¼ cup dry bread crumbs
2 eggs, slightly beaten
¼ cup freshly grated Parmesan
  cheese

½ teaspoon minced garlic
¼ teaspoon dried thyme
¼ teaspoon salt
⅛ teaspoon freshly ground pepper
8 large thick (about ½-inch)
  slices tomato
½ teaspoon garlic salt
Watercress to garnish

Preheat oven to 350°. Cook spinach according to package directions; drain well. In a small skillet, melt ½ tablespoon of the butter. Add scallions and sauté until soft. Combine spinach with bread crumbs, sautéed scallions, eggs, cheese, garlic, remaining butter, thyme, salt, and pepper. Arrange tomato slices in a shallow buttered baking dish. Sprinkle with garlic salt. Spoon ¼ cup of spinach mixture on each tomato slice and shape it into a dome. Bake 15 to 20 minutes or until heated through. Garnish with watercress.

Cauliflower-Carrot-Celery Almondine

Easy   Yield: 4 to 6 servings
Do ahead   Preparing: 10 minutes
Cooking: 20 minutes
May be doubled

Q E D

1 head cauliflower, broken
  into flowerets
2 cups diagonally sliced carrots
2 cups one-inch chunk celery
¼ teaspoon sugar
¼ cup butter or margarine

⅓ cup slivered, blanched almonds
2 teaspoons lemon juice
Coarsely ground pepper
Sprigs of fresh parsley
Lightly sautéed red pepper,
  for color (optional)

In a small amount of water (salted to taste), cook cauliflower, carrots, and celery, sprinkled with sugar, until tender-crisp (about 10 to 15 minutes). Adjust time to suit vegetables — celery will take the least amount of time. Drain and place vegetables in a casserole. In a small skillet, melt butter or margarine; stir in almonds and sauté for 1 to 2 minutes until lightly browned. Remove from heat and stir in lemon juice. Pour almond/lemon mixture over vegetables. Sprinkle generously with ground pepper. Garnish with fresh parsley sprigs. May be made ahead and reheated in a microwave.

Layered Carrot Spinach Soufflé

Average
Do ahead

Yield: 8 to 10 servings
Preparing: 30 minutes
Baking: 1 hour
Standing: 30 minutes

Carrot Soufflé:
1½ pounds carrots, cooked
   and puréed
1 cup milk
1½ cups shredded sharp
   Cheddar cheese
½ cup melted butter or margarine

¼ cup finely chopped onion
1¼ teaspoons salt
⅛ teaspoon pepper
Dash cayenne pepper
⅛ teaspoon nutmeg
3 eggs, beaten

Spinach Soufflé:
1¾ pounds spinach cooked and
   puréed, or 3 (10-ounce) packages
   frozen, chopped spinach, thawed
   and squeezed dry.

All ingredients, other than carrots,
   as in carrot soufflé

¾ cup cornflake crumbs

Garnishes:
Chopped parsley

Cooked baby peas

Preheat oven to 350°. Use two large mixing bowls. Prepare carrot soufflé first. Mix all ingredients together for each soufflé. Lightly grease a 14-cup ring mold (springform pan) and dust with crumbs. Layer carrot mixture and spinach in pan. Bake, uncovered, for 1 hour. Allow to stand for 30 minutes, then invert on a large platter and sprinkle with chopped parsley. Fill cavity with baby peas. To serve, slice like a cake. Serve warm.

Easy Baked Carrots

Easy
Do ahead

Yield: 4 servings
Preparing: 15 minutes
Baking: 1 hour
May be doubled or tripled

12 carrots, peeled, and cut on the bias
Fresh dill, chopped, to taste
3 heaping tablespoons good-quality
   marmalade (or more)

Salt and pepper to taste
Butter (optional)

Preheat oven to 400°. Place carrots into a casserole, add dill, and stir in marmalade. Season with salt and pepper. Bake, covered, for 1 hour.

Note: Best when made 1 day ahead and reheated in the microwave.

Bravo!

Corn-Zucchini Bake

Easy *Yield: 6 servings*
Preparing: 25 minutes
Cooking: 1 hour

1 pound zucchini
2 cups fresh corn, cut from 4 to 5
  cobs, cooked
½ cup chopped onion
1 tablespoon butter
2 eggs, beaten

1 cup (4 ounces) Jarlsberg
  cheese, grated
Salt and pepper to taste
¼ cup fresh bread crumbs
2 tablespoons grated
  Parmesan cheese
1 tablespoon melted butter

Wash zucchini, but do not peel. Cut into 1-inch slices. Cook in boiling water to cover for 15 to 20 minutes. Drain and mash. Cook corn and onion in butter until onion is transparent. Combine with zucchini. Add grated Jarlsberg, beaten eggs, and mix well. Put into a buttered casserole. Combine crumbs, Parmesan, and butter. Sprinkle over vegetable mixture. Bake at 350° for 40 minutes.

Iman Bayildi — A Variation

Average *Yield: 6 to 10 servings*
Preparing: 20 minutes
Cooking: 15 minutes
May be doubled

¼ cup (or more) olive oil
¾ cup finely diced onion
¾ cup finely diced green pepper
1 large clove garlic, minced
1 firm medium eggplant (about 1
  pound), peeled and cut into
  ½-inch dice
½ cup raisins
2 tablespoons fresh mint

1¾ cups cooked rice (separate grains
  — not sticky)
1 cup chopped parsley
½ cup toasted pine nuts
  or sliced almonds
1 cup diced, peeled, and seeded
  ripe tomatoes
Salt and pepper to taste

In a large heavy skillet over medium heat, sauté onion, pepper, and garlic until barely soft. Set aside. In the same pan, using more oil if necessary, sauté eggplant until it is soft. Remove from heat and add onion mixture, raisins, mint, rice, parsley, nuts, and tomatoes; gently combine. Taste for seasoning and add salt and pepper if necessary. Serve at room temperature.

Eggplant Parmigiana

Average
Partial do ahead

Yield: 6 servings
Preparing: 30 minutes
Cooking: 90 minutes (sauce)
Baking: 30 minutes

Sauce:
3 tablespoons olive oil
4 large garlic cloves, minced
8 plum tomatoes, peeled or
   1 (2 pound 3-ounce) can
   peeled tomatoes

1 (8-ounce) can tomato sauce
1 (6-ounce) can tomato paste
½ teaspoon oregano
½ teaspoon basil (or 2 fresh leaves)
Salt and pepper to taste

Eggplant:
1 large eggplant
2 jumbo eggs (or 3 large)
1 tablespoon water

2 cups bread crumbs
3 tablespoons vegetable oil

1 1-pound piece mozzarella cheese,
   thinly sliced (or less)

1 cup grated Parmesan
   or Romano cheese

Sauce: In a 2-quart pot, heat the olive oil and lightly sauté the garlic for 30 seconds. Add the plum tomatoes, tomato sauce, tomato paste, oregano, and basil and stir well. Bring to a boil, lower heat, cover, and allow to simmer for 90 minutes. Taste for seasoning and add salt and pepper to taste. Set aside.
Eggplant: Peel eggplant and cut into thin round slices. Mix the eggs with 1 tablespoon water. Dip the eggplant in the egg mixture and then in the bread crumbs. In hot vegetable oil, fry the slices until golden brown on each side and transfer them to a paper towel-covered platter to absorb any excess oil.
Assembly: In an 8 x 12 x 3-inch rectangular casserole, barely cover the bottom with a layer of tomato sauce. Cover with slices of eggplant, slices of mozzarella, and sprinkle with Parmesan cheese. Repeat this process until the eggplant is finished. Preheat the oven to 325° and bake the casserole for 30 minutes or until mozzarella is melted. Serve with pasta, salad, and antipasto.

The tomato sauce may be made ahead and refrigerated for several days.

Benita Valente

Bravo!

Baked Fennel

Easy   Yield: 6 servings
             Preparing: 30 minutes
             Baking: 10 minutes

3 bulbs fennel, trimmed
Butter or margarine
Salt and pepper

3 tablespoons grated
Parmesan cheese

Preheat oven to 400°. Cut fennel bulbs into eighths. Sprinkle with salt and steam until tender. Arrange fennel in a single layer in a well-greased gratin dish. Dot with butter and sprinkle with pepper. Sprinkle with cheese. Bake until cheese is golden brown (approximately 10 minutes).

Leeks Parmesan

Easy   Yield: 4 servings
             Preparing: 20 minutes
             Baking: 1 hour
             May be doubled

6 leeks, 1½ inches in diameter
3 tablespoons honey
Juice of 1 lemon
Pinch of nutmeg

Salt and pepper to taste
3 tablespoons Parmesan cheese
Lemon slices to garnish

Preheat oven to 350°. Remove coarse and/or damaged outer leaves of leeks and, using the light green and white parts only, cut stalks into 1½-inch pieces. Place in a bowl of cold water and allow to stand for 10 to 20 minutes to remove grit and/or sand. Remove carefully from water and transfer to a shallow, heat-proof casserole. Add cold water to barely cover leeks. Add honey, lemon juice, nutmeg, salt, and pepper. Place over medium heat and bring to a boil. Boil, uncovered, for 5 minutes. Place casserole in oven and bake, uncovered, for 30 minutes. Turn leeks over and continue cooking for another 30 minutes. Transfer to serving dish and sprinkle with Parmesan cheese.
Garnish with lemon slices.

Mushroom Casserole

Easy　Yield: 6 servings
Preparing: 25 minutes
Baking: 30 minutes

1½ pounds mushrooms	¼ teaspoon coarsely ground
¼ cup butter or margarine	black pepper
2 tablespoons flour	½ cup fresh bread crumbs
2 beef bouillon cubes	½ cup grated Parmesan cheese
¼ cup hot water	½ teaspoon onion salt
½ cup half-and-half cream	

Preheat oven to 350°. Wipe mushrooms well, slice, and place in a lightly greased 2-quart casserole. In a saucepan, melt the butter and blend in the flour. Dissolve the bouillon cubes in the hot water and add the half-and-half and the pepper. Remove from heat and whisk the bouillon mixture into the butter/flour. Return to moderate heat and, stirring constantly, heat until thickened. Pour this sauce over the mushrooms. Mix together the bread crumbs, Parmesan, and onion salt; sprinkle over the mushrooms. Bake for 20 minutes; check to see if the casserole is sufficiently moist. If too dry, add a little milk. Return to the oven for another 10 minutes. Serve hot.

Note: A speedy way to clean mushrooms: Immerse them in a bowl filled with cold salted water. Drain and shake dry in a towel.

Baked Vidalia Onions

Easy　Yield: 6 servings
Preparing: 10 minutes
Baking: 1 hour
May be doubled

½ cup water	¼ cup cider vinegar
½ cup butter	5 large Vidalia onions, sliced
½ cup brown sugar	

Preheat oven to 350°. Bring water to a boil, add butter, sugar, and vinegar; stir to mix thoroughly. Place onions in a casserole and pour hot mixture over them. Bake, uncovered, for 1 hour. A very good side dish with meats.

Potatoes, Leeks, and Tomatoes

Easy
Do ahead

Yield: 8 servings
Preparing: 20 minutes
Cooking: 30 minutes

3 large garlic cloves, finely chopped
4 medium-size leeks, cleaned and
sliced (white part only)
2 tablespoons olive oil
3 tablespoons fresh dill, chopped

1 teaspoon dried tarragon
6 large new potatoes, chopped
1 can (1 pound, 12 ounces) whole
tomatoes, drained and chopped

Sauté garlic and leeks in olive oil until transparent. Add all other ingredients. Cover and cook until potatoes are tender (about 25 minutes).

Grated Potato Casserole

Easy
Partial do ahead

Yield: 6 servings
Preparing: 30 minutes
Chilling: Overnight
Baking: 1 hour

6 medium-size potatoes
1 ounce chopped onion
Chopped parsley to taste

Salt and pepper to taste
½ pint heavy cream

Cook potatoes in water to cover until tender. Refrigerate overnight. Peel and grate into a shallow casserole. Add onion, parsley, salt, and pepper. Chill. Before baking, add cream. Bake at 325° for 1 hour.

Potatoes Anna

Easy

Yield: 6 servings
Preparing: 30 minutes
Baking: 1½ hours

6 tablespoons butter, melted
2 pounds russet or Idaho potatoes,
peeled and thinly sliced

Salt and pepper to taste

Preheat oven to 375°. Lavishly butter a 10-inch Pyrex dish. Dry potatoes thoroughly and place one layer in a decorative pattern in the bottom of the dish. Brush lavishly with melted butter, and season to taste. Make layers of potato, butter, salt, and pepper until the pan is filled. Cover dish and bake for 1 hour. Uncover and continue baking for another 30 minutes or until nicely browned. Turn upside down on heated platter and serve in wedges, as a pie.

Spinach with Fresh Rosemary

Easy Yield: 4 servings
Preparing: 15 minutes
Cooking: 5 minutes
May be doubled

2 pounds spinach leaves, preferably
  the flat variety
2 bunches green onions
1 to 2 tablespoons butter

1 teaspoon fresh rosemary, chopped
  (or ½ teaspoon dried)
¼ cup fresh parsley, chopped
Salt and pepper to taste

Wash and (if desired) chop spinach. Chop green onions. Melt butter in a large heavy pot and add remaining ingredients. Stir to coat with melted butter. Cover and cook over medium heat for 4 to 6 minutes, or until done. Serve immediately.

Pommes de Terre Savoies

Easy Yield: 4 to 6 servings
Preparing: 10 minutes
Baking: 45 to 60 minutes

1 pound new potatoes, peeled and
  thinly sliced

1 wheel Brie
Butter

In a shallow buttered casserole lay potato slices in an even layer. Slice Brie lengthwise (through entire circle so that you end up with additional circles). Cover potatoes with Brie, skin side down. Bake at 350° for 45 to 60 minutes, until nicely browned and bubbly.

Jeffrey Brillhart

Roasted New Potatoes and Shallots with Caraway

Easy Yield: 8 servings
Preparing: 10 minutes
Baking: 45 minutes
May be doubled or tripled

24 small red new potatoes,
  quartered lengthwise
20 large shallots, peeled

8 tablespoons olive oil
2 teaspoons caraway seeds
Salt and pepper

Mix together all ingredients in a shallow baking pan. Preheat oven to 375°. Bake potatoes, stirring occasionally, for 45 minutes, or until tender.

Bravo!

New Potatoes with Bay Leaves and Lemon

Easy
Do ahead

Yield: 8 servings
Preparing: 10 minutes
Baking: 45 minutes

2 pounds red new potatoes, quartered
¼ cup plus 2 tablespoons fresh lemon juice
1½ teaspoons dried oregano, crumbled

1 teaspoon grated lemon peel
1 teaspoon salt
¼ teaspoon freshly ground pepper
½ cup olive oil
20 small bay leaves

Preheat oven to 375°. Lightly oil a shallow baking dish. Add potatoes to dish. In a bowl mix lemon juice, oregano, lemon peel, salt, and pepper. Whisk in oil. Pour over potatoes; toss well. Tuck bay leaves around potatoes. Bake, stirring every 10 minutes, until potatoes are brown and a knife easily pierces the center (about 45 minutes). Discard bay leaves; adjust seasonings.

Individual Potato Soufflés

Easy
Partial do ahead

Yield: 4 servings
Preparing: 10 minutes
Baking: 1 hour plus 30 minutes

3 baking potatoes
2 tablespoons butter
¾ cup sour cream
⅓ cup grated Parmesan cheese

4 tablespoons sour cream
Parmesan cheese
Paprika
Salt and pepper to taste

Preheat oven to 400°. Prick potatoes in several places with a fork and bake in preheated oven for 1 hour. When cool enough to handle, cut potatoes in half and scoop out insides. Mash. Add butter, ¾ cup sour cream, ⅓ cup Parmesan cheese, and salt and pepper to taste. Divide mixture into individual greased baking dishes or custard cups. Spread 1 tablespoon of sour cream over each portion; sprinkle with cheese and paprika. Can be made ahead to this point. Increase oven temperature to 450° and bake, uncovered, for 30 minutes or until brown. Serve immediately.

Tomatoes McFadden

Easy   Yield: 6 servings
         Preparing: 20 minutes
         Baking: 3 hours
         May be doubled

6 large tomatoes
2 medium yellow onions
¾ cup dark brown sugar

½ stick (4 ounces) butter
¾ cup water

Preheat oven to 300°. Wipe tomatoes with a damp cloth. With a sharp knife make a hole in the stem end of each tomato 1 inch in diameter and 1 inch deep. Place tomatoes in roasting pan, cut side up. Peel and quarter onions and purée in a food processor or blender. Cut butter into 6 equal slices. Fill the hole in each tomato with 1 or more tablespoons of puréed onion. Place a slice of butter over the onion. Cover the top of the tomato with brown sugar. Sprinkle any remaining brown sugar around each tomato. Add ⅓ cup of water to the pan. Bake, uncovered, in the middle of the oven, basting occasionally, for 3 hours.

Note: If all the liquid boils off well before cooking is complete, add a small amount of additional water. However, there should be very little liquid in the pan by the end of the 3 hours. Avoid the temptation to decrease the cooking time by increasing the oven temperature.

The Rabbit, Philadelphia, PA

Cheese Custard Squash

Average   Yield: 4 to 6 servings
            Preparing: 30 minutes
            Baking: 30 minutes

4 medium zucchini or yellow squash
1 cup (4 ounces) grated
** Cheddar cheese**
2 eggs

½ teaspoon dill weed
½ teaspoon salt
¼ teaspoon pepper
½ cup buttered bread crumbs

Preheat oven to 350°. Cut squash lengthwise and boil in salted water to cover for just 5 minutes. Drain; carefully scoop out seeds, making a boat. Mix together the cheese, eggs, dill, salt, and pepper and spoon into the boats. Do not mound. Bake for 25 minutes. Sprinkle buttered bread crumbs over the tops and return to the oven for 5 minutes or until golden.

Bravo!

Cheesy Squash

Average Yield: 6 to 8 servings
Do ahead Preparing: 15 minutes
Baking: 90 minutes plus 45 minutes

---

3 (1-pound) butternut squash
½ cup heavy whipping cream
1 egg, beaten

¼ cup brown sugar
1 cup grated Swiss cheese
½ teaspoon salt

Preheat oven to 350°. Cut each squash in half, scoop out the seeds, and place, cut side down, in a flat baking pan that has about ½ inch of water in the bottom. Bake for 45 minutes. Turn the squash, cut side up, and bake for another 45 minutes, or until fork-tender. When cool enough to handle, scoop the cooked squash out of the skin; in a large bowl, mix it with the cream, egg, brown sugar, and salt. Using a hand mixer, beat for a few minutes to make sure all ingredients are combined. Place in a lightly greased baking dish; if desired, sprinkle a little more brown sugar on the top.
Bake at 350° for 45 minutes or until hot.

Note: Good with ham or as an addition to the Thanksgiving meal.

Red Cabbage

Easy Yield: 8 servings
Do ahead Preparing: 30 minutes
Marinating: Overnight
Baking: 2 hours

---

2 pounds red cabbage, shredded
1 medium onion, grated
2 Granny Smith apples, peeled
** and grated**
1 Bartlett pear, peeled and grated
½ cup raisins
½ cup red currant jelly

1 teaspoon salt plus ½ teaspoon
** ground pepper**
4 cloves
6 peppercorns
1 cinnamon stick
1 bay leaf
1 bottle (750 milliliters) dry red wine
1 teaspoon ground nutmeg

In a large pot, place cabbage, onion, apple, and pear. Tie cloves, peppercorns, bay leaf, and cinnamon stick in cheesecloth and add to the pot. Add all remaining ingredients, mix, and cover. Refrigerate overnight. Place uncovered pot over medium/low heat and bring to a simmer, stirring occasionally, until cabbage is tender and liquid has reduced and thickened. Remove cheesecloth bag of herbs and spices. Add salt to taste and serve hot.

Vegetable Casserole

Easy	Yield: 8 to 10 servings
Do ahead	Preparing: 1 hour
	Baking: 45 minutes

1 butternut squash, peeled
  and cut in ¼-inch cubes
3 teaspoons oil
1 cup ¼-inch dice carrots
1 cup ¼-inch dice leeks

1 cup ¼-inch dice unpeeled zucchini
1 cup ¼-inch dice unpeeled apple
½ cup minced shallots
1 cup chicken broth
Salt and pepper to taste

Preheat oven to 375°. Coat butternut squash with 2 teaspoons oil and roast, uncovered, for 20 minutes or until just tender. Heat remaining 1 teaspoon oil in large skillet and toss roasted squash and carrots for 3 to 5 minutes. Add leeks and cook 1 minute. Add zucchini, apples, and shallots, and cook for 2 more minutes. Stir in chicken broth and simmer until all are tender (about 10 minutes). Adjust seasonings and serve warm.

Note: This dish is easily reheated in the microwave in a covered casserole. The colors are wonderful.

Roasted Medley of Vegetables

Easy	Yield: 6 servings
	Preparing: 10 minutes
	Baking: 45 minutes to 1 hour
	May be doubled

8 medium red-skinned potatoes
2 large red peppers, seeded
  and deveined
2 Vidalia onions

Salt and pepper
¼ cup olive oil
1 teaspoon thyme

Preheat oven to 450°. Thoroughly wash, but do not peel, potatoes; cut them into quarters or eighths. Cut peppers into 1-inch strips. Slice onions. Lightly grease bottom of a large, low-sided casserole (lasagna pan) and scatter potatoes, peppers, and onions in the dish. Sprinkle with salt, several grindings of pepper, oil, and thyme. Place in preheated oven; immediately reduce heat to 400°. Roast for about 1 hour, or until vegetables are tender when pierced with a knife, turning 2 or 3 times.

Note: Very good accompaniment for fish, beef, or chicken.

Bravo!

Winter Squash Purée

Easy   Yield: 4 servings
Preparing: 30 minutes

QED

**2 pounds winter squash
    (butternut or acorn)
2 tablespoons butter
1 sweet red pepper, seeded
    and chopped**

**½ cup chopped onions
¼ teaspoon ground cumin
Salt and pepper to taste**

Cut squash in half; remove seeds and fibers. Place cut pieces in 1 layer in a microwaveable dish; cover tightly with plastic wrap and cook on high until tender (approximately 15 minutes). Drain thoroughly; when cool enough to handle, remove skin. Purée in food processor. In a large non-stick pan heat butter; add red pepper, onions, cumin, salt, and pepper. Cook, stirring occasionally, for about 5 minutes. Add puréed squash and mix thoroughly; reheat while stirring.

Spaghetti Squash Monterey

Easy   Yield: 6 servings
Preparing: 30 minutes
Baking: 30 minutes

**1 spaghetti squash (2 pounds)
1 large onion, chopped
¼ cup butter
½ cup sour cream**

**2 cups shredded
    Monterey Jack cheese
Salt and pepper to taste**

Cut squash in half and remove seeds. Place, cut side down, in a pot with 2 inches of water. Bring water to a boil; cover and simmer for 20 minutes. Remove squash from water and allow to cool. With a fork, gently remove spaghetti-like strands from the shells and reserve. Sauté onion in butter until soft and lightly browned. Fold onion, sour cream, and 1 cup of cheese into the squash, season with salt and pepper and place in a lightly greased casserole. Sprinkle with remaining cheese. (May be made ahead to this point.) Bake in a preheated 325° oven for 30 minutes.

Note: An alternative way to cook the spaghetti squash is to steam it, whole, for 30 minutes or until the skin gives when finger-pressed. Allow to cool, cut in half, remove seeds, and scrape out strands.

Pasta

and RICE

con Gusto

Bravo!

Educational Outreach

With the goal of making classical music accessible and understandable to the general community, The Philadelphia Orchestra has programs to accommodate all ages, from preschoolers to high school and college students. It has long captured the imagination of young people by opening rehearsals to students and by performing concerts specifically for children, families, and students throughout the year. As a special gift to the school children of the city of Philadelphia, the Orchestra performs one student concert for them annually.

The Orchestra's cultural diversity initiative develops projects to include a broad range of the city's population as a growing part of its audience. Through the cooperation of the Orchestra's Department of Education, the Orchestra performs a series of concerts that bring approximately 25,000 children to the Academy of Music each year. Often, these concerts feature young guest artists who have won the annual Philadelphia Orchestra Albert M. Greenfield Student Competition. Special written materials and question-and-answer sessions increase the understanding of the young audiences, drawn from a wide geographic area.

Not only do school children come to the Academy, but musicians and volunteer docents also visit schools to help prepare students for the concert experience. All these programs that reach out to the broad community give children and adults the opportunity to develop their understanding of the language of music.

Pasta con Vitello Verdi

Easy	*Yield: 2 servings*
Do ahead	*Preparing: 25 minutes*
	Cooking: 1¾ hours
	May be doubled

1 tablespoon butter
2 tablespoons olive oil
3 tablespoons chopped prosciutto
¼ cup minced onion
½ pound veal tenders julienned (see note)
1 red bell pepper, julienned
2 large fresh white mushrooms, julienned

½ cup dry white wine
1 whole bay leaf, broken in half
½ teaspoon dried thyme
¼ teaspoon cracked black pepper
1½ cups very lightly seasoned tomato sauce (preferably homemade)
8 ounces fresh spinach fettucine
Freshly grated Parmesan cheese

In a large saucepan, sauté the prosciutto in the butter and oil until it is crisp and browned. With a slotted spoon remove prosciutto from pan and reserve for later use. Sauté veal and onion in the remaining fat until the meat is no longer pink. Add red pepper, mushrooms, wine, and seasonings to pot and simmer over medium heat for 5 minutes. Return the cooked prosciutto to the pot and add the tomato sauce. Mix gently. Turn heat down to very low and cook, uncovered, very slowly for 45 minutes. Cover and cook for an additional 45 minutes, or until very thick, stirring occasionally. Serve over fresh spinach fettucine and sprinkle with freshly grated Parmesan cheese. With garlic bread, a green salad, and a good dry white wine, you have a delicious meal!

Note: Freeze veal slightly and then julienne into ¼-inch x 4-inch strips.

Bravo!

Tortellini with Gorgonzola Sauce

Easy Yield: 4 to 6 servings
Preparing: 10 minutes
Cooking: 20 minutes
May be doubled

Q E D

1½ cups dry white vermouth
2¼ cups heavy cream
Freshly ground pepper
Pinch grated nutmeg
1½ pounds tortellini

½ pound sweet Gorgonzola cheese
1½ tablespoons grated Parmesan
cheese
1 large red bell pepper, cored, seeded,
and diced

In a heavy saucepan, bring vermouth to a boil; reduce by half. Add the heavy cream, freshly ground pepper, and nutmeg. Bring to a boil, lower heat, and simmer, uncovered, for approximately 15 minutes until reduced by one third. In a large pot of salted, boiling water, cook pasta according to directions. Drain and return to pot. Remove cream sauce from heat and stir in Gorgonzola and Parmesan. Pour over tortellini and mix thoroughly. Over medium heat cook gently, stirring constantly, for 5 to 8 minutes or until cream has thickened slightly. To serve, divide onto plates and sprinkle with red pepper.

Rigatoni with Smoked Chicken and Ricotta

Average
Partial do ahead

Yield: 6 servings
Preparing: 45 minutes
Cooking: 20 minutes
May be doubled

1 tablespoon olive oil
1 pound rigatoni
11 ounces smoked chicken,
  finely chopped
4 ounces ricotta cheese
¼ cup grated Romano cheese
2 eggs, beaten
3 tablespoons minced fresh basil
1 tablespoon minced fresh oregano

Salt and pepper
1 (26-ounce) can chicken stock
2 cups tomato or marinara sauce
1 large red pepper, cored,
  seeded, diced
1 large yellow pepper, cored,
  seeded, diced
1 large orange pepper, cored,
  seeded, diced

To a large pot of boiling water add oil and pasta. Cook 12 minutes until pasta is still firm to bite. Drain. Rinse under cold water and drain well. In a medium bowl combine chicken, ricotta, Romano, eggs, basil, and oregano. Season with salt and pepper. With a narrow spoon fill each rigatoni with 1½ teaspoons of cheese mixture. Set on paper-lined baking sheet. Cover and refrigerate. Heat tomato sauce. In a large skillet bring stock to a simmer. Carefully lower rigatoni into stock and cook 5 minutes. Spoon sauce onto plates. With slotted spoon remove rigatoni. Place them on top of sauce. Sprinkle with peppers.

Note: Large shells may be substituted for rigatoni.

Fettucine all'Ortolana
(Fettucine with Grilled Vegetables)

Average Yield: 4 servings
Partial do ahead Preparing: 30 minutes
Cooking: 15 minutes

Vegetables for grilling:
1 zucchini, halved lengthwise, then
  cut across into 4 pieces
1 medium onion, cut into 4 slices
1 medium tomato, cut into 4 slices
  (do not core)
1 head radicchio, cut into quarters
1 Belgian endive, cut in half

1 red bell pepper, cut
  into 2-inch squares
1 yellow bell pepper, cut
  into 2-inch squares
1 medium eggplant, peeled
  and cut into 2-inch cubes

Olive oil to coat vegetables
Salt and pepper to taste
1 pound fresh fettucine
4 ounces olive oil

4 ounces dry white wine
1 sprig fresh rosemary,
  about 30 leaves

The vegetables should be cut into large pieces for grilling so that they do not fall through the grates. Brush the vegetables with olive oil; season with salt and pepper. Grill for about 10 minutes, turning frequently. (Tomatoes will take less time.) When cool, chop into large dice (may be made ahead to this point). Bring a large pot of salted water to the boil. Meanwhile, in a large skillet, heat 4 ounces olive oil and add grilled vegetables. Sauté over high heat for about 1 minute, add white wine, and boil for another minute. Transfer to a large serving bowl and keep warm. Drop the pasta into the boiling water and boil until pasta is al dente. Drain and plunge directly into the hot sauce. Sprinkle with rosemary leaves and serve at once.

Daniel J. Butler, Chef, Griglia Toscana, Wilmington, DE

179

Bravo!

Meat Cannelloni with Grilled Tomato Sauce and Morel Mushroom Cream Sauce

Complicated
Partial do ahead

Yield: 10 to 12 servings
Preparing: 2 hours
Cooking: 2 hours

Meat Filling:
2 tablespoons olive oil
2 medium onions, cut into
    ¼-inch julienne
2 pounds veal stew meat, cut
    into 1-inch cubes
1 pound skinless chicken thigh meat,
    cut into 1-inch cubes

15 whole garlic cloves
¼ cup fresh rosemary
½ bottle white wine
Salt and pepper to taste
1 cup grated Parmesan cheese
2 cups ricotta cheese
8 egg yolks

Crepes:
2¼ cups flour (1 cup whole wheat;
    1¼ cups unbleached all-purpose)
1 tablespoon sugar
7 eggs

3 cups skim milk
3 tablespoons melted,
    unsalted butter

Sauces:
3 cups Grilled Tomato Sauce

2 cups Morel Mushroom Cream
Sauce

Preheat oven to 400°. Using a heavy braising pan large enough to hold all the meat, over moderately high heat, sauté the onions in the olive oil until the onions begin to turn amber. Add garlic cloves and meats and continue cooking until ingredients begin to turn caramel in color. Add rosemary, wine, and salt and pepper to taste. Roast in the oven for 1½ hours, stirring once. Remove meat and reserve the defatted liquid for later use. When the meat has cooled slightly, put into the food processor a batch at a time, and mince. To the ground mixture add the Parmesan and ricotta cheeses and egg yolks; taste for seasoning. Add salt and pepper if necessary, and possibly some reserved broth. (May be made ahead and stored in the refrigerator for up to 2 days.) Crepes: Divide all ingredients for the crepes (except the melted butter) into 2 equal amounts. In a food processor thoroughly blend two batches separately. Transfer both batches to 1 bowl, combine, and add butter. Blend well. The batter should be a little thicker than heavy cream. Heat a heavy-duty 9-inch crepe pan, lightly greased, until it is really hot but not burning. Quickly pour 2 to 3 ounces of batter onto the pan and tilt it in every direction so that the batter forms an even layer all over the bottom of the pan. Cook the first side for 1 minute and carefully turn it over to cook the second side for 30 seconds. Transfer to a tea towel and cover. Repeat until all batter is used. There should be about 30 9-inch crepes. Filling the Crepes: Divide the meat mixture among the crepes. Fold the ends of the crepes onto the filling, then fold them up like tidy little burritos. Cover tightly and refrigerate until final cooking. Preheat oven to 400°. Place cannelloni on a lightly oiled sheet pan and cover them loosely with foil. Cook for 17 minutes. Warm the tomato sauce, the mushroom sauce, and the serving plates. Cover the bottom of the plates with tomato sauce (3 or 4 tablespoons). Place 2 cannelloni on each plate, with a strip of mushroom sauce over each. Sprinkle with grated Parmesan cheese, chopped parsley, and a rosemary sprig.

Grilled Tomato Sauce

Average
Do ahead

Yield: 4 cups
Preparing: 30 minutes
Cooking: 25 minutes
Cooling: 15 minutes

20 ripe plum tomatoes
1 (12-ounce) can tomato paste
3 tablespoons minced garlic
1 red onion, sliced in ¼-inch cross-cut

Olive oil
Kosher salt and black pepper to taste
1 cup fresh basil, gently rough
  chopped

In a large mixing bowl, combine the tomatoes, garlic, and enough olive oil to lightly coat the tomatoes. Massage the oil and garlic over the tomatoes, and generously season with the salt and pepper. Rub oil and seasoning on the onion slices, but keep intact for easier grilling. Grill the tomatoes and onions until 50% of the tomato skins are black and the onions have nice grill marks and are beginning to soften. Thoroughly purée the grilled tomatoes and onions with the tomato paste and basil. Let the sauce cool for 15 minutes so the basil flavor can be released. Sauce can be kept in this coarse state or put through a fine-bowl sieve for a smooth and thinner texture.

Morel Mushroom Cream Sauce

Easy

Yield: 4 to 5 cups
Preparing: 30 minutes
Cooking: 30 minutes

2 tablespoons thin, julienned shallots
Olive oil
1 pound morel mushrooms, washed,
  sliced lengthwise (¼-inch)
2 cup white wine
½ teaspoon ground fennel seed

Kosher salt and pepper to taste
1 quart heavy cream
2 tablespoons fresh chopped thyme
2 tablespoons fresh chopped
  Italian parsley

In a tall sauce pot, sauté the shallots in a splash of olive oil until they begin to soften. Add the mushrooms and continue cooking, on medium-high heat, stirring often, until the morels have released their water and the water has been reduced to nearly dry. Season with salt and pepper, add the wine, and reduce to half. Add the cream and reduce the volume of liquid to desired sauce consistency. Season and serve immediately.

Chris Kastner, Evergreen Restaurant, Ketchum, ID

181

Tagliatelle alla Toscana

Average Yield: 4 servings
Baking: 1 hour
Preparing: 20 minutes

½ cup fresh broccoli rabe
3 tablespoons extra virgin olive oil
6 cloves garlic, roasted
2 shallots, diced

8 large shrimp, peeled and deveined
1 cup sliced portabella mushrooms
Salt and pepper to taste
1 pound fresh tagliatelle

Steam the broccoli rabe until it is just tender (5 minutes) and set aside. Heat the olive oil in a large skillet. Squeeze roasted garlic into skillet and add shallots, shrimp, and mushrooms. Season to taste with salt and pepper. Sauté for about 2 to 3 minutes or until mushrooms are soft. Add the steamed broccoli rabe and heat through. Transfer sauce to a large serving bowl and keep warm. Bring a large pot of salted water to the boil and add tagliatelle. Boil for 1 minute or until pasta is cooked al dente. Drain and plunge directly into the waiting sauce.

Daniel J. Butler, Chef, Griglia Toscana, Wilmington, DE

To roast garlic, lop the top off the head of garlic. Drizzle a teaspoon or two of olive oil into the top, allowing it to seep between the cloves. Wrap tightly in aluminum foil and bake at 400° for 1 hour.

Easy Thai Pasta

Easy Yield: 4 servings (2½ cups sauce)
Do ahead Preparing: 35 minutes
Chilling: Several hours

1 (13-ounce) can coconut milk
1 (8-ounce) can satay peanut sauce
3 large garlic cloves, minced
1 tablespoon minced fresh
   ginger root

¼ teaspoon red chili pepper flakes
1 pound linguine
Chopped scallions for garnish

Combine coconut milk, satay sauce, garlic, and ginger root; mix well. Cover and refrigerate for several hours to allow the flavors to blend. When ready to serve, heat to boiling and pour over linguine that has been prepared al dente according to the directions on the package. Garnish with chopped scallions. This quantity would serve 4 as a first course or 6 to 8 as an accompanying side dish.

Linguine Lepic

Easy Yield: 4 lunch or 6 appetizer servings
Preparing: 20 minutes
Cooking: 15 minutes

½ tablespoon butter
½ tablespoon olive oil
1 canteloupe
1 pint heavy cream

1 tablespoon tomato paste, or more
1 tablespoon fresh lemon juice,
  or more
1 pound linguine

Cut flesh of melon into small chunks. In a large skillet heat oil and butter. Add melon and sauté over moderately high heat until the melon begins to dissolve. Add cream and continue cooking, stirring, until sauce thickens. Add tomato paste and lemon juice; taste for seasoning. Adjust if desired. Cook linguine according to directions, al dente. Drain and stir gently into sauce.
Serve immediately.

Jeffrey Brillhart

Italian Shrimp Pasta

Easy Yield: 4 to 6 servings
Preparing: 20 minutes
Cooking: 15 minutes

8 ounces uncooked fettucine
2 tablespoons butter or olive oil
½ cup chopped onion
1 cup sliced carrots
1 cup sliced mushrooms
1 cup broccoli flowerets
1 teaspoon finely chopped garlic

1 teaspoon dried basil
½ teaspoon salt
¼ teaspoon freshly ground
  black pepper
12 ounces shrimp, shelled
  and deveined
1½ cups shredded mozzarella cheese

Cook fettucine according to directions (al dente). Drain. Set aside. In a large skillet heat butter; sauté onion until it is translucent (about 5 minutes). Add carrots, mushrooms, broccoli, and garlic. Sauté until tender-crisp (5 minutes). Stir in basil, salt, and pepper. Increase heat to high, and add shrimp. Toss until shrimp turn pink. Add cooked fettucine and mozzarella, and mix gently. Heat only until cheese has melted. Serve immediately.

Bravo!

Pasta with Mussels and Shrimp

Average   Yield: 4 to 6 servings
Preparing: 45 minutes
Cooking: 45 minutes
May be doubled

3 tablespoons olive oil
2 cloves garlic, pressed
¼ cup chopped onions
1 can (28 ounces) Italian plum
  tomatoes, drained and chopped
1 tablespoon capers, drained
½ teaspoon salt
1 to 2 teaspoons white pepper

1 teaspoon chopped parsley
½ pound black olives, sliced
½ cup dry white wine or vermouth
12 or more large mussels,
  thoroughly scrubbed
1 pound shrimp, shelled and deveined
¼ teaspoon crushed red pepper
1 pound linguine or angel hair pasta

In a large skillet, heat 1 tablespoon oil over moderate heat. Sauté onions and garlic until translucent. Add tomatoes, capers, salt, and pepper. Simmer uncovered for 20 minutes. Add parsley and olives. In a separate saucepan, heat 2 tablespoons olive oil over high heat. Add wine and mussels, and steam until the mussels open (approximately 7 to 10 minutes). With a slotted spoon, remove mussels from liquid and discard the shells. In the same liquid, steam the shrimp until barely done (approximately 2 minutes). Remove from liquid. Combine the shrimp and mussels with the sauce, and add any cooking liquid if the sauce seems too thick. Cook pasta according to directions (al dente). Combine sauce and pasta and serve immediately.

Thaw frozen fish in milk to restore that fresh-caught flavor.

Pasta Pescara

Easy Yield: 6 servings
Preparing: 30 minutes
Cooking: 20 minutes

1 medium onion, chopped
2 cloves garlic, crushed
¼ cup crushed red pepper
   (or to taste)
2 tablespoons green olive oil
½ cup Italian dry white wine
2 cups fresh tomatoes, peeled,
   seeded, and diced

1 teaspoon Italian herb seasoning
1 cup fresh Italian parsley, chopped
3 cups fresh seafood: chopped
   calamari, mussels, clams, shrimp,
   crabmeat, lobster, cod, bass,
   or swordfish
2 tablespoons chopped fresh basil
1 pound linguine

In a large (5-quart) pot, bring salted water to a boil to cook the pasta. In a frying pan, sauté the onion, garlic, and crushed red pepper in the olive oil for 2 minutes. Add the tomatoes, Italian herb seasoning, and parsley. Cook over moderate heat for 5 minutes. Stir in the chopped seafood and cook, stirring constantly, for 3 to 4 minutes. (Do not overcook.) Stir in basil, and remove from heat. Cook the linguine al dente and drain. Place pasta in a large bowl and mix in the seafood. Serve immediately.

Günther Herbig

Bow Tie Pasta Salad

Easy Yield: 8 to 10 servings
Do ahead Preparing: 15 minutes
Marinating: 1 hour
Cooking: 20 minutes
May be doubled

1 (16-ounce) box bow tie pasta
½ cup olive oil
½ cup salad oil
½ cup good white wine vinegar
1 teaspoon Dijon mustard
½ teaspoon white pepper

1 cup Parmesan cheese
Salt to taste
1 bunch broccoli flowerets,
   blanched and cooled
½ cup sliced fresh roasted
   red peppers

Cook pasta as directed on the package. Drain and plunge into cold water to stop cooking. Drain again and set aside. In a jar with a lid, mix together the oils, vinegar, Dijon mustard, pepper, and Parmesan cheese. Shake thoroughly, add salt if necessary, set aside. At least 1 hour before serving, pour the dressing over the pasta, add the broccoli, and toss. Just before serving, add the red peppers and toss.

Bravo!

Warm Pasta Salad

Easy — Yield: 4 servings
Partial do ahead — Preparing: 15 minutes
Cooking: 10 minutes
May be doubled

½ red bell pepper, diced
½ jalapeño pepper, minced
½ red onion, diced
8 cherry tomatoes, quartered
1 celery stalk, diced
2 carrots, chopped

8 ounces capellini
½ bottle sun-dried tomato
  vinaigrette, fat-free
4 leaves romaine lettuce, torn
  into small pieces

In a large pot, cook pasta according to directions. Drain and return to pot. Toss with vegetables and vinaigrette. Add lettuce, toss again, and serve immediately.

Note: Vegetables may be prepared ahead and set aside.

Pasta with Pesto Sauce, Macadamia Nuts, and Roasted Peppers

Average — Yield: 4 servings
Partial do ahead — Preparing: 30 minutes
Baking: 25 minutes

3 cups loosely packed fresh basil
  leaves (about 2 ounces)
1 cup olive oil
¾ cup roasted macadamia nuts
  (3 ounces)
6 garlic cloves, minced

1¼ cups freshly grated Parmesan
  cheese (5 ounces)
2 large red bell peppers
1 pound linguine
2 tablespoons olive oil
Chopped macadamia nuts
Additional Parmesan cheese

In a processor, purée the basil, olive oil, and macadamia nuts. Add the Parmesan cheese and process until incorporated. Season with salt and pepper to taste. (If made ahead, transfer mixture to a jar, pour olive oil over to cover completely, cover the jar and refrigerate for up to 1 week. Pour off excess oil before using.) Char red peppers over a gas flame, or cut in half, flatten with your hand, and put under the broiler until blackened. Wrap charred peppers in a paper bag and allow them to steam for 15 minutes. Remove skins and cut into thin slices. Keep warm. Cook linguine in a large pot of boiling salted water until just tender but still firm to the bite, stirring occasionally to prevent overflow and/or sticking. Drain well. Return to the same pot and mix with 2 tablespoons olive oil. To serve, divide pasta among 4 plates, spoon some pesto over, then the roasted peppers. Garnish with chopped roasted macadamia nuts and Parmesan cheese. A wonderful summer dish.

Tortellini Salad

Easy
Do ahead

Yield: 12 servings
Preparing: 1 hour
Cooking: 15 to 20 minutes
Chilling: Several hours
May be doubled

Dressing:
½ cup green onions, chopped
⅓ cup red wine vinegar
⅓ cup vegetable oil
2 tablespoons chopped fresh parsley
2 cloves garlic, minced
2 teaspoons dried basil

1 teaspoon dried dill weed
1 teaspoon salt
½ teaspoon freshly ground pepper
½ teaspoon sugar
½ teaspoon dried oregano
1½ teaspoons Dijon mustard

Salad:
2 cups fresh snow peas
2 cups broccoli flowerets
 (1 large head)
2 cups cherry tomatoes, halved
1 (7¾-ounce) can whole, pitted, black
 olives, drained

2 cups sliced fresh mushrooms
2 (8-ounce) packages cheese-stuffed
 tortellini
2 tablespoons Parmesan cheese

Place all dressing ingredients into a jar with a lid and shake vigorously. Set aside. Into a 2-quart pot of boiling salted water, drop the snow peas and cook for 1 minute. Remove with a slotted spoon to a large bowl. Into the same boiling water, drop the broccoli and cook for 1 minute. Remove with a slotted spoon and combine with the peas. Add the tomatoes, olives, and mushrooms; toss. Set aside. In a large pot of boiling salted water, cook the pasta al dente, according to directions. Drain and allow to cool slightly. Combine pasta with vegetables and Parmesan cheese. Shake the dressing well and add to the pasta. Toss well. Refrigerate, covered, for several hours. Serve at room temperature.

Note: Different vegetables may be interchanged. It looks nice to have a variety of colors.

Bravo!

Penne with Asparagus and Artichoke Hearts

Average | *Yield: 4 servings*
Preparing: 45 minutes
Cooking: 35 minutes
May be doubled

2 tablespoons olive oil
2 tablespoons butter
½ small onion, sliced
¼ pound regular or smoked
  pancetta, thinly sliced
4 fresh artichoke hearts, washed and
  coarsely chopped

1 pound tender skinny asparagus,
  cleaned but not dried
4 sprigs fresh parsley
Salt and pepper to taste
⅓ cup white wine
1 cup heavy cream
1 pound dry small penne
½ cup grated Parmesan cheese

In a large heavy frying pan, heat the olive oil and butter over moderate heat
and sauté onions and pancetta until onions are translucent. Add artichoke
hearts and asparagus. Add parsley, salt, and pepper to taste. Continue to
sauté, stirring constantly, for 5 minutes. Add wine, cover, and simmer over low
heat for approximately 20 minutes. Add heavy cream. Simmer for 2 minutes.
Set aside. In boiling, salted water, cook pasta al dente. Drain and pour into a
prewarmed serving dish. Cover with sauce and a sprinkle of Parmesan.
Serve immediately and pass additional Parmesan.

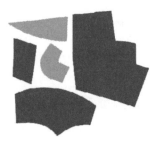

 How much to buy? Whole fish —
1 pound per person;
dressed/cleaned fish —
⅓ to ½ pound per person.

Ralph's Fettucine alla Caprese

Easy   Yield: 2 to 4 servings
Preparing: 20 minutes
Cooking: 25 minutes
May be doubled

3 quarts lightly salted water
¾ pound fettucine
1 tablespoon olive oil
2 tablespoons butter
1½ tablespoons finely
  chopped shallots
1½ tablespoons finely
  chopped scallions
10 cherry tomatoes, quartered
¼ cup vodka

1 tablespoon dried basil
1 teaspoon green
  peppercorns, crushed
1 cup chicken broth
2 egg yolks
¼ cup Parmesan cheese,
  and more to pass
2 tablespoons finely chopped
  fresh parsley

In a large pot, bring salted water to a boil. Add fettucine and cook according to directions, until al dente. Drain and reserve. In a skillet, heat oil and butter. Add shallots and scallions and cook, stirring, until they are wilted. Add tomatoes and cook, stirring, for 3 minutes. Add vodka, and carefully ignite it. When flames subside, add basil, peppercorns, and broth. Simmer for 5 minutes. Add pasta to sauce. Stir in egg yolks and Parmesan cheese. Toss and allow to simmer until thickened. Stir in parsley and serve
with additional Parmesan cheese.

*Use dry-curd or low-fat
cottage cheese instead of
ricotta in lasagna or manicotti.*

Chicken Romano over Linguine

Average   Yield: *4 servings*
Preparing: *45 minutes*
Cooking: *30 minutes*

4 boneless skinless chicken breasts,
   pounded to ⅛-inch thickness
Flour for dredging
3 eggs, beaten
4 tablespoons Romano cheese
2 tablespoons butter
2 tablespoons oil
1½ cups chicken stock

1 cup dry white wine
1½ cups sliced mushrooms
1 cup grated mozzarella cheese
1 teaspoon garlic powder
Juice of 1 lemon
Parsley or watercress as garnish
1 pound linguine

Dredge chicken in flour. Make a batter with the beaten eggs and Romano cheese. Coat chicken pieces in batter. In a large skillet over moderately high heat, melt the butter and oil, and sauté chicken in batches, 1 layer at a time, until golden brown on each side. Remove chicken and keep warm. Deglaze skillet with chicken stock and wine; simmer for 5 minutes. Add mushrooms and chicken; simmer for 5 minutes. Add garlic powder and lemon juice; mix thoroughly. Sprinkle the mozzarella over the top. Continue cooking over low heat until the mozzarella melts. Cook linguine according to directions. To serve, place a portion of cooked linguine on each plate, top with chicken and sauce, and garnish with chopped parsley or watercress.

Orange Rice

Easy   Yield: *4 servings*
Preparing: *5 minutes*
Cooking: *20 minutes*

Q E D

1 tablespoon unsalted butter
1 cup white rice (not quick-cooking)
1 cup freshly squeezed orange juice

1 cup water
1 teaspoon salt

Melt butter in a 2-quart saucepan. Add rice and stir until every grain is coated. Add juice, water, and salt. Bring to a boil. Reduce heat to simmer. Cover and cook for 20 minutes. Very good when served with Pecan Chicken (page 109).

Rice Salad with Peas and Pepper

Average
Do ahead

Yield: 6 to 8 servings
Preparing: 30 minutes
Cooling: 30 minutes to 1 hour
Cooking: 45 minutes

2 sweet red peppers (about ¾ pound)
2 quarts water, lightly salted
1½ cups long grain rice
¼ cup thinly sliced green onions
1½ cup peas, fresh or frozen, cooked
¾ cup pitted black olives, quartered

1 tablespoon chopped, fresh parsley
2 teaspoons capers, drained
2 tablespoons white wine vinegar
6 tablespoons extra virgin olive oil
Freshly ground pepper

Cut red peppers in half and lay, cut side down, on broiling rack. Broil 2 inches from heat until blistered and charred, about 10 to 15 minutes. Transfer to a covered container or brown bag and allow to stand for 15 minutes. Peel, remove cores, pat dry, and dice. In a large saucepan, bring the salted water to a boil. Add rice and boil, uncovered, until just tender, about 12 to 14 minutes. Drain. Rinse in cold water and drain again. Combine rice, roasted peppers, onions, peas, olives, parsley, and capers; mix well. To make vinaigrette, whisk thoroughly vinegar and oil with salt and pepper to taste. Add to rice mixture and toss gently. Adjust seasonings. Serve cool or at room temperature.

Lemon Rice

Easy
Do ahead

Yield: 6 to 8 servings
Preparing: 10 minutes
Baking: 50 minutes

6 cups water
2 cubes chicken bouillon
2½ cups long grain rice
Black pepper

2 tablespoons minced onion
2 tablespoons butter (optional)
Juice of 1 lemon
½ cup finely chopped Italian parsley

Preheat oven to 400°. Add bouillon to 6 cups water and bring to a boil. Lightly grease a 3-quart casserole. Pour boiling water into casserole, add rice, black pepper, onion, and optional butter. Stir to mix. Cover and bake for 50 minutes. Add lemon juice and parsley. Mix well.

Note: This dish may be made ahead and reheated in the microwave.

Bravo!

Arborio Rice Salad
with Sun-Dried Tomatoes and Saffron

Easy　　*Yield: 6 servings*
Do ahead　　*Preparing: 20 minutes*
　　　　Cooking: 1 hour

1½ cups arborio rice
2 tablespoons extra virgin olive oil
1 large yellow onion, chopped
3 cloves garlic, sliced
Pinch of saffron

10 sun-dried tomatoes
¼ cup Madeira
½ cup chicken stock, fat removed
Salt and pepper
Mint leaves

Boil rice in a large pot of salted water until tender, about 15 minutes. Drain well and transfer to a bowl. Sauté onion, saffron, and garlic in olive oil over moderate heat, until golden and soft. Add to rice. Cut sun-dried tomatoes into julienne strips and boil for 5 minutes in the mixture of Madeira and chicken stock. Add tomatoes and liquid to rice. Allow rice mixture to cool. Toss with chopped mint leaves, leaving some whole leaves for garnish.

Bud Bruno, Greenfield Grocer, Ardmore, PA

Baked Orzo Casserole

Easy　　*Yield: 4 servings*
　　　　Preparing: 15 minutes
　　　　Baking: 15 minutes

1 cup orzo
1 cup grated Monterey Jack cheese
½ cup diced red pepper
⅓ cup diced, canned green chilies

1 cup sour cream
½ cup grated Parmesan cheese
2 tablespoons butter (optional)

Preheat oven to 350°. Cook the orzo according to directions on the package. Lightly grease a 1½-quart soufflé dish. In a bowl, thoroughly mix the pasta, Monterey Jack cheese, red pepper, and chilies. Place in baking dish and top with sour cream. Sprinkle with Parmesan cheese and dot with butter. Bake for 10 to 15 minutes or until golden and heated through.

Risotto with Sun-Dried Tomatoes

Average   Yield: 4 to 6 servings
Preparing: 25 minutes
Cooking: 30 minutes

**1 ounce sun-dried tomatoes
   (not packed in oil)
1 cup water
2½ cups chicken broth
4 tablespoons olive oil
1 cup finely chopped onion**

**1 garlic clove, minced
1 cup arborio rice
¼ cup grated Parmesan cheese
Finely chopped parsley to garnish
Salt and pepper to taste**

In a small saucepan, simmer the tomatoes and water for 1 minute. Drain (reserve liquid) and chop finely. In a 1-quart saucepan, combine the reserved tomato liquid and the broth. Bring to a simmer and keep it there. In a large skillet, sauté the onion and garlic in olive oil until translucent. Do not brown. Add rice and tomatoes. Add ½ cup of hot liquid and cook, stirring over moderate heat, until liquid is absorbed. Continue adding liquid, ½ cup at a time, stirring and allowing each portion to be absorbed before adding the next, until rice is tender but still al dente (approximately 20 minutes). Add salt and pepper to taste. Sprinkle with Parmesan cheese and freshly chopped parsley.

Seafood and Vegetable Risotto

Average   Yield: 4 servings
Preparing: 20 minutes
Cooking: 40 minutes

**4 teaspoons olive oil
½ pound medium shrimp, shelled,
   deveined, and each cut into 3
½ pound sea scallops, quartered
½ teaspoon salt
½ cup dry white wine**

**2 cups reduced-sodium chicken broth
½ cup minced onion
1⅓ cups arborio rice
2 cups frozen peas, thawed
1 cup finely shredded radicchio
2 tablespoons chopped fresh parsley**

In a saucepan over medium heat, warm 2 teaspoons olive oil. Stir in shrimp, scallops, and salt. Cook for 1 minute or until shrimp are pink. Add wine and cook 2 minutes longer. Remove seafood with slotted spoon to a plate, cover with foil, and set aside. Add broth and 2 cups water to saucepan. Cover. Reduce heat to low to keep liquid hot. Heat remaining 2 teaspoons oil in a large heavy saucepan over medium heat. Stir in onion. Cover and cook 5 minutes or until onions are soft. Add rice, stirring to coat. Using a ladle, add about ½ cup of hot broth mixture to rice. Cook, stirring constantly, until liquid is fully absorbed, about 5 minutes. Repeat, adding ½ cup of hot broth at a time, until rice is tender and creamy but not mushy, about 25 minutes. Stir in seafood, peas, radicchio, and parsley. Cook 2 minutes longer. Serve immediately.

Bravo!

Green Rice

Easy   *Yield: 6 to 8 servings*
           Preparing: 10 minutes
           Cooking: 30 minutes

2 tablespoons olive oil
4 tablespoons butter or margarine
1 cup minced green onions
1 cup chopped parsley
1½ cups chopped spinach

2 cups short grain rice
3½ cups hot chicken stock
1½ teaspoons salt (optional)
Grated Parmesan cheese (optional)

In a 2-quart saucepan, heat oil and 2 tablespoons butter. Add green onions, parsley, and spinach. Stir and cover. Cook on low for 5 minutes. Remove cover, add rice, and stir until rice is translucent (about 5 minutes). Add 2 cups hot chicken stock. Season if necessary. Cover and cook 10 minutes. Add remaining broth, stir. Cover and cook 15 minutes more or until liquid is absorbed. Lightly mix in remaining 2 tablespoons butter with a fork. Sprinkle with Parmesan if desired.

Wild Rice in a Casserole

Easy   *Yield: 6 servings*
Do ahead   *Soaking: Overnight*
               Preparing: 15 minutes
               Baking: 30 to 40 minutes

1 cup wild rice, soaked overnight
1 (10½-ounce) can consommé, undiluted
4 tablespoons butter
¾ pound mushrooms, sliced
1½ cups finely chopped celery

1 bunch green onions, sliced
1 (6-ounce) can water chestnuts, drained and sliced
½ cup vermouth
Butter

Rinse wild rice well and drain. Combine with consommé in a large saucepan and simmer, covered, until liquid is absorbed (about 30 minutes). In a skillet, melt butter and sauté mushrooms, celery, and green onions until they are limp. Combine vegetables with rice in a buttered 2-quart casserole. Cover and refrigerate until ready to use. Preheat oven to 350°. Add vermouth and dot with butter. Bake, covered, for 30 to 40 minutes or until heated through.

Couscous Salad

Easy
Do ahead

Yield: 6 to 8 servings
Preparing: 20 minutes
Cooking: 5 minutes
May be doubled

2 cups chicken broth
2 tablespoons butter
1½ cups couscous
½ cup currants (or dried cranberries)
1 tablespoon freshly grated orange
   zest
½ cup chopped parsley

2 cups drained mandarin oranges
   (about 2 11-ounce cans)
⅓ cup fresh orange juice
⅓ cup extra virgin olive oil
3 tablespoons fresh lemon juice
Salt and pepper to taste
2 cups chopped pecans, toasted
   slightly

Bring broth and butter to boil and stir in couscous. Remove from heat and allow to stand, covered, for 5 minutes. Fluff with a fork. Transfer to a large bowl and add currants (or cranberries), zest, parsley, mandarin oranges, orange juice, lemon juice, and oil. Toss gently and taste for seasoning. Add salt and pepper if desired. Just before serving, fold in the chopped pecans.

Note: This is an excellent accompaniment to Cornish game hens or baked ham.

Bravo!

Low-Fat Garlicky Cheese Grits

Easy   *Yield: 6 servings*
Preparing: 30 minutes
Baking: 1 hour
May be doubled

1 cup uncooked grits
4 cups water
1 beaten egg or ¼ cup egg substitute
1 pound low-fat Cheddar cheese,
   shredded
2 ounces Gorgonzola cheese
   (a high-fat option)

¼ cup liquified Butter Buds mix
½ cup 1% milk
6 cloves garlic, crushed
¼ teaspoon Tabasco sauce
1 teaspoon salt, or to taste
1 egg white
Paprika

Preheat oven to 350°. Grease a 2-quart casserole. Bring 4 cups water to a boil, add grits, and cook according to directions. Drain. Mix 1 tablespoon of cooked grits with beaten egg. Return this mixture to the grits, and mix thoroughly. Add the cheese (or cheeses), butter mix, milk, garlic, Tabasco, and salt, stirring until the cheese melts. Beat the egg white until fluffy and fold in. Pour into casserole, dust with paprika, and bake, uncovered, for 50 minutes, or until lightly puffed. Allow to stand for 5 minutes before serving.

Sesame Noodles

Easy   *Yield: 8 servings*
Do ahead   *Preparing: 10 minutes*
Cooking: 20 minutes

1 pound linguine noodles
¼ cup sesame oil
3 tablespoons soy sauce
¼ teaspoon freshly ground pepper

½ cup diced sweet red pepper
¼ cup chopped watercress
½ teaspoon finely chopped garlic
Sesame seeds, toasted

Cook linguine according to directions. (Do not overcook.) Drain and submerge in cold water to stop the cooking. Drain again and set aside. Mix together the sesame oil, soy sauce, and ground pepper; toss with the noodles. Add the red pepper, watercress, and garlic; toss again. Put into a serving bowl and sprinkle generously with toasted sesame seeds. Cover and refrigerate.
Best when served at room temperature.

Rhapsodies

Desserts
cookies
and
candies

Bravo!

Volunteers for The Philadelphia Orchestra

Philadelphia, long known as the "Cradle of Liberty," may also be called the "Cradle of Orchestra Volunteerism!" A Women's Committee was formed in 1904 to "Save the Orchestra" from financial disaster. Its efforts were successful, and this early group continued on to become the first permanent organization of its kind in the world.

Today, the Governing Board of The Volunteer Committees serves 600 volunteers who work, both in separate committees and collectively, to provide education, service, and fundraising support for The Philadelphia Orchestra. Significant joint projects include the annual Opening Night Gala, The Philadelphia Orchestra/WFLN Radiothon, an Orchestra Boutique and Shop, and the Museum of the Academy of Music and The Philadelphia Orchestra.

Each year the volunteers honor Orchestra members with special parties and the presentation of gold watches to musicians commemorating 25 years of service. Numerous gifts and endowment funds have resulted from the volunteers' dedication to The Philadelphia Orchestra.

Volunteer Committees

Central Committee: organized in 1904
Chestnut Hill Committee: organized in 1905
West Philadelphia Committee: organized in 1905
Main Line and Delaware Committee: organized in 1911
New Jersey Committee: organized in 1938
Old York Road Committee: organized in 1938
Rittenhouse Square Committee: organized in 1954
Greater Philadelphia Committee: organized in 1992

Associate Committees

Old York Road Associates: organized in 1961
Chestnut Hill Musical Cocktails: organized in 1964
Main Line Associates: organized in 1971
Overtures: organized in 1995

Fallen Chocolate Soufflé with Crème Anglaise

Complicated *Yield: 16 servings*
Do ahead *Preparing: 1 hour*
May be halved
Baking: 25 to 30 minutes
Chilling: 12 to 24 hours

**16 ounces bittersweet chocolate
 (Tobler or Lindt)
2 sticks (½ pound) sweet butter,
 cut into pieces
2 tablespoons dark rum**

**9 large eggs, separated
1¾ cups sugar
Crème Anglaise
2 quarts raspberries**

Soufflé: In top of double boiler, set over barely simmering water, melt chocolate and butter, stirring until mixture is smooth. Remove and cool to room temperature. Stir in rum. In a large bowl, beat egg yolks and sugar with an electric mixer for 10 minutes. Eggs should be pale in color and form a ribbon when beaters are lifted. In another large bowl, beat egg whites until they form stiff peaks. Fold one third of chocolate mixture into yolk mixture, fold in one third of egg whites; then fold in remaining yolks and whites in the same manner. Turn mixture into a buttered and floured 12-inch springform pan (put buttered parchment on bottom of pan) and bake soufflé at 350° for 25 to 30 minutes, or until edge has puffed but center is not set. If pan is lightly shaken, soufflé should jiggle. Let cool on a rack. It will fall. Chill, covered loosely, for 12 to 24 hours. Run a knife around edge of pan and remove side carefully. Cut fallen soufflé with a knife that has been dipped in hot water. It should be somewhat uncooked when cut. Serve with crème anglaise and raspberries.

**Crème Anglaise
1 cup milk
1 cup cream (light is fine)
½ vanilla bean
4 large egg yolks**

**½ cup sugar
½ teaspoon flour (optional)
¼ cup whipped cream (optional)**

Scald milk and cream with the vanilla bean in the top of a double boiler. Whip yolks with sugar until very light. Combine with milk and cream, stirring vigorously with a whisk. Cook over gently boiling water, stirring constantly, until thick like a custard. It should coat the back of a spoon lifted from the mixture. Strain through a fine sieve or cheesecloth. Cool, whipping from time to time with a whisk to keep smooth. (If a thicker sauce is preferred, add the flour with the sugar and egg yolks. This sauce can be kept a few days, tightly covered, in the refrigerator. If a lighter, richer sauce is desired, fold in optional whipped cream just before serving.) Tip: Like any custard, mixture curdles easily. Because of this, be sure to mix some of the hot milk with the egg yolk and sugar mixture; then stir all together, briskly, and continue stirring while sauce is over heat. The minute it thickens, remove from heat and set pan in cold water to prevent further cooking and possible curdling. Stir frequently as sauce cools to prevent formation of a skin.

Bravo!

Danish Rice Pudding

Easy — Yield: 6 servings
Do ahead — Preparing: 1 hour
May be doubled or tripled

1 cup white rice	**½ pint whipping cream, whipped**
5 cups milk	**½ cup blanched almonds (optional)**
2 tablespoons sugar	

In a saucepan, bring rice and milk to a boil, stirring constantly. Simmer 5 minutes. Turn off heat and let stand, covered, 10 minutes. Reheat; simmer another 5 minutes, stirring constantly. Add sugar and stir. Add almonds. Cool completely. Add whipped cream. Serve plain or with strawberry or raspberry sauce.

Anne's Barbados Rum Cream

Average — Yield: 6 to 8 servings
Do ahead — Preparing: 25 minutes
Chilling: At least 2 hours

1 envelope (¼ ounce) plain gelatin	**½ cup dark rum**
½ cup water	**1 pint heavy cream, whipped**
4 eggs, separated	**⅛ teaspoon salt**
⅔ cup sugar	**¼ cup grated dark chocolate**

Dissolve gelatin in water by heating 5 minutes over hot water in a double boiler. Cool. In a large bowl whip egg yolks until they are pale yellow. Add sugar, 1 tablespoon at a time, continuing to whip. Gradually whip dissolved gelatin into egg-yolk mixture. Add rum, a little at a time. Fold in heavy cream. In large bowl add salt to egg whites; beat until stiff. Fold into yolk mixture. Pour into a pretty 6-to-8-cup bowl or soufflé dish, and sprinkle with grated chocolate. Refrigerate at least 2 hours. Serve chilled. If desired, top with additional whipped cream.

Grapes Juanita

Easy — Yield: 8 servings
Do ahead — Preparing: 10 minutes
Chilling: 2 hours

2 pounds seedless grapes	**½ cup light brown sugar**
1 cup low-fat (or no-fat) sour cream	**Grated orange rind**

Remove grapes from stems. Combine grapes and sour cream. Sprinkle with brown sugar. Chill 2 hours. Garnish with grated rind.

C-String Fantasy

Easy Yield: 6 to 8 servings
Preparing: 15 to 20 minutes
Refrigerating: Several hours

½ pound good-quality
  semisweet chocolate
½ pound butter
2 eggs
¼ cup sugar

2 ounces glacé cherries, chopped
½ cup walnuts, chopped
4 ounces brandy or sherry (optional)
½ pound sweetmeal biscuits, crushed

Melt together chocolate and butter over low heat. In a bowl beat together eggs and sugar until creamy. Beat in chocolate/butter mixture. Fold in three quarters of the cherries and walnuts. Add brandy, if desired, and biscuits. Place ingredients in a buttered springform cake pan. Decorate the top with remaining cherries and walnuts. Refrigerate until firm.

Byron Janis

Rice Pudding Glazed with Crème Brûlée

Complicated Yield: 6 to 8 servings
Partial do ahead Preparing: 1 hour
Baking: 20 to 25 minutes

Crème Brûlée:
6 egg yolks
6 tablespoons sugar
Rice Pudding:
3 cups milk
¾ cup rice
½ cup sugar

1 pint heavy cream
1 vanilla bean pod

1 teaspoon grated fresh ginger root
½ cup candied orange peel

Crème Brûlée: Whisk egg yolks and sugar in a stainless steel bowl until the yolks are pale. Split vanilla bean and remove seeds. In a pot over medium heat, bring cream to a boil with the vanilla bean seeds. Pour the boiled cream over the egg yolk mixture. Stir slowly and strain to remove seeds. Set aside to cool.
Rice Pudding: In a pot over low heat, cook rice with milk, sugar, and ginger until soft, stirring from time to time to prevent sticking (about 30 minutes). Remove from heat and add candied orange peel. Cool to room temperature. In a gratin dish spread a ½-inch layer of rice pudding on the bottom. Fill to the top with the crème brûlée mix. Place dish in a deep pan and pour water halfway up. Preheat oven to 300°. Bake for 20 to 25 minutes, until barely set. The center should be soft. Remove from water bath and allow to cool for 1 hour before refrigerating. When the crème brûlée is cold, spread a thin layer of dry sugar on top and brown under a broiler. Serve immediately.

Four Seasons, Philadelphia, PA

Bravo!

English Bread-and-Butter Pudding
with Vanilla Custard Sauce

Average
Partial do ahead

Yield: 6 servings
Preparing: 90 minutes
Soaking: Overnight
Standing: 1 hour
Baking: 50 minutes

Pudding:

3 ounces raisins
2 tablespoons amaretto
1 cup milk
2 ounces sugar
1 teaspoon vanilla
3 eggs
½ cup heavy cream

8 thin slices white bread, generously
    buttered (crusts trimmed)
4 tablespoons apricot jam
1 package (2½ ounces)
    toasted slivered almonds
Confectioners' sugar for dusting
Blackberries or raspberries as garnish

Soak raisins in amaretto overnight. Preheat oven to 325°. In a large saucepan combine milk, sugar, and vanilla. Slowly bring mixture to a boil; cool. Beat eggs with cream until well blended. Gradually blend in milk mixture. Make sandwiches of bread using 2 tablespoons of apricot jam on well-buttered slices. Cut each sandwich diagonally into fourths. Arrange bread triangles in layers in a buttered ovenproof dish. Sprinkle each layer with soaked raisins and some of the toasted almonds. Gradually pour cream mixture over bread, making sure all bread is coated. Let pudding stand for 1 hour to allow bread to absorb the liquid. It will become light and crisp during cooking. Place dish in a roasting pan. Fill with hot water to a depth of 1 inch. Bake for 50 minutes to 1 hour, until top is crisp and golden. Meanwhile, add 1 tablespoon of water to the remaining 2 tablespoons of apricot jam. Gently melt in a saucepan. Brush jam over pudding as a glaze and sprinkle with remaining toasted almonds. Lightly dust top with confectioners' sugar. Serve warm or at room temperature, with slightly warm vanilla custard sauce and a dollop of whipped cream on each serving. Garnish with blackberries or raspberries.

Vanilla Custard Sauce:

2 cups half-and-half
⅔ cup whole milk
1 teaspoon vanilla

5 egg yolks
⅔ cup sugar
Pinch salt

Combine half-and-half with milk in a heavy saucepan. Bring to a simmer; add vanilla. Whisk egg yolks with sugar and salt in a bowl. Blend well. Bring half-and-half mixture to a second boil. Gradually whisk about ½ cup into the yolks. Return to saucepan and stir over low heat until custard thickens and coats the back of a spoon (6 to 8 minutes). Cover and refrigerate until ready to serve. Microwave 1 minute to warm.

Naughty Chocolate Pudding

Average Yield: 12 servings
Do ahead Preparing: 35 minutes
Steaming: 2½ hours

⅓ cup butter	1 teaspoon vanilla
⅔ cup sugar	¼ cup orange liqueur
1 egg	¼ cup orange marmalade, warmed
2¼ cups flour	1 cup heavy cream, whipped stiffly
4 teaspoons baking powder	Orange flavored chocolate bar,
Pinch salt	shaved
¾ cup milk	Peppermint leaves, borage flowers
2 squares baking chocolate	(optional garnish)

Cream butter and sugar. Beat in egg. Sift together flour, baking powder, and salt; add this mixture to the butter mixture, alternating with the milk. Melt the chocolate squares over hot water (or in the microwave). Add melted chocolate, vanilla orange liqueur to the batter and mix thoroughly. Lightly grease a 2-quart baking mold and cover with foil. In a covered kettle large enough to hold the baking mold insert a rack to hold the mold off the bottom. Add enough water to just reach the rack and bring the water to a boil. Insert the pudding, cover the kettle, and steam for 2½ hours, checking occasionally to make sure the water does not boil away. Add water if needed. After 2½ hours, unmold the pudding onto a wire rack; while still warm, drizzle warmed orange marmalade over pudding. When cooled, decorate with whipped cream and shaved chocolate bar. Before serving, add some fresh peppermint leaves and blue borage flowers to the plate.

Note: You may substitute raspberry liqueur and warmed raspberry seed-less jam for the orange. Decorate with whipped cream and fresh raspberries instead of shaved orange chocolate.

Hummer

Easy Yield: 6 (5-ounce) servings
Preparing: 5 minutes

1 pint vanilla ice cream	4½ ounces (3 jiggers) fine brandy
4½ ounces (3 jiggers) dark rum	4½ ounces (3 jiggers) Kahlua

Put ice cream and other ingredients in a blender or mixer and blend until smooth, but still cold. Serve immediately in 9- or 10-ounce wine glasses or stemmed equivalent.

Note: If a thicker dessert is desired, add more ice cream.

Bravo!

Champagne, Peach, and Mint Sherbet

Complicated   Yield: 6 to 8 servings
Do ahead   Preparing: 30 minutes
Freeze   Freezing: 7 hours

4 egg whites
1 cup sugar
1½ cups heavy cream
1 cup puréed fresh peaches

1 cup water
1¼ cups Champagne
¼ cup finely chopped fresh mint
Mint sprigs (garnish)

Beat egg whites until soft peaks are formed. Gently beat in sugar. Fold in cream, peaches, water, Champagne, and mint. Put mixing bowl, covered with plastic wrap, into the freezer. After 2 or 3 hours, when mixture is partially set, remove bowl from freezer. Beat vigorously; mixture will increase in volume and lighten in color. Cover bowl and freeze again for 1 hour. Beat vigorously again. Cover and freeze for several more hours before serving. Allow to soften in the refrigerator for 30 minutes before serving in a tuile cup, garnished with mint sprigs or edible flowers. May also be served with a fresh fruit coulis.

Sweet Daddy's, Wayne, PA

Fresh Pear Alaska

Easy   Yield: 6 servings
Preparing: 15 minutes
Broiling: 2 minutes

Q E D

3 large fresh pears
1 tablespoon crème de menthe or
   mint jelly
1 egg white

Dash salt
2 tablespoons extra-fine sugar
1 pint vanilla ice cream

Pare, core, and halve pears. Cut thin slices from bottom so that pears will sit up straight. Place on a baking sheet and spoon ½ teaspoon of crème de menthe into the center of each pear. Beat egg whites with salt until soft peaks form. Gradually beat in sugar. Continue beating until very stiff. Spoon a scoop of ice cream into the center of each pear. Frost with meringue.
Broil 2 minutes or until brown. Watch closely!

Pears in Port Wine

Easy
Do ahead

Yield: 4 servings
Preparing: 25 minutes
May be doubled or tripled

4 large ripe pears	Rind of 1 lemon, grated
¼ pint port wine	2 tablespoons red currant jelly
¼ pint water	Cream or whipped cream
3 ounces sugar	

Peel and core pears. Make a syrup of wine, water, sugar, and lemon rind. Add pears; simmer gently until tender. Remove the fruit, add jelly, and boil rapidly until well reduced. Place pears in a clear bowl and strain the syrup over them. Cool and serve with cream or whipped cream.

Gingered Pears

Easy
Do ahead

Yield: 12 servings
Preparing: 30 minutes
Cooking: 40 minutes

2¼ cups sugar	3 tablespoons Grand Marnier
3 cups water	3 to 4 tablespoons chopped candied
1 tablespoon ground ginger	ginger
1½ teaspoons orange-flower water	Juice of 1½ lemons
Peel or zest from 1½ oranges	2 tablespoons cornstarch dissolved in
12 small Anjou pears, not too ripe, peeled and quartered	3 tablespoons cold water

Boil sugar and water until sugar is dissolved. Add ground ginger, orange-flower water, and peel. Bring to a boil and simmer 10 minutes. Add pears. Simmer, covered, 30 minutes, or until tender but not soft. Remove pears and peel. Sliver the peel, return to syrup, and add Grand Marnier, candied ginger, lemon juice, and dissolved cornstarch. Simmer until thickened.
Pour over pears. Chill. Refreshing and different.

Bravo!

Cranberry-Apple Crisp

Easy
Partial do ahead

Yield: 4 to 6 servings
Preparing: 20 minutes
Baking: 45 to 50 minutes
May be doubled

2 cups tart apples, peeled, cored, and sliced
2 cups cranberries

Topping:
¼ cup sugar
¼ cup dark brown sugar
½ cup rolled oats
¼ cup toasted wheat germ
5 tablespoons flour
Pinch salt

3 tablespoons light brown sugar
½ teaspoon cinnamon
2 tablespoons lemon juice

⅓ cup butter, at room temperature, cut up
¼ teaspoon cinnamon
⅛ teaspoon nutmeg
Ice cream

Preheat oven to 350°. Butter a casserole or pie plate (9-inch). Add to it sliced apples and cranberries; sprinkle with sugar, cinnamon, and lemon juice. Combine topping ingredients, cutting in butter. Spread topping over fruit and pat it flat with the palm of your hand. Bake 45 to 50 minutes. Serve warm with ice cream.

Note: Topping may be prepared in advance and stored for several days in a tightly fitting covered container, refrigerated. Double the amount of fruit for a deep-dish pie.

Bananas Foster

Easy

Yield: 6 servings
Preparing: 10 minutes
Cooking: 3 to 4 minutes

QED

4 small ripe bananas
Lemon juice
⅔ cup brown sugar, packed
6 tablespoons butter

Cinnamon
3 tablespoons banana liqueur
3 tablespoons light rum
Vanilla ice cream

Peel bananas and cut in half across the middle. Cut in half lengthwise. Brush bananas with lemon juice. In a low copper pan, cook sugar and butter over direct heat until melted. Add bananas. Cook for 3 to 4 minutes, turning once. Sprinkle lightly with cinnamon. Pour the banana liqueur on top. Place light rum in a ladle and hold over low heat until it almost simmers. Ignite the rum and pour over the bananas. Serve over ice cream.

Ovocne Knedliky (Czech Fruit Dumplings)

Average

Yield: 12 servings
Preparing: 30 minutes
Standing: 30 minutes
Cooking: 10 minutes

5 tablespoons butter, melted
1 cup (8 ounces) drained, sieved,
  cottage cheese
Salt
2 eggs, slightly beaten
2 cups flour

1½ pounds fresh apricots,
  plums, or cherries
12 to 15 sugar cubes
2½ quarts water
⅓ cup butter or margarine
1 cup fine dry bread crumbs
3 tablespoons granulated sugar

In a large bowl combine butter, cottage cheese, a pinch of salt, eggs, and enough flour to make a soft dough. Shape into a roll; cover and let stand 30 minutes. Wash and dry apricots, plums, or cherries. Remove pits. Place 1 sugar cube between each pair of apricot halves or plum halves. Set aside. On a lightly floured board roll out dough about ½ inch thick. Cut into 2-inch squares. In a large pot bring water to a boil. While water is heating, finish dumplings by placing the fruit in the center of each square. Press dough around fruit, covering it completely. Add to the gently boiling water and cook for 8 to 10 minutes. Meanwhile, in a medium skillet melt butter or margarine. Add bread crumbs and sugar. Sauté until golden brown. When dumplings are cooked, remove them gently with a slotted spoon, drain, and serve with the sugar/bread crumb mixture sprinkled over them.

Zdenek Macal

Mousse à la Framboise

Easy
Do ahead

Yield: 8 servings
Preparing: 30 minutes
Chilling: 4 hours
May be doubled or tripled

4 cups fresh or frozen raspberries
⅓ cup sugar
Juice of half lemon
3 tablespoons framboise
  (raspberry liqueur)

¼ cup cold water
1⅓ tablespoons unflavored gelatin
2 cups whipping cream, whipped

Purée raspberries in a blender or food processor. Force the purée through a sieve (discard seeds) into a large bowl. Whisk in sugar, lemon juice, and framboise. Adjust the flavor, if necessary, depending on the sweetness of the berries. Set aside. Put ¼ cup cold water into a small dish. Sprinkle gelatin over the water and let it soften. Heat until dissolved. Stir gelatin into purée; fold in the whipped cream, and pour into a soufflé dish. Refrigerate for at least 4 hours before serving.

Bravo!

Lemon Soufflé with Raspberry Sauce

Complicated
Partial Do ahead

Yield: 6 servings
Preparing: 1 hour
Baking: 35 minutes

¾ cup sugar
2 tablespoons cornstarch
¼ cup water
⅓ cup fresh lemon juice
2 tablespoons fresh orange juice
1½ teaspoons grated lemon zest

2 tablespoons orange liqueur
5 large egg whites,
   at room temperature
¼ teaspoon cream of tartar
Pinch of salt

Raspberry Sauce (Make ahead):
2 cups fresh or unsweetened frozen
   raspberries
2 tablespoons sugar
1 tablespoon cornstarch

2 tablespoons water
3 tablespoons Chambord liqueur or
   crème de cassis

In a small heavy saucepan whisk together ¼ cup sugar and cornstarch. Gradually whisk in water, lemon juice, orange juice, and zest. Bring to a boil over medium heat, stirring constantly. Cook, stirring, for 30 to 45 seconds, until slightly thickened and clear. Remove from heat and allow to cool for 15 minutes. (Can be refrigerated at this point for up to 2 days. Bring back to room temperature before proceeding.) Preheat oven to 350°. Lightly coat sides and bottom of a 1½-quart soufflé dish with vegetable oil and sprinkle with sugar. Tap out excess. Beat egg whites at medium speed until foamy. Add cream of tartar and salt. Increase speed; beat until soft peaks form. Gradually add remaining ½ cup sugar; beat until stiff, but not dry. Stir the lemon mixture well. Whisk in one quarter of the egg-white mixture until smooth. Fold in remaining egg-white mixture; turn into prepared dish. Place dish in a roasting pan. Fill pan with hot water to about one third of the way up the sides of the dish. Bake for 35 minutes until puffed and top feels firm to the touch. Dust with confectioners' sugar and serve with raspberry sauce.

Raspberry Sauce: Bring raspberries and sugar to a boil in a small heavy saucepan. In a small bowl dissolve cornstarch in water. Add raspberries and cook, stirring, 30 seconds, until thick and clear. Remove seeds by straining mixture through a fine-meshed sieve. Serve at room temperature.

To soften brown sugar, place it in a glass bowl. Add a slice of soft bread or an apple wedge. Cover with plastic wrap turned back slightly, and microwave on high 30 to 40 seconds. Let stand for 30 seconds; stir.

Chocolate Soufflé

Complicated	*Yield: 6 servings*
	Preparing: 20 minutes
	Baking: 30 minutes

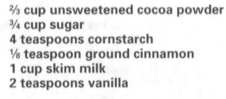

⅔ cup unsweetened cocoa powder
¾ cup sugar
4 teaspoons cornstarch
⅛ teaspoon ground cinnamon
1 cup skim milk
2 teaspoons vanilla

7 large egg whites,
 at room temperature
¼ teaspoon cream of tartar
Pinch salt
½ ounce unsweetened
 chocolate, grated

Blend cocoa, ¼ cup sugar, cornstarch, and cinnamon in a small, heavy sauce-pan. Whisk in milk. Bring to a boil over medium heat, stirring constantly. Cook, stirring, for 1 minute, or until thickened. Remove from heat and stir in vanilla. Allow to cool. Preheat oven to 350°. Lightly oil a 2-quart soufflé dish and dust with sugar. In a large bowl, beat egg whites at medium speed until foamy. Add cream of tartar and salt. Increase speed to high and beat until soft peaks form. Gradually beat in remaining ½ cup sugar and beat until stiff but not dry. Whisk one quarter of egg-white mixture into the cocoa mixture. Sprinkle in grated chocolate, then fold in remaining egg-white mixture. Transfer to soufflé dish. Place dish in a roasting pan. Fill pan with hot water one third of the way up the sides of the soufflé dish. Bake for 30 minutes, or until puffed and firm to the touch. Dust with confectioners' sugar and serve immediately, as is or with raspberry sauce. (See preceding recipe for Raspberry Sauce.)

Chocolate-Mocha Mousse

Easy	*Yield: 6 servings*
Do ahead	*Preparing: 30 minutes*
	Chilling: 1 hour

¼ cup strong black coffee,
 preferably espresso
2 tablespoons rum or brandy

1 cup (6 ounces) semisweet
 chocolate bits
¼ cup sugar
1 cup whipping cream, whipped

Combine coffee, rum, and chocolate in a 4-cup glass bowl. Microwave on high for 2 minutes or until chocolate is melted, stirring once during cooking. Add sugar and continue stirring until smooth and glossy. Cool. (May be placed in freezer for 15 minutes to speed cooling.) Fold whipped cream into chocolate mixture. Spoon into glasses or demitasse cups and chill at least 1 hour.

Bravo!

Joan Specter's Chocolate Pecan Cake

Easy Yield: One 9-inch cake
Preparing: 20 minutes
Baking: 30 minutes

1 stick (¼ pound) butter, divided
½ cup dark brown sugar
½ cup coconut
⅔ cup chopped pecans
½ cup semisweet chocolate bits
2 tablespoons milk
1 cup flour

½ cup sugar
1½ teaspoons baking powder
¼ teaspoon salt
½ teaspoon vanilla
⅓ cup water
1 egg
Vanilla ice cream

Preheat oven to 350°. Melt ½ stick butter in a small saucepan. Remove from heat. Stir in brown sugar, coconut, pecans, chocolate bits, and milk; blend well. Spread mixture on bottom of a 9-inch round cake pan. Set aside. Stir together flour, sugar, baking powder, and salt in a mixing bowl. Add the remaining ½ stick butter, vanilla, water, and egg; beat until batter is thoroughly blended and smooth. Pour over the coconut-pecan mixture and bake for 30 minutes, or until a toothpick inserted in the center comes out clean. Cool in pan 5 minutes. Turn onto a serving plate, with the coconut-pecan mixture on top. Serve warm or cold with vanilla ice cream.

Joan Specter

Decadent Chocolate Sauce

Easy Yield: 3 cups
Do ahead Preparing: 30 minutes
May be doubled

6 ounces bittersweet chocolate chips
2⅔ sticks unsalted butter,
 cut into pieces
1 cup unsweetened cocoa powder

1 cup white sugar
1 cup dark brown sugar, packed
1⅓ cups heavy cream
Dash salt

In a heavy saucepan melt butter and chocolate over medium-low heat, stirring occasionally. When melted, blend in cocoa, sugars, and cream. Stirring constantly, bring mixture just to a boil — be sure the sugars have dissolved. Remove from heat; add salt and mix well. Store in a covered container in the refrigerator. Will last for months if undiscovered by chocolate lovers! When needed, reheat, as much as is needed, in a pan over low heat or in a double boiler, stirring constantly. Do not reheat in the microwave.

Chocolate Finale

Easy   Yield: 8 to 10 servings
Do ahead   Preparing: 15 minutes
        May be doubled or tripled

Q E D

2 (12-ounce) packages
   semisweet morsels
2 (½-ounce) packages chopped
   walnuts

½ pound butter, cut into small pieces
Vanilla, coffee, or peanut butter
   ice cream

In top of double boiler melt chocolate, stirring occasionally. Add butter and nuts. Stir while melting. While this is heating, fill sherbet glasses with ice cream, leaving enough room for chocolate sauce. Place glasses in freezer. To serve, heat chocolate mixture slowly in a saucepan. Remove glasses from freezer and pour hot chocolate mixture over ice cream. Chocolate will harden immediately. Serve on a small plate with a pretty cookie.

Pumpkin Roll

Average   Yield: 10 servings
Do ahead   Preparing: 30 minutes
        Baking: 15 minutes

3 eggs
1 cup sugar
⅔ cup canned pumpkin
1 teaspoon lemon juice
¾ cup flour

Filling:
1 cup confectioners' sugar
8 ounces cream cheese, softened

½ teaspoon baking powder
2 teaspoons cinnamon
1 teaspoon ginger
½ teaspoon nutmeg

4 tablespoons butter, at room
   temperature
½ teaspoon vanilla

Preheat oven to 375°. In a large bowl beat eggs very well. Add remaining ingredients, one at a time, combining well. Pour batter into a greased and floured 15½ x 10½ x 1-inch jelly-roll pan. Bake 15 minutes. Remove from heat; cover with a kitchen towel and roll. Prepare filling by combining all ingredients with a mixer. Unroll dough, spread with filling, then reroll (without towel). Wrap in plastic and refrigerate. Chill well. Slice and serve.

Bravo!

Coconut Candy Bar Cheesecake

Complicated　　Yield: 16 to 20 servings
Do ahead　　Preparing: 1½ hours
　　　　　　　Baking: 1 hour and 10 minutes
　　　　　　　Chilling: 4 hours

Crust:
26 chocolate wafer cookies,
　broken into pieces
1 cup lightly packed flaked coconut

¼ cup sugar
¼ cup chilled unsalted butter, diced

Filling:
5 ounces unsweetened
　chocolate, chopped
1 pound cream cheese,
　at room temperature
1¾ cups sugar

3 tablespoons light corn syrup
1 teaspoon vanilla extract
1 large egg, at room temperature
2 large egg yolks, at room
　temperature

Topping:
3 cups lightly packed sweetened
　flaked coconut
6 tablespoons sour cream
2 ounces cream cheese, at room
　temperature

¼ cup confectioners' sugar
¼ cup canned cream of coconut
¼ teaspoon coconut extract
⅓ cup sweetened flaked coconut,
　toasted

Crust: Preheat oven to 350°. Wrap the outside of a 9-inch springform pan with
2¾-inch high sides with heavy duty aluminum foil. In a food processor,
coarsely grind cookies, coconut, and sugar. Add butter; process until moist
crumbs form. Press firmly onto bottom and 2 inches up the sides of pan. Bake
10 minutes. Cool on rack.
Filling: Melt chocolate in top of double boiler, stirring constantly. Cool. In
processor, blend cheese and sugar until thoroughly combined. Add melted
chocolate, corn syrup, and vanilla. Blend well, scraping down sides occasionally. Add egg and yolks; blend 5 seconds. Scrape down sides; blend 5 seconds.
Spoon batter into crust. Bake 40 minutes or until outer 2 inches are puffed and
set; center will be only softly set. Transfer to a rack and cool 5 minutes.
Topping: Blend coconut, sour cream, cream cheese, confectioners' sugar,
cream of coconut, and extract in processor. Mix until coconut is finely
chopped, scraping down sides occasionally (about 1 minute). Gently press
cheesecake to flatten any raised edges. Pour topping over cheesecake. Bake
until topping is just set and coconut begins to brown (about 20 minutes). With
a small knife, cut around cake to loosen crust from pan sides. Cool. Refrigerate
until very cold (about 4 hours). Can be prepared 2 days ahead. Cover and keep
refrigerated. Sprinkle toasted coconut over cake before serving.

Apricot Strudel

Average	*Yield: 24 pieces (¾-inch)*
Partial do ahead	*Preparing: 45 minutes*
Freeze	*Baking: 40 minutes*

Dough:
8 ounces butter
1 egg
8 ounces sour cream

1 tablespoon vinegar
2 cups flour

Filling:
1 cup sugar
1 cup golden raisins
½ cup chopped nuts
12 ounces apricot preserves

1 teaspoon cinnamon
4 teaspoons sugar mixed with 1
   teaspoon cinnamon

Dough: 24 hours ahead of time cream the butter, egg yolk (reserving the white), sour cream, and vinegar. Blend in the flour. Divide dough into 4 equal pieces. Wrap each in plastic and refrigerate overnight.

Filling: Blend the sugar, raisins, nuts, apricot preserves, and cinnamon. Preheat oven to 350°. Roll out each piece of dough to a rectangle approximately 6 x 9 inches. Place one fourth of the filling along the 9-inch end and roll up tightly. Refrigerate while preparing the other 3 rolls. Place on a lightly greased pan and score each roll every ¾ inch just through the dough. Brush with the reserved egg white and sprinkle with cinnamon sugar. Bake for 40 minutes. Cool completely before slicing.

Note: Dough can be frozen, unbaked. Strudel also freezes well. Make sure it is well wrapped.

Chase's Original Specialty Bakery, Philadelphia, PA

Mocha-Macaroon Dessert

Easy	*Yield: 4 servings*
Partial do ahead	*Preparing: 15 minutes*
	May be doubled or tripled

8 almond macaroons
⅓ cup dark rum
1 pint coffee ice cream

1 cup heavy cream, whipped
1 to 2 macaroons, crumbled

Place macaroons in a flat dish large enough to hold them in one layer. Sprinkle with rum. Turn macaroons to moisten both sides and allow them to stand until all the rum is absorbed. May be done ahead to this point. Just before serving, line an attractive 6- or 7-cup bowl with the rum-soaked macaroons. Spoon ice cream over macaroons. Cover with whipped cream; sprinkle crumbs over top.

Bravo!

Raspberry Roll

Average Yield: 10 servings
Do ahead Preparing: 1¼ hours
Baking: 12 to 15 minutes
Chilling: 1 to 4 hours

½ cup flour
½ teaspoon baking powder
¼ teaspoon salt
4 eggs, separated
1 tablespoon cold water
½ cup and ⅓ cup sugar

½ teaspoon vanilla
⅓ cup confectioners' sugar
½ cup red raspberry preserves
1 teaspoon lemon juice
1 cup heavy cream, whipped

Preheat oven to 350°. Grease and flour a 15½ x 10½ x 1-inch jelly-roll pan. Sift together flour, baking powder, and salt. In a large bowl, combine egg whites and water. Beat on high speed until frothy. Gradually beat in ½ cup sugar; continue to beat until glossy. In a small bowl, beat yolks until thickened (about 3 minutes). Gradually add ⅓ cup sugar. Add vanilla; beat 2 minutes longer. Fold into egg whites, then fold in dry ingredients; mix just until blended. Do not overmix. Spread batter evenly in pan. Bake 12 to 15 minutes, until lightly browned and center springs back when lightly touched with finger. Meanwhile, sprinkle a dish towel with confectioners' sugar. Turn out cake on towel. While cake is still hot, roll up cake and towel together, starting from the short end. Let stand 1 minute; unroll to allow steam to escape. Reroll; let cool on wire rack. Unroll; spread with preserves mixed with lemon juice. Top with whipped cream. Spread filling to within ½ inch of edges. Reroll (without towel); trim off ends. Cover and chill at least 1, or up to 4, hours before serving. Dust with confectioners' sugar before slicing.

 Self-rising flour loses its potency if stored too long. Here's a great substitute: For each cup of self-rising flour called for in a recipe, use 1 cup of all-purpose flour, 1¼ teaspoons of baking powder, and ½ teaspoon of salt.

Chocolate Cake

Easy   Yield: 8 to 10 servings
Do ahead   Preparing: 30 to 45 minutes
             Baking: 40 to 50 minutes

1 cup boiling water
3 ounces unsweetened chocolate
1 stick (4 ounces) butter
1 teaspoon vanilla
2 cups sugar
2 large eggs, separated.

1 teaspoon baking soda
½ cup sour cream
2 cups minus 2 tablespoons flour
1 teaspoon baking powder
¾ cup chocolate morsels
Confectioners' sugar or frosting

Preheat oven to 350°. Grease and flour a 10-inch tube pan. Pour boiling water over chocolate and butter. Let stand until melted. Stir in vanilla and sugar; then whisk in egg yolks. Mix together soda and sour cream; whisk into chocolate. Sift together flour and baking powder; add to batter and mix thoroughly. Beat egg whites until stiff but not dry. Stir one fourth of egg whites into batter. Scoop remainder on top of batter, and fold together. Fold in chocolate bits. Pour batter into the 10-inch tube pan. Bake for 40 to 50 minutes, or until edges have pulled away from the sides and tester comes out clean. Cool in pan 10 minutes. Frost when cool, or serve dusted with confectioners' sugar.

Chocolate Frosting

Easy   Yield: 1½ cups
             Preparing: 15 minutes

2 tablespoons butter (1 ounce)
¾ cup semisweet chocolate bits
6 tablespoons heavy cream

1¼ cups confectioners' sugar
1 teaspoon vanilla

Place all ingredients in a heavy saucepan. Cook over low heat, whisking until smooth. Cool slightly. If too thin to spread, add more sugar.

Bravo!

Red, White, and Blueberry Shortcakes

Average
Partial do ahead

Yield: Fifteen 2½-inch shortcakes
Preparing: 30 minutes
Baking: 20 minutes

1¼ cups blueberries
Juice of ½ lime
1⅔ cups flour
½ cup sugar
2 teaspoons baking powder
¾ cup heavy cream
1 extra large egg

4 tablespoons butter, melted
1 pint raspberries
1 quart strawberries, halved
1 pint heavy cream
2 tablespoons confectioners' sugar
1 teaspoon vanilla

Clean blueberries. Mix gently with lime juice. In a bowl mix together dry
ingredients. Melt butter; cool slightly. In a bowl combine heavy cream, egg,
and butter; beat with a fork. Make a well in the dry ingredients. Mix in cream
mixture. Stir in blueberries carefully. Some will break. At this point, mixture
may be covered tightly and refrigerated up to 3 days. To bake, preheat oven to
400°. Cover cookie sheet with aluminum foil, oil lightly, and spoon 2-inch
spoonfuls onto foil, leaving space between them. Bake for 20 minutes on
middle oven rack. Remove from oven, slide foil onto rack, and cool slightly.
Whip cream until soft peaks form. Add sugar and vanilla.
Serve with berries over warm shortcakes.

Apple Walnut Cake from the Islands

Easy

Yield: One 8-inch or 9-inch Bundt cake
Preparing: 30 minutes
Baking: 1 hour

2 eggs
¾ cup vegetable oil
2 teaspoons vanilla
½ cup chopped walnuts
4 cups Granny Smith apples,
   cut into chunks, skin left on
2 cups sugar

2 cups flour
1½ teaspoons baking soda
2 teaspoons cinnamon
1 teaspoon salt
Confectioners' sugar
   for dusting (optional)
Brandy-flavored whipped cream

Preheat oven to 350°. Grease an 8-inch or 9-inch Bundt pan; set aside. Combine and stir together eggs, oil, vanilla, and walnuts. Add apples, but do not
mix. Add sugar, but do not stir. In a separate bowl stir together flour, soda,
cinnamon, and salt. Add to the apple mixture and stir everything together.
Batter will be sticky and hard to stir. Pour into Bundt pan; press down. Bake at
350° for 1 hour. Dust with confectioners' sugar. Serve with brandy-flavored
whipped cream.

Cloud Nine Torte

Easy — Yield: 8 servings
Preparing: 20 minutes
Baking: 1 hour 10 minutes

6 egg whites
2 cups sugar

1 tablespoon vinegar
1 teaspoon vanilla

Icing:
1 cup heavy cream, whipped
Vanilla and sugar, to taste

1 to 2 packages frozen raspberries or
strawberries, thawed and crushed

Preheat oven to 400°. Beat egg whites until very stiff. Add 2 cups sugar, the vinegar, and 1 teaspoon of vanilla. Beat again, until very stiff. Pour into an ungreased 10-inch springform pan. Bake at 400° for 3 minutes. Decrease oven temperature to 200° and continue baking for 7 minutes. Turn off oven, but allow torte to remain in oven for 1 hour longer.
Icing: Add vanilla and sugar to whipped cream. Spread over cooled cake. Serve with crushed strawberries or raspberries.

Note: This cake is equally delicious, and low in cholesterol, served without the whipped cream.

Chocolate Chip Cake

Easy
Do ahead
Yield: One 9-inch cake
Preparing: 25 minutes
Baking: 50 minutes

½ cup butter
1 cup light brown sugar
¾ cup sugar
2 eggs
½ cup boiling water
½ cup sour cream

1 teaspoon baking soda
2 cups flour
1 cup chocolate chips
Cinnamon sugar
Confectioners' sugar

Preheat oven to 350°. Grease a 9-inch tube pan and sprinkle with cinnamon sugar. Cream butter with both sugars. In separate bowl, add boiling water to eggs. Beat until light and fluffy. Mix sour cream with soda; let stand several minutes. Combine egg mixture with butter mixture. Fold in flour and sour cream. Add chocolate chips. Pour into prepared pan. Bake for 50 minutes. Cool on rack. Dust with confectioners' sugar.

Bravo!

Harp and Fiddle Cake

Easy   Yield: 8 to 10 servings
Do ahead   Preparing: 10 to 15 minutes
Freeze   Baking: 30 minutes

4 eggs
1 package (3 ounce) lemon Jell-O
1 package (18¼ ounce)
  lemon cake mix

¾ cup vegetable oil
¾ cup water
Juice of 2 lemons
2 cups confectioners' sugar

Preheat oven to 350°. Beat together eggs, Jell-O, cake mix, water, and oil. Pour into a greased 9 x 13-inch pan. Bake for 30 minutes. While cake is baking, combine lemon juice and confectioners' sugar. When cake is done, remove from oven and pierce top in several spots with a fork. Drizzle with juice/sugar combination. Variation: Use orange cake mix with orange or lemon Jell-O, or substitute orange juice for lemon juice in this recipe.

Marilyn Costello and Norman Carol

Jeanne's Fruit Nut Cake

Easy   Yield: Four 1-pound cakes
Do ahead   Preparing: 1 hour
Freeze   Baking: 2 hours

1 pound golden raisins
1 pound chopped pecans
3 cups flour
1 teaspoon salt
1 pound butter, at room temperature

2 cups sugar
6 eggs, separated
1 teaspoon baking soda
1 tablespoon warm water
¼ cup Grand Marnier

Preheat oven to 250°. In a very large bowl, mix together with your hands raisins, pecans, flour, and salt, making sure raisins are separated from one another. Blend butter and sugar in a food processor; add egg yolks, one at a time. Dissolve soda in water, mix with Grand Marnier, and add to processor. Blend well. Add sugar mixture to the large bowl and blend thoroughly. In a separate bowl beat egg whites until stiff. Stir one third of beaten egg whites into batter. Evenly fold in the remainder of the egg whites; do not overmix. Divide among 4 8½ x 4½ x 2½-inch loaf pans, greased. Bake 2 hours, or until tester comes out clean. Cool in pans 20 minutes. Remove from pans. Cool. Store in airtight containers.

Note: Serve with sorbet and fruit sauce, ice cream, or frozen yogurt.

Scotch Apricot Bars

Average
Do ahead

Yield: 50 squares (1-inch)
Preparing: 30 minutes
Crust Baking: 25 minutes
Final Baking: 30 minutes
May be doubled

---

1 cup butter or margarine (room temperature)
2 cups flour + ⅔ cup flour
½ cup white sugar
1⅓ cups dried apricots
4 eggs
2 cups light brown sugar

½ teaspoon salt (optional)
1 teaspoon baking powder
1 cup chopped black walnuts (or pecans or almonds)
1 teaspoon vanilla
Confectioners' sugar for dusting

Preheat oven to 350°. In a bowl mix with the hands the butter, 2 cups of flour, and the white sugar. Pat this mixture into a buttered 9 x 13-inch pan and bake for 25 minutes, until light brown. Meanwhile, boil the apricots in water to cover for 10 minutes. Drain apricots and chop finely. Beat the eggs until light and fluffy. Add the apricots, brown sugar, ⅔ cup of flour, optional salt, and baking powder; mix well. Add the nuts and vanilla; mix. Spread the apricot mixture over the crust as evenly as possible and bake for 30 minutes. When cool, cut into 1-inch square bars and sprinkle with confectioners' sugar.

Apfelpfannkuchen — Apple Pancake

Average
Partial do ahead

Yield: 4 servings
Preparing: 45 minutes

Batter:
3 eggs, lightly beaten
4 tablespoons flour

Pinch of salt
3 to 4 tablespoons milk

In a bowl mix eggs, flour, and salt. Blend well. Add 3 to 4 tablespoons milk and beat. Allow batter to rest for 30 minutes.

Filling:
2 apples (½ apple per person)
8 teaspoons butter

Sugar
Powdered sugar

Allow one pancake per person. Peel and remove apple cores. Cut each apple in half, and each half into ¼-inch slices. Melt 2 teaspoons butter in a 6-inch omelette pan. Arrange apple slices from one-half apple in a single layer, sprinkle with sugar, and allow to cook gently — sugar may caramelize. Carefully pour batter into the pan, just enough to cover the apples. When the underside is golden, turn carefully to finish baking. Put on a warmed plate, sprinkle with powdered sugar and serve immediately.

Mrs. Wolfgang Sawallisch

Bravo!

Oatmeal Raisin Cookies

Easy Yield: 3 dozen
Do ahead Preparing: 15 minutes
Freeze Baking: 10 minutes

2 sticks butter
2 tablespoons maple syrup
2 tablespoons water
1 cup sugar
1 cup flour

½ teaspoon baking soda
1 teaspoon baking powder
2½ cups quick-cooking oats
1 cup raisins soaked in 2 tablespoons
rum or orange juice

Preheat oven to 350°. In a saucepan combine butter, maple syrup, and water. Cook slowly until butter melts; remove from heat. Add sugar, flour, soda, and baking powder. Add oats and raisins. Cool dough slightly. Drop by teaspoon onto ungreased baking sheets. Bake 10 minutes.

Macadamia Nut Brownies

Easy Yield: 18 to 24 bars
Do ahead Preparing: 45 minutes
Freeze Baking: 30 minutes
May be doubled

2 cups sugar
½ teaspoon salt
2¼ sticks butter, at room
temperature
¼ cup light corn syrup

1 cup flour
1 cup unsweetened cocoa
4 eggs
2 cups macadamia nuts, chopped

Preheat oven to 325°. Hand mix sugar, salt, butter, and corn syrup. Add flour, cocoa, and eggs; mix well. Spread on bottom of a greased 11 x 17-inch pan. Top with chopped nuts. Bake 30 minutes. Serve warm with vanilla ice cream.

Chocolate Pecan Toffee Bars

Average	*Yield: 48 squares (1-inch)*
Do ahead	*Preparing: 20 minutes*
	Baking: 20 to 25 minutes
	May be doubled or tripled

¾ cup canola oil
1 cup light brown sugar
1 egg yolk
2 cups flour

1 teaspoon vanilla
1 cup semisweet chocolate bits
½ cup coarsely chopped pecans

Preheat oven to 350°. In a medium bowl, cream oil and sugar. Add egg yolk, beating well. Stir in flour and vanilla. Lightly grease an 11 x 14-inch baking sheet. Press dough evenly onto the sheet. Bake 20 to 25 minutes. Cool. In top of a double boiler, melt chocolate bits. Spread over cooled toffee and sprinkle with chopped pecans. Cut into squares.

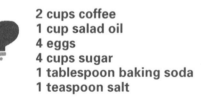

Chocolate Cupcakes

Easy	*Yield: 36 cupcakes*
Do ahead	*Preparing: 20 minutes*
Freeze	*Baking: 25 minutes*

2 cups coffee
1 cup salad oil
4 eggs
4 cups sugar
1 tablespoon baking soda
1 teaspoon salt

1½ cups milk
Splash vinegar
2 cups cocoa powder
3½ cups flour
2 teaspoons baking powder

Preheat oven to 350°. In a large bowl, mix thoroughly all the ingredients. Lightly grease three (12 unit) cupcake pans or use paper cups and fill them to the ¾ mark. Bake for 20 to 25 minutes or until an inserted toothpick comes out clean. Allow to cool and store in an airtight container, or wrap well and freeze.

The Skippack Roadhouse and 4022 Rotisserie, Skippack, PA

Bravo!

Surfers' Squares

Easy
Do ahead

Yield: 16 to 25 squares
Preparing: 15 minutes
Baking: 25 minutes
May be doubled

1 cup (6 ounces) butterscotch bits
¼ cup light brown sugar
¼ cup butter
1 egg
¾ cup flour
1 teaspoon baking powder

¼ teaspoon salt
1 cup (6 ounces) semisweet chocolate bits
1 cup miniature marshmallows
½ cup chopped walnuts
1 teaspoon vanilla

Preheat oven to 350°. In a saucepan over medium heat melt butterscotch bits, sugar, and butter, stirring constantly. Remove from heat; cool 3 or 4 minutes. Add egg and beat well. Add flour, baking powder, and salt. Stir in remaining ingredients. Pour into a greased 8-inch square pan. Cool; cut into squares.

Note: In hot weather it may be necessary to refrigerate before cutting into squares.

Choco-Crispy Clusters

Easy
Do ahead

Yield: 3 dozen
Preparing: 20 minutes
Chilling: 1 hour or more

1 package (6 ounces) semisweet chocolate
1 package (6 ounces) butterscotch bits

⅔ cup smooth peanut butter
4 cups crispy rice cereal

In a double boiler, melt chocolate chips, butterscotch bits, and peanut butter. Stir often. Remove from heat when the mixture is smooth. Add cereal and mix well to coat. Drop by spoon onto wax paper lined cookie sheets. Chill for at least 1 hour. Cookies may be kept refrigerated. Kids love these!

Chocolate-Dipped Fruit Balls

Average Yield: 40 to 50 balls
Do ahead Preparing: 30 minutes
Resting: 24 hours
Chilling: 1 hour

2 pounds (about 5 cups) raisins, figs,
    apricots, or any combination
    of dried fruits
1 cup walnuts
2 tablespoons orange juice

2 tablespoons apricot brandy (or
    other fruit flavored liqueur)
1 cup (more or less)
    confectioners' sugar
4 ounces semisweet chocolate
1 teaspoon butter or margarine

In a food processor chop finely the dried fruit and walnuts. Transfer to a
mixing bowl. Mix together orange juice and liqueur and add just enough to the
fruit and nuts to hold the mixture together. Shape into 1-inch balls and roll
them in confectioners' sugar to coat. Arrange in one layer on a cookie sheet
and allow to stand for 24 hours. In the top of a double boiler melt the chocolate with the butter; stir until well blended. Dip each fruit ball into the chocolate
and place on a wax-paper covered cookie sheet. Chill until the chocolate
hardens. Stored in an airtight container, these snacks
will keep for up to 1 month (if undiscovered)!

Poached Pears with Chocolate and Raspberry Coulis

Average Yield: 6 servings
Preparing: 30 minutes
Cooking: 20 minutes

6 pears, stems attached
Fresh lemon juice
¼ cup sugar
2 pints fresh raspberries
⅓ cup sugar

Juice of 1 lemon
Melted chocolate
Fresh mint to garnish
Vanilla ice cream (optional)

Pears: Peel pears, leaving stems attached. Rub with fresh lemon juice. Soak
pears in water and lemon juice for 5 to 10 minutes. In a 4-quart saucepan cook
pears in water and lemon juice along with sugar. Simmer for 20 minutes, or
until pears are tender. Allow pears to cool in the juice.
Raspberry Coulis: In a blender or food processor, purée raspberries. Strain into
a bowl. Add sugar and lemon juice. Whisk until thoroughly blended.
To Serve: Cover the bottom of dessert plate with the raspberry coulis. Place a
pear in the center. Drizzle melted chocolate over the pear. Garnish with fresh
mint. If desired, serve with small scoops of vanilla ice cream
surrounding the pears.

Jacques Vitré Catering, Wayne, PA

Bravo!

Raspberry Bars

Easy	Yield: 24 bars
Do ahead	Preparing: 30 minutes
Freeze	Baking: 50 minutes
	May be doubled

½ cup butter, at room temperature
½ cup margarine, at room temperature
1 cup sugar
2 egg yolks
2 cups all-purpose flour
1 cup chopped walnuts
½ cup raspberry preserves

Preheat oven to 325°. Cream butter and margarine. Gradually add sugar, beating until light and fluffy. Add egg yolks and blend well. Add flour and mix thoroughly. Stir in walnuts. Spread one third of the batter evenly in a greased 9-inch square pan. Drop preserves by the spoonful over the batter and spread almost to the edges. Completely cover preserves with remaining two thirds of the batter. Bake for 50 minutes, or until golden. Cool and cut into 24 bars.

Butterscotch Brownies

Easy	Yield: 16 squares (2-inch)
Do ahead	Preparing: 15 minutes
Freeze	Baking: 25 minutes
	May be doubled

¼ cup vegetable oil
1 cup light brown sugar, firmly packed
1 egg, lightly beaten
¾ cup sifted flour
1 teaspoon baking powder
½ teaspoon salt
½ teaspoon vanilla
½ cup coarsely chopped walnuts or pecans

Preheat oven to 350°. Blend oil and sugar. Stir in egg. In a separate bowl sift together flour, baking powder, and salt; combine with the egg mixture. Add vanilla and nuts; mix well. Spread into a lightly greased 8-inch square pan. Bake for 25 minutes. Cool slightly and cut into 2-inch squares.
Do not overbake!

Mother's Rum Balls

Easy   Yield: 4 dozen
Do ahead   Preparing: 10 minutes

**Q E
D**

40 vanilla wafers, crushed to crumbs
3 tablespoons unsweetened
   cocoa powder
2½ tablespoons light corn syrup

1 cup chopped walnuts or pecans
6 to 8 tablespoons dark rum
2 pounds (or more) confectioners'
   sugar

Mix together all ingredients except the sugar. Add enough confectioners' sugar to allow chocolate mixture to be rolled into walnut-sized balls. Roll balls in confectioners' sugar. Store in airtight container, covered with confectioners' sugar. Will keep at least 1 month in the refrigerator.

Raisin Bars

Average   Yield: 1 dozen
Do ahead   Preparing: 25 minutes
    Baking: 40 minutes

1 cup plus 2 tablespoons flour
1¼ cups sugar
⅓ cup butter
2 eggs, lightly beaten
½ teaspoon baking powder

¼ teaspoon salt
1 tablespoon orange peel, grated
2 tablespoons orange juice
¾ cups raisins, chopped

Glaze:
1½ teaspoons orange juice
1½ teaspoons lemon juice

1½ teaspoons butter
¾ cup confectioners' sugar

Preheat oven to 350°. Place 1 cup flour and ¼ cup sugar in a bowl. Work in butter until crumbly. Press into bottom of greased 9-inch square baking pan. Bake 15 minutes. Meanwhile, combine eggs, remaining flour and sugar, baking powder, and salt. Stir until smooth. Stir in orange peel, orange juice, and raisins. Pour over baked layer; bake 20 to 25 minutes.
Glaze: Combine orange and lemon juices, butter, and enough sugar to make a thin frosting. Spread over cooled mixture. Cut into bars.

Bravo!

Fishers Spice Cookies

Easy	Yield: 7 dozen
	Preparing: 15 minutes
Freeze	Baking: 10 to 12 minutes

¾ cup shortening
1 cup sugar
¼ cup dark molasses (generous)
1 egg
2 cups sifted flour

2 teaspoons baking soda
1 teaspoon cinnamon
1 teaspoon ground ginger
1 teaspoon ground cloves

Preheat oven to 350°. Cream shortening and sugar. Add egg, molasses, and remaining ingredients, sifted together. Dough will be stiff and slightly sticky. Form into balls the size of a walnut. Roll balls in granulated sugar. Place 2½ inches apart on greased cookie sheets. Bake for 10 to 12 minutes.

Note: For a crisp cookie, cool on wire rack; for a chewy cookie, cool on cookie sheets.

Cinnamon Stars

Easy	Yield: 30
Do ahead	Preparing: 20 minutes
	Baking: 10 minutes
	Chilling: Several hours or overnight

4 egg whites
1 cup sugar

1 pound almonds
1 tablespoon cinnamon

Beat together egg whites and sugar for 15 minutes. Set aside 1 scant cup for icing. Grind almonds 3 times in blender or processor, and add them to the egg mixture. Add cinnamon. Chill thoroughly. On a board coated with a mixture of half confectioners' sugar and half flour, roll out dough to ½-inch thickness. Cut into stars. Place on a baking sheet and cover with wax paper. Refrigerate several hours or overnight. Ice with reserved egg mixture.
Bake at 325° for 10 minutes.

Chinese Chews

Easy Yield: 24 bars
Preparing: 15 minutes
Baking: 30 minutes

1 cup flour	½ cup shortening, melted
1½ cups sugar	½ teaspoon vanilla
1¼ teaspoon salt	1 cup dates, chopped
1 teaspoon baking powder	1 cup walnuts or pecans, chopped
4 eggs	Confectioners' sugar

Preheat oven to 350°. Mix flour, sugar, salt, and baking powder. Add eggs, one at a time, beating well. Add shortening and vanilla. Fold in dates and nuts. Pour into a 9 x 9-inch pan. Bake for 30 minutes. Cool. Cut into bars and roll in confectioners' sugar.

Raspberry Squares

Easy Yield: 25 bars
Preparing: 15 minutes
Baking: 30 to 35 minutes

1½ cups flour	1½ cups quick-cooking oats
1 teaspoon baking powder	1 (10-ounce) jar red
¼ teaspoon salt	raspberry preserves
½ cup sugar	¼ cup chopped almonds
½ cup light brown sugar	Confectioners' sugar to dust
1 cup butter	

Preheat oven to 375°. In a bowl combine flour, baking powder, and salt. Stir in sugars; cut in butter until mixture is crumbly. Stir in oats. Press two thirds of batter into a lightly greased 9 x 9-inch pan. Spread with preserves. Add almonds to remaining batter and sprinkle over preserves, patting down lightly. Bake for 30 to 35 minutes. Cool. Sprinkle with confectioners' sugar. Cut into squares.

Bravo!

Zuppa Inglese

Easy   *Yield: 6 to 8 servings*
Do ahead   *Preparing: 30 minutes*

Custard:
3 or 4 egg yolks
¼ cup sugar

2 cups milk
1 teaspoon vanilla

Cake mixture:
**1 sponge cake or good quality
    pound cake**
1 (8-ounce) jar raspberry jam or jelly

**¼ cup brandy mixed with
    ¼ cup sherry**
Almond paste (optional)

Topping:
1 cup heavy cream
1 teaspoon sugar or to taste

1 to 3 drops almond extract (optional)
Toasted sliced almonds

Custard: Beat egg yolks with sugar. Scald 2 cups milk in a saucepan (heat until just bubbling at the edges). Add milk in a thin stream to the egg/sugar mixture, stirring constantly. Pour all into the top pan of a double boiler and cook over simmering water, stirring constantly, until the custard thickens and coats the back of the spoon. Add vanilla. Cool and refrigerate until ready to use.

Cake: Slice cake thinly. Begin making layers, starting with cake slices, lining the bottom of the serving bowl. Cut or break them to fit. Spread with jam and sprinkle liberally with liquor mixture. Add chunks of almond paste if desired, and add some custard. Continue making layers, ending with custard. Depending on the size of the bowl there should be 4 or 5 layers. Top with sweetened whipped cream, flavored with optional almond extract, and sprinkle almonds over the top.

Note: May be refrigerated for 24 hours to allow the flavors to meld.

Note: A glass serving bowl is recommended to show the various layers.

Robert B. Driver

Heavenly Hash Cake

Average
Do ahead

Yield: 25 squares
Preparing: 15 minutes
Baking: 30 minutes

Cake:
¼ pound butter (1 stick)
1 cup sugar
4 eggs
1 can (16 ounces) chocolate syrup

1 cup flour
1 teaspoon baking powder
1 small (10½-ounce) package
   miniature marshmallows

Frosting:
¼ pound butter (1 stick)
4 squares unsweetened chocolate,
   melted
1 egg

2 cups confectioners' sugar
1 teaspoon vanilla
1 cup chopped nuts (walnuts or
   pecans)

Cake: Preheat oven to 350°. Cream butter and sugar. Beat in eggs, one at a time, chocolate syrup, flour, and baking powder. Pour into a lightly greased 9 x 13-inch pan and bake in a preheated 350° oven for 28 to 30 minutes. Remove from oven and, while cake is still hot, cover with marshmallows.
Frosting: Melt butter and chocolate together. Off heat, beat in egg, sugar, vanilla, and nuts. Spread frosting over marshmallow layer. Cool. Cut into 2-inch squares.

Pinchas Zukerman

Chocolate Cheesecake

Average
Do ahead

Yield: 12 servings
Preparing: 1 hour
Chilling: 4 hours or overnight

10 chocolate cookie wafers,
   finely crumbled
1 tablespoon butter, melted
1 container (15 ounces) part skim
   milk ricotta cheese
⅓ cup unsweetened cocoa powder
Pinch salt

½ cup sugar, divided
1 envelope unflavored gelatin
½ cup 1% milk
1 teaspoon vanilla
2 egg whites, at room temperature
½ cup non-dairy dessert topping

Preheat oven to 350°. In an 8-inch springform pan, combine chocolate wafer crumbs and butter; pat onto bottom. Bake 5 minutes. Cool. In blender or food processor purée ricotta with cocoa and salt until smooth. Set aside. In a small saucepan, combine ¼ cup sugar and gelatin; stir in milk and let stand for 1 minute. Heat over medium-low heat, stirring constantly, for 5 minutes, until gelatin is dissolved. Add to ricotta mixture in blender, and process until smooth. Blend in vanilla. Transfer to a bowl and refrigerate, stirring occasionally, until mixture mounds slightly when dropped from a spoon (about 30 to 40 minutes). In a bowl beat egg whites until foamy. Gradually beat in remaining ¼ cup sugar, until soft peaks form. Fold into ricotta mixture. Pour into prepared pan. Refrigerate until set (4 hours or overnight). Remove sides of pan. Spoon topping into a pastry bag and decorate top of cake.

Bravo!

Fruit Tart

Easy
Do ahead

Yield: 10 to 12 servings
Preparing: 45 minutes
Baking: 15 minutes
Chilling: 1 hour

Crust:
½ cup confectioners' sugar
¾ cup butter

1½ cup flour

Filling:
8 ounces cream cheese, at room
**   temperature**
1 cup confectioners' sugar

1 teaspoon vanilla
Fruit, such as kiwi, strawberries,
**   peaches, grapes**

Glaze:
1 tablespoon cornstarch
½ cup pineapple juice

¼ cup sugar
2 teaspoons lemon juice

Preheat oven to 300°. Mix together ingredients for crust until crumbly. Pat into a 12-inch pizza pan; bake 15 minutes. Cool.
Filling: Mix together cream cheese, 1 cup confectioners' sugar, and vanilla. Spread over cooled crust. Cut fruit and arrange decoratively over filling.
Glaze: Combine all ingredients in a saucepan. Cook until thick. Drizzle over fruit. Chill until set.

Frozen Key Lime Pie

Easy
Do ahead
Freeze

Yield: 8 servings
Preparing: 1 hour
Baking: 10 minutes
Freezing: At least 4 hours

Crust:
1½ cups graham cracker crumbs
1 tablespoon sugar

4 tablespoons butter, melted

Filling:
1 can (14 ounces) sweetened
**   condensed milk**

½ cup key lime juice
1 cup whipping cream, whipped

Crust: Preheat oven to 350°. Combine crumbs, sugar, and butter; press into a 9-inch pie plate. Bake 10 minutes. Cool completely.
Filling: Combine sweetened condensed milk and lime juice. Fold whipped cream into milk/lime juice mixture. Pour into pie shell. Freeze at least 4 hours. Let stand 10 minutes at room temperature before serving. Garnish with whipped cream and lime slices.

Cranberry Nut Pie

Easy
Do ahead

Yield: 8 servings
Preparing: 15 minutes
Baking: 45 minutes

2 cups cranberries, fresh or frozen	1 cup sugar
½ cup walnuts, chopped	¾ cup margarine or butter, melted
½ cup sugar	2 large eggs, slightly beaten
1 cup flour	2 teaspoons almond extract

Preheat oven to 325°. In a mixing bowl gently combine cranberries, walnuts, and the ½ cup of sugar. Spread into a lightly greased 10-inch pie plate. In a bowl mix together flour, the 1 cup of sugar, margarine, eggs, and extract. Pour over cranberry mixture. Bake 45 minutes. Serve warm or at room temperature with whipped cream, vanilla ice cream, or vanilla frozen yogurt topped with fresh cranberries.

Peppermint Pie with Fudge Sauce

Easy
Do ahead
Freeze

Yield: One 10-inch pie
Preparing: 30 minutes
Baking: 5 minutes
Freezing: Overnight

12 ounces chocolate wafers, crushed	1 quart pink peppermint-stick ice cream, softened
¼ stick (2 ounces) butter, melted	
2 tablespoons sugar	6 Heath Bars
Sauce:	
2 ounces unsweetened chocolate	1 cup sugar
1 tablespoon butter	2 tablespoons light corn syrup
⅓ cup boiling water	1 teaspoon vanilla

Preheat oven to 350°. Combine wafer crumbs with melted butter and sugar. Press into a 10-inch pie plate. Bake 5 minutes. Process Heath Bars in food processor until chunky. Mix with ice cream. Spread over baked crust and freeze. Make sauce: In double boiler, over hot water, melt chocolate. Add butter and boiling water, stirring constantly. Add sugar and corn syrup; boil 5 minutes and add vanilla. Pour over individual servings of pie. Sinfully delicious!

Bravo!

Pecan Tart

Average Yield: 2 tarts (9-inch)
Do ahead Preparing: 40 minutes
Baking: 25 minutes

6 tablespoons dark brown sugar
6 tablespoons granulated sugar
¼ cup Frangelico (hazelnut liqueur)
¾ cup light corn syrup
1 tablespoon unsalted butter, melted

Sweet Pastry:
2¾ cups flour
8 ounces unsalted butter
½ cup sugar

1 vanilla bean, split and scraped
2 egg yolks
1 egg
7 ounces pecan halves
1 recipe Sweet Pastry

¼ cup heavy cream
2 egg yolks

Preheat oven to 375°.
Filling: In a large bowl combine sugars and liqueur; beat in corn syrup. In a saucepan heat butter and vanilla until bubbles subside and mixture turns light brown. Add to sugar mixture while hot. Whisk together. In another bowl mix egg yolks and egg. Add to cooled sugar mixture; beat vigorously.
Pastry: Mix together flour and butter by hand. In a small bowl mix sugar, cream, and egg yolks. Combine and form into a ball. Add extra cream, if needed. Roll out and place on bottom and sides of 2 9-inch tart pans. Arrange pecan halves in a circular pattern around the tart shell. Spoon in filling to cover pecans. Bake for 25 minutes, until underside is brown.

Jake's, Manayunk, PA

Utterly Deadly Pecan Pie

Easy Yield: 8 servings
Preparing: 10 minutes
Baking: 45 to 50 minutes

1 cup sugar
1¼ cups dark corn syrup
4 eggs, slightly beaten
4 tablespoons (½ stick) butter
1 teaspoon vanilla

¼ teaspoon salt
1½ cups pecan halves
1 pie shell, unbaked
Ice cream or heavy cream

Preheat oven to 350°. In a saucepan boil sugar and corn syrup for 2 to 3 minutes. Pour over eggs. Add butter, vanilla, salt, and pecans. Turn into pie shell. Bake 45 minutes. Serve warm with ice cream or whipping cream.

Chocolate Mousse Ladyfinger Pie

Average
Do ahead
Freeze

Yield: 16 to 18 servings
Preparing: 45 minutes
Chilling: Overnight

4 ounces unsweetened chocolate
6 eggs, separated
¾ cup sugar
⅓ cup milk
⅛ teaspoon salt

1½ cups butter
1 cup confectioners' sugar
1 teaspoon vanilla
30 ladyfingers, split

Topping:
1 cup heavy cream
1 teaspoon instant coffee

1 teaspoon confectioners' sugar

Melt chocolate in top of double boiler over hot water. Cool. In a large bowl beat egg yolks until lemon colored. Gradually beat in sugar until smooth and thick. Beat in milk. Add egg mixture to chocolate. Cook over hot water, stirring, until well blended (5 to 10 minutes). Transfer to a large bowl. Cool for 30 minutes. In a medium bowl beat egg whites with salt until stiff but not dry. Beat in ½ cup confectioners' sugar, 1 tablespoon at a time. Set aside. Cream butter. Gradually beat in remaining ½ cup confectioners' sugar. Add to chocolate mixture and stir until well blended. Gently fold in beaten egg whites and vanilla. Line bottom and sides of a 3-quart springform pan with ladyfingers. Pour in a generous one third of batter. Spread neatly to the edges. Add a layer of ladyfingers, then another third of batter. Repeat with remaining ladyfingers and batter. Refrigerate overnight. Wrap and freeze the following day. On serving day, thaw in refrigerator 8 to 10 hours, or overnight. Two hours before serving, remove from springform pan. Whip cream with coffee and sugar, and spread over top and sides of cake. Refrigerate until served.

Note: To serve without freezing, remove from springform pan and spread with flavored whipped cream. Refrigerate until served.

To toast and skin hazelnuts, place them in one layer in a baking pan. Bake in a preheated 350° oven for 10 to 15 minutes or until they are lightly colored and the skins blister. Wrap nuts in a dish towel and allow them to steam for 1 minute. Rub the nuts in the towel to remove the skins. Cool.

Bravo!

Peanut Butter Pie

Average	Yield: One 9-inch pie
Do ahead	Preparing: 1 hour
	Baking: 10 to 12 minutes
	Chilling: 1 hour

Pastry:

1½ cups sifted cake flour
½ teaspoon salt
2 tablespoons sugar

½ cup shortening
2½ to 3 tablespoons ice water
¼ cup chocolate chips

Filling:

2 cups milk
¾ cup sugar
6 tablespoons cornstarch
3 eggs
1 egg yolk

1 ounce butter
½ cup peanut butter
2 cups whipped cream
⅓ cup sliced almonds, toasted

Pastry: Preheat oven to 450°. Sift together flour, salt, and sugar. Cut in shortening until mixture resembles cornmeal. Add water, 1 tablespoon at a time, tossing with a fork, until moist enough to hold together. Shape into a ball. Wrap in waxed paper. Refrigerate 1 hour. Roll out dough. Fit into a 9-inch pie plate, prick with a fork, and bake for 10 to 12 minutes. Cool. Melt chocolate and brush evenly over pie shell. Filling: Boil milk. Combine sugar, cornstarch, and eggs; add to milk. Bring to a boil, and boil for 2 minutes, stirring constantly. Remove from heat; add butter and peanut butter. Mix well and cool. Pour mixture into pie shell. Chill thoroughly. Garnish with whipped cream and almonds.

Morgan's Restaurant, Philadelphia, PA

Blueberry Pie

| Easy | Yield: 6 to 8 servings |
| Do ahead | Preparing: 30 minutes |

1 tablespoon butter or margarine
½ cup dark brown sugar
½ cup sugar
1 tablespoon lemon juice
¼ teaspoon salt

¼ teaspoon nutmeg
3½ tablespoons flour
4 cups blueberries, divided
1 fully baked 9-inch pie shell

In a medium saucepan melt butter. Add the sugars, lemon juice, salt, nutmeg, and flour. Stir. When thoroughly mixed, add 2 cups of the blueberries. Cook, stirring occasionally, until slightly thickened. Remove from heat and stir in remaining 2 cups of blueberries. Allow to cool. Pour into pie shell.

Sauces

Relishes

and
Beverages

Embellishments

Bravo!

Cranberry Orange Relish

Easy	Yield: 6 cups
Do ahead	Preparing: 10 minutes
	May be doubled

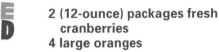

2 (12-ounce) packages fresh
   cranberries
4 large oranges

1 cup orange juice concentrate
1 tablespoon lemon juice
½ cup very fine sugar

Wash and remove stems of cranberries. Peel and quarter oranges, removing seeds. Place half of the cranberries, half of the oranges, ½ cup orange juice concentrate, ½ tablespoon lemon juice, and ¼ cup sugar in food processor and pulse so that the mixture is roughly chopped. Repeat with remaining ingredients. Store, covered, in the refrigerator until ready to use. Will keep for up to 2 weeks, refrigerated.

The Skippack Road House & 4022 Rotisserie, Skippack, PA

Cranberry Orange Relish with Grand Marnier

Easy	Yield: 3 cups
Do ahead	Preparing: 10 minutes
	Cooking: 30 minutes

2 cups cranberries, washed and
   picked over
2 navel oranges, quartered
   (not peeled)
1½ cups sugar

¾ cup water
2 tablespoons minced candied ginger
¼ teaspoon ground cloves
¼ teaspoon cinnamon
¼ cup Grand Marnier

In a food processor chop the cranberries and quartered oranges until fine. In a saucepan combine this mixture with the sugar, water, candied ginger, cloves, and cinnamon. Bring to a boil, stirring; lower heat and simmer, uncovered, for 30 minutes. Cool. Add Grand Marnier. Store, covered, in the refrigerator.

Note: Will keep for several months, refrigerated.

Cranberry Relish

Easy
Do ahead

Yield: 2 cups
Preparing: 10 minutes
Cooking: 7 minutes

Q E D

1 cup cranberry juice cocktail
  concentrate
⅓ cup sugar
1 (12-ounce) package fresh
  cranberries

½ cup dried cranberries
2 tablespoons fresh orange juice
2 teaspoons minced orange peel
¼ teaspoon allspice

In a 1½-quart saucepan mix juice concentrate and sugar; bring to a boil. Add fresh and dried cranberries and cook, uncovered, until the berries pop, about 7 minutes. Add orange juice and orange peel; mix. Pour into a serving bowl and chill until ready to serve.

Cranberry, Cherry, and Walnut Chutney

Easy
Do ahead

Yield: 12 servings
Preparing: 30 minutes
Cooking: 20 minutes

2 cups dried tart cherries
1 cup fresh cranberries
1 cup raisins
1 cup sugar
½ cup cider vinegar
⅓ cup chopped celery

6 tablespoons apple juice
½ teaspoon crushed red pepper flakes
1 tablespoon chopped lemon zest
1 cup toasted, coarsely chopped
  walnuts (black or English)

Combine all ingredients in a 2-quart saucepan and cook for 20 minutes over medium heat, stirring constantly. Cool to room temperature, cover tightly, and refrigerate. The chutney thickens as it cools and will keep for up to 2 weeks in the refrigerator.

Note: Out of cranberry season, frozen cranberries may be substituted. If dried tart cherries are hard to find, dried apricots may be used instead.

Bravo!

Apple Chutney

Easy Yield: 3 quarts
Do ahead Preparing: 20 minutes
Cooking: 1 hour

8 medium cooking apples, peeled,
    cored, and diced (about 5 cups)
1 can (15 ounces) tomato sauce
2 cups dark brown sugar, packed
1½ cups dark raisins

⅔ cup white vinegar
½ cup chopped onion
½ cup fresh lemon juice
1 tablespoon freshly grated
    ginger root

Place all ingredients in a large heavy-bottomed saucepan. Bring to a boil over medium heat, stirring occasionally. Reduce heat; simmer approximately 45 minutes until thickened, stirring occasionally. Pour into hot clean jars.
Cover and refrigerate.

Note: In addition to curry, this chutney is wonderful served with fish, poultry, or a vegetarian meal.

Albertson's Cooking School, Wynnewood, PA

Cumberland Sauce

Easy Yield: 1½ cups
Do ahead Preparing: 15 minutes
Resting: 1 hour

2 oranges
2 lemons
½ cup currant jelly

1 cup port wine
1 tablespoon cornstarch
2 tablespoons water

Remove the zest from the oranges and lemons, and squeeze their juice. Add zest and juice to currant jelly and bring to a boil. Simmer, uncovered, for 3 to 5 minutes. Add port. Set aside for at least 1 hour to allow flavors to blend. Strain. Mix cornstarch with 2 tablespoons water and stir into sauce.
Heat, stirring, until sauce thickens.

Note: May be used with venison, ham, or other "wild" things.

Horseradish Sauce

Easy   Yield: 10 servings
Do ahead   Preparing: 10 minutes

½ pint heavy cream, whipped
4 tablespoons prepared horseradish
1 tablespoon sugar
½ teaspoon salt

2 teaspoons prepared mustard
1 teaspoon vinegar
Paprika to taste

Combine all ingredients and whip until stiff. May be refrigerated for several hours before served.

Note: An excellent accompaniment for a roasted beef filet.

Sweet Hot Mustard

Easy   Yield: 1 cup
Do ahead   Preparing: 10 minutes
              Standing: 4 hours
              May be doubled

½ cup dry mustard
½ cup white vinegar

¼ cup sugar
1 egg yolk

Combine mustard with vinegar in a small bowl. Cover and allow to stand at room temperature for 4 hours. In a small saucepan mix sugar and egg yolk. Add mustard mixture, and cook over low heat, stirring constantly, until slightly thickened. Remove from heat and allow to cool, covered. Refrigerate in a covered container until ready to use. Best served at room temperature.

Note: Excellent with spinach balls or whenever good mustard is required.

Swordfish Marinade

Easy   Yield: Enough to marinate a 1-pound swordfish steak
Do ahead   Preparing: 5 minutes

2 tablespoons soy sauce
2 tablespoons orange juice
1 tablespoon olive oil
1 tablespoon tomato paste

1 tablespoon minced parsley
½ teaspoon lemon juice
¼ teaspoon oregano
¼ teaspoon freshly ground pepper

Combine all ingredients. This quantity will marinate a 1-pound swordfish steak.

Bravo!

Marinade for Tuna, Swordfish, Chicken, or Vegetables

Easy   Yield: 1¼ cups
Do ahead   Preparing: 10 minutes

Q E D

1 tablespoon honey
½ cup rice wine vinegar
1 2-inch piece fresh ginger root, diced
3 tablespoons tamari

1 teaspoon dark sesame oil
3 cloves garlic, minced
2 tablespoons lime juice
¾ cup olive oil

Combine all ingredients. Marinate fish several hours before barbequing, grilling, or broiling.

Note: In addition to fish, chicken, and vegetables, try marinating slices of firm tofu.

Mustard-Dill Sauce

Easy   Yield: 1 cup
Do ahead   Preparing: 3 minutes
               Chilling: 1 to 2 hours
               May be doubled

1 cup mayonnaise
1 tablespoon horseradish
2 tablespoons Dijon mustard

1 tablespoon fresh lemon juice
1 tablespoon dried dill weed

Mix all ingredients together in a small bowl. Refrigerate 1 to 2 hours ahead of serving. Serve chilled as a sauce for poached or grilled salmon, tuna, or chicken.

Grand Marnier Sauce for Fresh Strawberries

Easy   *Preparing: 30 minutes*

QED

5 egg yolks	**⅓ to ½ cup Grand Marnier**
½ cup sugar	**1 cup heavy cream**

Beat egg yolks with a whisk or electric mixer and gradually add the sugar. Place bowl over a pan of simmering water, or use a double boiler. Be sure the bottom of the bowl does not touch the hot water. Continue beating for approximately 10 minutes, until the yolks are thick and pale yellow. Chill, setting the bowl over iced water, stirring occasionally. Stir in the Grand Marnier. Whip the cream until it is moderately thick and blend it into the yolk mixture. Chill. Serve over strawberries or raspberries, or both.

Mint-Curry Salad Dressing

Easy   *Yield: 2 cups*
Do ahead   *Preparing: 5 minutes*
              Chilling: 2 hours
              May be doubled

¾ cup mayonnaise	**Dash nutmeg**
¾ cup plain yogurt	**½ teaspoon ground cumin**
2 tablespoons honey	**¼ teaspoon cayenne pepper**
1 teaspoon curry powder	**¼ cup fresh mint leaves, chopped**
½ teaspoon ground ginger	**1 tablespoon soy sauce**

Combine all ingredients in a food processor or blender. Chill 2 hours, for flavors to blend, before serving.

Note: Serve with any mixed salad of lettuce and vegetables; add shrimp or chicken to make it even more of a meal.

Honey of a Raspberry Vinaigrette

Easy   *Yield: 1 cup*
Do ahead   *Preparing: 10 minutes*

QED

1 clove garlic	**3 tablespoons walnut oil**
2 teaspoons Dijon mustard	**⅓ cup vegetable oil**
2 to 3 teaspoons honey, to taste	**¼ teaspoon salt**
½ cup raspberry vinegar	**½ teaspoon white pepper**

Combine all ingredients in a blender or food processor. Mix thoroughly. If made ahead, refrigerate; just before serving, shake well to combine.

Albertson's Cooking School, Wynnewood, PA

Bravo!

Harry's Salad Dressing/Marinade

Easy   *Yield: 3 cups*
Do ahead   *Preparing: 5 minutes*

4 teaspoons sugar
2 teaspoons salt
1 teaspoon dry mustard
1 teaspoon Hungarian paprika
15 drops Worcestershire sauce
3 tablespoons ketchup

2 large cloves garlic, sliced
1 cup cider vinegar (flavored
   with sage leaves)
2 cups salad oil
10 grindings pepper

Mix all ingredients well and store in a covered glass jar in the refrigerator. Use as a marinade for meats; add to warm potatoes in potato salad; or use as a dressing for a mixed green salad.

Honey Vinaigrette

Easy   *Yield: 1¼ cups*
Do ahead   *Preparing: 10 minutes*

1 clove garlic
1 large shallot
2 tablespoons fresh dill, or herbs of
   your choice
¼ cup cider vinegar
3 tablespoons fresh lemon juice

2 teaspoons Dijon mustard
1 to 2 teaspoons honey, to taste
¼ teaspoon salt
½ teaspoon pepper
1 cup vegetable oil

In a food processor fitted with a steel blade, drop garlic through feed tube while motor is running. Add shallot and mince. Add all ingredients except oil; process several seconds to blend. With motor running, add oil through feed tube. Pour into bottles and refrigerate.

Albertson's Cooking School, Wynnewood, PA

Poppy Seed Dressing for Fruit Salad

Easy   *Yield: 1½ cups*
Preparing: 10 minutes

½ cup sugar
1 teaspoon dry mustard
1 teaspoon salt
⅓ cup cider vinegar

1 small onion, quartered
1 cup salad oil
1½ tablespoons poppy seeds
1 teaspoon paprika

Combine all ingredients and mix well in a blender. Serve over fruit.

Fat-Free Veggie Dip/Sandwich Spread/ Salad Dressing

Easy   *Preparing: 2 minutes*
Do ahead   *May be doubled or tripled*

1 (8-ounce) package salad dressing
   mix (Italian, honey mustard
   or zesty herb)
1 (16-ounce) container non-fat yogurt

Mustard (optional)
Dill (optional)
Paprika (optional)

Mix the first 2 ingredients thoroughly and allow to stand for a few minutes to thicken. Now consider adding the optional ingredients, mustard, dill, and/or paprika.

Chambord Flambé

Easy   *Yield: 3 to 4 cups*
Do ahead   *Preparing: 15 minutes*
            Cooking: About 30 minutes

½ cup Chambord liqueur
1 teaspoon freshly grated orange zest
½ cup orange juice
½ cup sugar

2 cups cranberries
2 teaspoons cornstarch
2 tablespoons orange juice, or water
¼ cup brandy, slightly warmed

In a heavy 3-quart saucepan, combine Chambord, orange zest, ½ cup orange juice, and sugar. Mix well. Bring to a boil; add cranberries and simmer until cranberries burst. Meanwhile, mix cornstarch with 2 tablespoons of orange juice. Stir, and add to the berry mixture. Simmer until mixture comes to a full boil and thickens (to use as a relish, simmer longer). Refrigerate; will keep several weeks. To flambé, warm mixture in saucepan. Carefully pour warmed brandy over the sauce mixture, dim the lights, and ignite. When flames subside, spoon over dessert (vanilla yogurt, ice cream, angel food cake, pound cake, or rice pudding) of your choice.

Albertson's Cooking School, Wynnewood, PA

Bravo!

Gracie's Summer Garden Tomato Sauce

Easy
Do ahead

Yield: 1 cup
Preparing: 10 minutes
Baking: 1 to 2 hours
May be doubled or tripled

4 large, ripe, garden tomatoes
12 peeled garlic cloves

3 tablespoons olive oil
Freshly ground pepper to taste

Preheat oven to 350°. Wash and dry tomatoes and cut off the stem end. Into the cut part of each tomato insert 3 garlic cloves (or more if desired). Place in a lightly oiled glass baking dish and drizzle each with olive oil and a few grindings of pepper. Bake, uncovered, for 1 to 2 hours (it depends on the size of the tomatoes, how juicy they are, etc.), until the tomatoes are mushy and slightly blackened, and most of the liquid has evaporated. Remove from oven and mash. (If the skin does not disintegrate, remove it.) The mixture should be thick. Store, covered, in the refrigerator or freezer. Excellent with pasta or meat loaf.

Note: This is a good way to use those excess tomatoes from the garden. The recipe can be expanded at will, but the time in the oven may need to be watched carefully.

Aunt Mabel's Freezer Sweet Pickles

Easy
Do ahead
Freeze

Preparing: 30 minutes
Chilling: 24 hours

2 cups sugar
1 cup 5% acidity vinegar
2 tablespoons pickling salt
(do not use regular salt)
1 teaspoon celery seed

7 cups thinly sliced cucumbers
3 medium onions, sliced
1 green bell pepper, chopped
(optional)

Combine sugar, vinegar, pickling salt, and celery seed in a large, non-reactive bowl and mix thoroughly. Add the cucumbers, onions, and optional green pepper. (The liquid at this point will not completely cover the vegetables.) Cover and refrigerate for 24 hours, stirring occasionally. There will now be enough liquid to cover. Place vegetables into plastic freezer containers (any size) and cover with liquid, leaving a ¾-inch space at the top. Put on lids and store in the freezer. The pickles may be eaten immediately.

Banana Rum Syrup (For French Toast, Pancakes, or Waffles)

Easy
Do ahead

Yield: 3 cups
Preparing: 5 minutes
Cooking: 5 minutes
May be doubled

2 cups maple syrup
4 tablespoons butter
1 teaspoon cinnamon
½ teaspoon ground ginger
Grated rind of 1 lemon

¼ cup Myers dark rum
Juice of ½ lemon
2 tablespoons chopped
   crystallized ginger
2 bananas, thinly sliced

In a 2-quart saucepan, over medium-low heat, warm the syrup and the butter until the butter is completely melted. Add the cinnamon, ground ginger, grated lemon rind, rum, lemon juice, and crystallized ginger; bring to a gentle boil. Remove from heat immediately. Add the bananas and gently stir them into the syrup mixture. Keep the sauce warm until ready to serve but do not cook it any longer or the bananas will become too soft.

Note: Sliced apples or fresh blueberries may be used in place of the bananas. May be prepared ahead, for up to 1 hour.

Champagne Punch

Easy
Do ahead

Yield: 20 cups
Preparing: 20 minutes
Freezing: Overnight
May be doubled or tripled

1 quart cran-raspberry juice (may use
   low-calorie)
2 cups orange juice
1 cup pineapple juice
¾ cup lemon juice
⅔ cup Chambord liqueur

1 large bottle Champagne or
   sparkling grape juice
Ice mold made from
   fruit juice or water
Whole fresh or frozen strawberries
½ pint raspberry sherbet (optional)

Mix all ingredients except Champagne, ice, strawberries, and sherbet. Chill. Ice Mold: Boil juice or water. Cool. Place whole fresh or frozen strawberries decoratively around the edge of a heart-shaped or ring mold. Pour in cooled juice or water. Freeze. (For a large party, prepare several molds and keep frozen.) When solid, transfer to a large Ziploc bag. Keep frozen. To serve, place chilled punch mixture in a large bowl. Just before serving add Champagne, ice, and sherbet. A beautiful holiday drink.

Albertson's Cooking School, Wynnewood, PA

Bravo!

Easy Margaritas

Easy · Do ahead

Yield: Variable
Preparing: 5 minutes
May be doubled or tripled

QED

1 can frozen lime juice, thawed
1 can water

1 can tequila
⅓ can triple sec

Combine all ingredients in a blender. Pour drinks over chopped ice. (The size of the can of lime juice in this recipe does not matter, because all the other ingredients are measured by whatever can size is used.)

Note: Particularly good on a hot summer evening

Helen's Iced Tea

Easy · Do ahead

Yield: 1 quart
Preparing: 20 minutes
May be doubled or tripled

QED

1 quart boiling water
3 tea bags
4 sprigs fresh spearmint

1 cup sugar
¼ cup lemon juice

Pour boiling water over the tea bags and mint and allow to stand for 15 minutes. Add sugar and lemon juice. Serve over ice cubes. (May be made with decaffeinated tea and a sugar substitute.)

Note: It is important that the mint be spearmint.

Chambord Cranberry Spritzers

Easy · Do ahead

Yield: 6 servings
Preparing: 15 minutes
Refrigerate: Up to 8 hours
May be doubled or tripled

1 (12-ounce) can cran-raspberry
concentrate, thawed, undiluted
½ cup Chambord liqueur
2 lemon slices

2 orange slices
2 lime slices
1 bottle (750 milliliters) Champagne,
chilled

In a large pitcher combine all ingredients except Champagne. Cover; refrigerate up to 8 hours. To serve, remove fruit slices with a slotted spoon. Place crushed ice in tall glasses, pour in punch mixture, and add Champagne. Stir gently. Garnish with fruit slices, if desired.

Albertson's Cooking School, Wynnewood, PA

Bravo!

Contributors

A very special thanks to those who so generously contributed recipes to the Committee. We regret that space constraints and content similarity prevented us from including each and every one. All recipes have been tested, and edited for clarity. We hope that many will become your favorites!

Jane T. Acton
Pam Adams
Alice Ahrens
Albertson's Cooking School
Dottebob Andes
Vladimir Ashkenazy
Baker Street
Mrs. Bertram Balch
Carol Barker
Joy P. Barrows
Mrs. Charles M. Bartler
Ruth P. Barton
Susan S. Becker
Mrs. Henry S. Belber II
Bob Benigni
Luke Block
Phyllis Pray Bober
Blair Bollinger
Kelly Bonn
Nancy Bowen
Patti Brecht
Jeffrey Brillhart
Mrs. John M. Brownback
Jean Brubaker
Bud Bruno
Elia Buck
Carolyn S. Burger
Beth Butler
Café Beaujolais
Martha Caesar
Joan Calhoun
Norman Carol
Connie Carroll
Lovina Carroll
Cookie Chase
The Cheese Company
Cheryl Cheston
Mary P. Chinappi
Anni Christiansen
City Market Café
DeAnn Clancy
Mrs. James E. Clark
Donald R. Clauser

Jeanne Coburn
Commander's Palace
Wayne Conner
Marian Conway
Rika Cornwell
Coventry Forge Inn
Samuel Crothers
Culinary Concepts
Alice Cullen
Karen Gordon Cunningham
Marilyn Costello
   Dannenbaum
Dorothy Davidson
Mrs. John C. Davis III
Evie Day
Van Deacon
Jean T. Dee
Anne Dibble
Winnie Doherty
Sonya Driscoll
Robert B. Driver
Jimmy Duffy & Sons, Inc.
Mrs. George W. Ebright
Kitty Ellis
Sandra T. Enck
Evergreen Restaurant
June Felley
Maureen Forrester
Four Seasons
Doris Frankel
Madeline Frantz
Mrs. Donald R. Frisch
Maria Gallagher
Helen Gannon
Lois Garaventi
Randy Gardner
Toni Garrison
Betsey Gibson
Jeffrey B. Gibson
Mrs. Robert D. Glennie
Mrs. Margaret Glennon
Gary Graffman
Laura Pratt Gregg

Esther Grier
Griglia Toscana
Mrs. James Halbkat
Richard Hamilton
Dorothy E. Hartley
Nancy Hastings
Teresa Heinz
Nancy Henry
Günther Herbig
Jean Herz
Mrs. Edward C. Hess
Mrs. A. Scott Holmes
Mrs. Kelly Holthus
Mrs. Louis Hood
David R. Horn
Mrs. D. W. Hostetler
Linda H. Hucke
J. Bridwell Ingleheart, Jr.
Rita Jacoby
Jake's
Mrs. Henry James, Jr.
Byron Janis
Edith H. Jones
Helen M. Justi
Mary Anne D. Justice
Emily Kaiser
Judith Kase
Chris Kastner
Peggy Kippax
Janet L. Klaus
Sandy Kress
Lynn A. Krivitsky
Anne Krout
Erich Kunzel
Carol Kuzmicki
Cleo Laine
Mary S. Leahy
Le Bec-Fin
Margery P. Lee
Mrs. Morgan Lefferdink
Mrs. David H. Lipson, Jr.
Barbara Little
E. Payson Little

Bravo!

Betty Lloyd
Mrs. David D. Longmaid
Holly Mayock Luff
Marnie Ludwig
Mrs. John Brockie Lukens
Theo Lumia
Sonja Lundgren
Zdenek Macal
Judy MacGregor
Polly P. Mackie
Grace L. Madeira
Cirel Magen
Matt Maher
Ethel Mallory
Muriel Manfrey
Rose Mark
Mrs. John Markle, Jr.
Nima Marsh
Margarette Marvin
Kurt Masur
Mary Mavor
Connie Mayock
Pat McCarter
Mrs. J. W. McConaghy
Esther Press McManus
Jeffrey Miller
Marian Mitchell
Patty Mitchell
Morgan's
Ingrid Morsman
Mrs. L. Naaker
Peter Nero
Maureen Nesbitt
June B. Newburger
New Orleans School of
   Cooking
Barbara A. Noone
Corrine A. Nyi
Judy Obbard
Orso Restaurant
Mary S. Page
Palladium
Phyllis Palmer
Charlotte Parker
Jill Pasternak
Rose Bampton Pelletier
Carol Roberts Pendergrass

March Pepper
Lois Perritt
Bette K. Peterson
Terry Petrella
John Alden Philbrick III
Kathryn Picht
The Pier
Cynthia Pierce
Virginia Pitrofsky
Lynn Early Pohanka
Linda Price
Queen of Hearts
The Rabbit
Betsy Rainey
Philip Randolph
John J. Reddish
Margaret A. Reese
Bee Reichel
Suzanne Reichel
Lois W. Renthal
Reunion Inn & Grill
Susan Rice
Polly Riggs
Alison Robb
Susie Robinson
Cackie Rogers
Renee Carol Rush
Janet Ryan
Mrs. Wolfgang Sawallisch
Mrs. Robert E. Schott
Susan Schubert
Scottsdale Princess
Guiseppina Seminara
Lynda Seminara
Mrs. J. Lawrence Shane
Jan Sharey, M.D.
Mrs. John E. Shaw
Catherine A. Shomaker
Dotty Shrier
Kathryn R. Simich
Mrs. John W. Simmons II
Skippack Roadhouse &
   4022 Rotisserie
Margot Smart
Mrs. A. Buford Smith
Deborah Carter Smith
William Smith

Club Soleil
Georg Solti
Joan Specter
Lyn Stallworth
Sydney Stevens
Mrs. Walter G. Stringer
Jeralyn T. Svanda
Alexander L. Taggart
Sue Talucci
Beb Thomson
Annie Thompson
Nathalie Thompson
Mary Hynson Thuroczy
Maud Tierney
William Tierney
Mrs. William Tilley
Barbara W. Trimmer
Mrs. Elizabeth Tusler
Kathryn Tusler
Jackie Tryon
21st Century Café
United States Hotel
Mrs. Edward W. Uthe
Benita Valente
Mary C. VanDervort
Mrs. Henry W. VanSciver
Jacques R. Vitré
Elizabeth Walker
Lorraine Wallace
Elizabeth Little Walsh
Dave Walti
Wilbur E. Wamsley
Dawn Warden
Holly Wendt
Renata Whitaker
Gayle Whittingham
Mrs. Thomas A. Williams
Ruth Winnick
Helen Wolck
Mrs. H. Palmer Woodcock, Jr.
Mrs. John S. Wynne
Yangming
David Zinman
Zocalo
Pinchas Zukerman
Aileen Farrell Zurka

Bravo!

Guide to Safe Food-Handling

Shopping

- Do not buy any food you will not consume before the "use by" date.
- Refrigerated foods should be cold to the touch.
- Frozen foods should be rock-solid.
- Do not buy cans that are dented, cracked, or bulging.
- Do not buy meat, fish, or seafood that could have touched raw food in a display case.
- Do not buy any food in packages that are broken or torn.
- Do not leave food in a hot car.

Storage

- Freeze meat, poultry, or fish immediately if it will not be used within 2 to 3 days.
- Refrigerate raw meat, poultry or fish on a plate so that the juices do not drip onto other foods.
- Refrigerate leftovers, even very hot foods, within 1 to 2 hours of serving.

Preparation:

- Wash hands in hot soapy water before handling food.
- Cut raw meat, fish, poultry on one side of a cutting board; flip board over to cut vegetables.
- To avoid the formation of bacteria, thaw food in the refrigerator or a microwave, not on the kitchen counter.
- Marinate food in the refrigerator.
- Wash aprons, kitchen towels and pot holders often.
- Replace sponges and wash cloths often.
- Place sponges and wash cloths in the top rack of your dishwasher whenever you run it.
- To disinfect your cutting board and counters, use a weak solution of bleach and water.

Serving:

- Serve grilled foods on a clean plate, not on the one that held raw or marinated food.
- Keep party food on ice, or serve from platters that have been kept refrigerated.
- Thoroughly heat leftovers; bring sauces, soups, and gravies to a boil before serving.

Microwaving:

- Do not allow plastic wrap to touch the food.
- Observe the standing time; food continues to cook during this period.
- Be sure there are no cold spots - bacteria can survive in them.
- Use a temperature probe or meat thermometer in several spots to check for doneness.

Bravo!

Useful Equivalents

3 teaspoons = 1 tablespoon
2 tablespoons = ⅛ cup
4 tablespoons = ¼ cup
5 tablespoons + 1 teaspoon = ⅓ cup
4 ounces = ½ cup
1 ounce liquid = 2 tablespoons
⅝ cup = ½ cup + 2 tablespoons
⅞ cup = ¾ cup + 2 tablespoons
1 jigger = 1½ fluid ounces = 3 tablespoons
8 to 10 egg whites = 1 cup
12 to 14 egg yolks = 1 cup
1 cup unwhipped cream = 2 cups whipped
1 pound shredded, Cheddar cheese = 4 cups
¼ pound crumbled, blue cheese = 1 cup
1 pound granulated sugar = 2 cups
1 pound unsifted, powdered sugar = 3½ to 4 cups
1 pound packed, brown sugar = 2¼ cups
1 pound sifted flour = 4 cups
1 pound unsifted, whole-wheat flour = 3½ cups
1 cup dry rice + 2 cups liquid = 3 cups cooked rice
28 saltine crackers = 1 cup crumbs
14 square graham crackers = 1 cup crumbs
22 vanilla wafers = 1 cup crumbs
3 medium bananas = 1 cup mashed
3 cups dry corn flakes = 1 cup crushed
1 pound whole dates = 1½ cups, pitted, and cut
⅛ teaspoon garlic powder = 1 small pressed clove of garlic
1 tablespoon instant minced onion, rehydrated = 1 small fresh onion
2 ounces compressed yeast = 3 (¼-ounce) packets dry yeast
1 teaspoon dry herbs = 1 tablespoon fresh herbs

Substitutions for a Missing Ingredient

1 square chocolate (1 ounce) = 3 or 4 tablespoons cocoa + ½ tablespoon fat
1 tablespoon cornstarch = 2 tablespoons flour (for thickening)
1 teaspoon baking powder = ¼ teaspoon baking soda + ½ teaspoon cream of tartar
1 cup sour milk = 1 cup sweet milk mixed with 1 tablespoon vinegar or lemon juice
1 cup sour cream or heavy cream = ⅓ cup butter + ⅔ cup milk

Index

Bravo!

Bravo!

Bravo!

Bravo!

Bravo!

Bravo!

Bravo!

Bravo!

Bravo!

Bravo!

THE PHILADELPHIA ORCHESTRA COOKBOOKS
PO Box 685
Bryn Mawr, PA 19010

BRAVO! The Philadelphia Orchestra Cookbook II

Please send _____ copies @ $19.95 each $ _____

The Philadelphia Orchestra Cookbook I

Please send _____ copies @ $16.00 each $ _____

Pennsylvania residents add 6% sales tax $ _____

Postage and handling @ $3.50 each $ _____

TOTAL ENCLOSED $ _____

Please make checks payable to The Philadelphia Orchestra Cookbooks

Name _____

Address _____

City _____ State _____ Zip _____

Proceeds from the sale of these books further the interests of The Philadelphia Orchestra. Please allow 4-6 weeks for delivery.

THE PHILADELPHIA ORCHESTRA COOKBOOKS
PO Box 685
Bryn Mawr, PA 19010

BRAVO! The Philadelphia Orchestra Cookbook II

Please send _____ copies @ $19.95 each $ _____

The Philadelphia Orchestra Cookbook I

Please send _____ copies @ $16.00 each $ _____

Pennsylvania residents add 6% sales tax $ _____

Postage and handling @ $3.50 each $ _____

TOTAL ENCLOSED $ _____

Please make checks payable to The Philadelphia Orchestra Cookbooks

Name _____

Address _____

City _____ State _____ Zip _____

Proceeds from the sale of these books further the interests of The Philadelphia Orchestra. Please allow 4-6 weeks for delivery.

Please send me information on ordering additional copies of
The Philadelphia Orchestra Cookbooks

Name _____

Address _____

City _____ State _____ Zip _____

Phone ( ) _____